SLIs and SLOs Demystified

A workshop approach to building and maintaining your service
level indicators and service level objectives

Alexandra F. McCoy

SLIs and SLOs Demystified

Copyright © 2025 Packt Publishing

Portfolio Director: Kartikey Pandey

Relationship Lead: Marylou De Mello

Book Project Manager: Sonam Pandey

Content Engineer: Sayali Pingale

Technical Editor: Arjun Varma

Copy Editor: Safis Editing

Indexer: Pratik Shirodkar

Production Designer: Vijay Kamble

First published: April 2025

Production reference: 1280325

Published by Packt Publishing Ltd.

Grosvenor House

11 St Paul's Square

Birmingham

B3 1RB, UK.

ISBN 978-1-83588-938-1

www.packtpub.com

To my daughter, Addison, thanks so much for being patient with Mom throughout this process. To my grandma, thanks for embedding the importance of books in me. To my family and friends who checked on me throughout this process; although you may not have known where my time was being invested, I appreciate you. To my former SRE colleagues, there's not a word in this book that was written where I did not think of "y'all!" ("Happy Engineering!")

– Alexandra F. McCoy

Acknowledgements

First and foremost, it is only appropriate to give praise to the higher being.

A huge thank you to my family and close friends (who I consider part of my family) for always showing up in the best way they know how when I need them the most.

There is a saying, "Give people their flowers while they are here." In my previous company, we personified this statement by showing appreciation after meetings, giving shoutouts in Slack channels, and through an organizational e-card system. So, it feels only right that I implement this important value here, too.

This book, for me, represents my challenges, growth, and learnings over the past few years. It's important to highlight that the process was more valuable than the outcome, in this instance. The outcome is a representation of my hard work and surrounding myself with people who see the potential in me on the days that I do not. Each word and diagram in the text is a reminder to me of the many words exchanged during my tenure as an SRE, and the many years prior spent navigating the cloud space.

While I am the author of this book, it is the summation of the knowledge of a few individuals, past and present, in SRE and Product Engineering that believe in providing people an opportunity and space to grow. If you've worked closely with me, then you'll be aware that I have a passion for learning and a knack for enabling and advocating for those around me. What I do not do well is advocate for myself and highlight the various ideas and opportunities that I leverage to increase my own knowledge.

When I started as an SRE, I had already worked closely with an SRE team filled with a few individuals who, in my opinion, were extremely smart and team-oriented, being there for the platform team when needed. In a later company, during my second week as an SRE, I found myself in a workshop with the internal support team, hosted by another staff engineer before even completing onboarding.

He ended up being one of the best engineers I've worked with, for reasons that others will not understand. I hope that he views each diagram and just smiles. On my first week of joining the org and working with him, I remember attending his workshop out of curiosity. We discussed sketches months later, and I eventually worked on my own soon after, with his support and encouragement. I won't mention how we got there, but it is what it is. Unfortunately, he left soon after.

I've had a few managers in my time. To the manager at this time, to this day, I have no idea how you managed a team of many headstrong engineers in a remote environment, but here we are. I'm positive there was so much more we could have accomplished as a team, and I hope each team member reads this paragraph and laughs out loud. I thank you for the time that was spent and the opportunity to immerse myself in the actual practice of SRE, while also developing healthier work habits.

Thank you to my former executives, for not only believing in me but also creating a people-centric culture developed for the people and by the people. This includes creating programs that teach individuals how to navigate and manage the good and the bad. This is something so many organizations miss! When I was in college, I explored HRIS. I started my masters in HR and transferred to information technology. Thank you for bringing back that memory and reminding me of the importance of investing in people, and not just financially.

Sometimes life will lead you astray, and it's a blessing in disguise to be able to get back on track. However, when you are back on track, you want to ensure you're moving not only quicker but also more efficiently. It's like that pitstop on the racetrack in the middle of a race. I also imagine that when you are at the top, it's hard to maintain accurate visibility of the goings-on of those handling the organization's daily operations. Each executives' initiatives taught me firsthand the importance of not losing sight of your people. It also afforded me the opportunity to connect with other executives and experience different leadership styles. A moment of transparency: I was not a fan of many executives until I participated in various initiatives during my tenure as an SRE and found ways to contribute in ways that felt meaningful to me.

TSRE, ugh. I love "y'all." I don't think there is much more to say. I grew so tired of inviting "y'all" to do things that I wanted to do and you all not agreeing. In my mind, I figured, "I will just write this on behalf of the team." I cringe thinking about the number of horrid meetings I would have had to join if we collaborated. But I would be a liar if I said I did not miss all of you, IPM, and our little karaoke stints for being late to meetings!

J.W., you are one of the worst and best managers. I am comfortable with saying I am probably the best and worst employee you've had. Sorry F., you were not the favorite child.

Sayali, I picked up Italian and Portuguese for moments when I became bored. I need to improve in one a bit more, to catch up to you! No time soon, though. I hope you're resting well! Brendan, you and I are "agree to disagree" personified! I continue to believe this enables more coverage, too!

Cheers to making work fun and looking like you're not working. You all owe me a beer and a trip to Ireland, too! Laying me off did not get you off the hook!

Contributors

About the author

Alexandra F. McCoy has worked within the software and technology industry, in various roles, for the last 12 years. She has spent a portion of that time as a site reliability engineer. Much of her experience has been in the cloud sector, including hybrid cloud and on-premises Kubernetes environments, implementing cloud-native solutions for container orchestration. She enjoys the practice of reliability engineering, cloud-native development, and container orchestration as they relate to architecting solutions for customers within various industries. She spends her free time with family and close friends, and dedicates time to mentoring junior engineers and professionals, with aspirational goals of successfully developing within the technology field.

I would like to thank my friends, family, and former colleagues who have positively poured into me throughout the years.

About the reviewers

Abirami Radhakrishnan is a seasoned engineering leader with deep expertise in **site reliability engineering** (**SRE**) and cloud-native architectures. With extensive experience in designing and optimizing resilient systems, she has been instrumental in implementing high-availability infrastructure and improving service reliability at scale.

She has contributed significantly to observability, automation, and cost optimization strategies in complex cloud environments. Her work includes designing robust monitoring frameworks, introducing **service-level objectives** (**SLOs**) for critical platforms, and optimizing infrastructure performance. She is also a mentor and technical speaker, sharing insights on Kubernetes, reliability engineering, and automation best practices.

As a reviewer of *SLOs and SLIs Demystified*, she brings a practical perspective on balancing performance, reliability, and operational efficiency.

Luke Rotta has been in the financial services industry for 23 years as both an engineer and a leader of global teams at firms ranging from 300 to 32,000 people. In these roles, Luke has led SRE transformations, SLO implementations, and incident management redesigns. In addition, he has built 24x7 follow-the-sun teams that support highly scaled trading systems. Luke is passionate about SRE, enhancing the client experience, building global teams, and increasing software velocity. He believes establishing an inclusive, collaborative, and autonomous culture is key to faster innovation with fewer outages.

Table of Contents

4

Observability and Monitoring Are a Necessity and a Must   57

5

The Financial Impact of Not Adopting Indicators   73

Part 2: The Tough Stuff – Kickstarting the SLI and SLO Conversation

6

Workshop Preparation: Structuring the SLI and SLO Conversation   89

7

Scenario 1: SLIs and SLOs for Web Applications   109

8

Scenario 2: SLIs and SLOs for Distributed Systems   129

9

Scenario 3: Optimizing SLIs and SLOs for Database Performance   151

10

Scenario 4: Developing SLIs and SLOs for New Features   175

Part 3: Help! We've Identified Our SLIs and SLOs... Now What?

11

SLO Monitoring and Alerting   199

12

Service Level Performance Metrics: Daily Operations   221

13

SLO Preservation and Incident Management   233

14

SLIs and SLOs as a Service   251

Preface

Reliability engineering, or **Site Reliability Engineering** (**SRE**), is the practice used to improve the reliability of software systems through automating IT operations. The practice consists of a set of hierarchal layers, each incorporating its own principles and guidelines to build upon one another. Within this practice, **Service Level Indicators** (**SLIs**) and **Service Level Objectives** (**SLOs**) are used to measure how well services are performing. These measurements help an organization make informed technical decisions, fostering accountability for commitments made to customers within a **Service Level Agreement** (**SLA**).

This book focuses on establishing and running a workshop to create SLIs and SLOs with your engineering teams. It is also filled with information that integrates concepts such as observability, "as-a-service" offerings, and structuring an SRE team to encourage the usage of other practices and get the mind prepared for pre- and post-concepts that are key to the long-term success of the work done within the workshops.

Who this book is for

This book is intended for experienced SRE and DevOps engineers invested in the practice of SRE. This includes other development or software engineering personas dedicated to embedding reliability into their services and seeking technical and process-related implementation examples for building and managing SLIs and SLOs.

In more detail, the target audience of this book is as follows:

- **SRE teams**: SRE engineers tasked with the responsibility of implementing SLIs and SLOs.
- **DevOps engineering**: DevOps engineers looking to understand SLIs and SLOs with regard to SRE.
- **Development/software engineering teams**: Other development roles looking to understand SLIs and SLOs with regard to SRE and seeking a starting point.

If starting the process for implementing SLIs within the next few weeks or months is the goal for you or your organization, then this book is for you. There's a little something for everyone, including you executives!

What this book covers

Chapter 1, SLIs and SLOs at the Heart of Reliability, provides a brief overview and introduction to the hierarchy of reliability engineering and the relationship between service level metrics used to measure system performance.

Chapter 2, Establishing an SLI and SLO Team, provides guidelines for building a team dedicated to creating SLIs and SLOs if required, while establishing a relationship with stakeholders and product engineering teams.

Chapter 3, Things to Consider When Crafting Your SLIs and SLOs, introduces the concept of a persona and persona journey used in the SLI and SLO process to ensure your focus remains on customer versus consumption.

Chapter 4, Observability and Monitoring Are a Necessity and a Must, provides information related to observability, monitoring, and the relationship to visibility to improve reliability engineering practices. This chapter also introduces observability as a layer within the hierarchy of reliability.

Chapter 5, The Financial Impact of Not Adopting Indicators, provides insights related to the benefits of incorporating reliability engineering and SLIs and SLOs into your organization. It also provides insights regarding the risk of not investing.

Chapter 6, Workshop Preparation: Structuring the SLI and SLO Conversation, provides an introduction and outline of the steps to create and implement SLIs and SLOs. The chapter also discusses the steps necessary prior to creating your workshop.

Chapter 7, Scenario 1: SLIs and SLOs for Web Applications, provides an example of a workshop for SLIs and SLOs centered around web applications.

Chapter 8, Scenario 2: SLIs and SLOs for Distributed Systems, provides an example of a workshop for SLIs and SLOs centered around distributed systems.

Chapter 9, Scenario 3: Optimizing SLIs and SLOs for Database Performance, provides an example of a workshop for SLIs and SLOs centered around database performance.

Chapter 10, Scenario 4: Developing SLIs and SLOs for New Features, provides an example of a workshop for SLIs and SLOs centered around new features within a system.

Chapter 11, SLO Monitoring and Alerting, provides information and examples related to configuring monitoring and alerting for SLOs. It also provides insights into deploying your SLOs into dashboard management platforms.

Chapter 12, Service Level Performance Metrics: Daily Operations, provides insights into managing SLOs daily. It also includes approaches to help facilitate iterating and adjusting your indicators and objectives over time.

Chapter 13, SLO Preservation and Incident Management, provides a workshop example for creating SLIs and SLOs dedicated to incident management. It also highlights the importance of extending accountability to engineering teams.

Chapter 14, SLIs and SLOs as a Service, provides information related to packaging your SLIs and SLOs as a service offering internally and externally. It also outlines the product lifecycle for SLOs.

To get the most out of this book

The goal of this book is to work through workshop examples for creating SLIs and SLOs. Terminology and concepts related to other domains within the technology are mentioned. However, you will need to understand the following:

- Application architecture and terminology
- Networking terminology
- Infrastructure-related concepts
- Have a basic understanding of SLAs

There are no requirements related to software or code downloads. However, I will challenge you to think of an application, infrastructure, or platform to flow through the workshop chapters.

Conventions used

There are a number of text conventions used throughout this book.

`Code in text`: Indicates code words in text, database table names, folder names, filenames, file extensions, pathnames, dummy URLs, user input, and Twitter handles. Here is an example: "It is important to not confuse redirection at this stage with receiving a `301` or `308` response code that is provided to the customer."

Bold: Indicates a new term, an important word, or words that you see onscreen. For instance, words in menus or dialog boxes appear in **bold**. Here is an example: "Select **System info** from the **Administration** panel."

> **Tips or important notes**
> Appear like this.

Get in touch

Feedback from our readers is always welcome.

General feedback: If you have questions about any aspect of this book, email us at `customercare@packtpub.com` and mention the book title in the subject of your message.

Errata: Although we have taken every care to ensure the accuracy of our content, mistakes do happen. If you have found a mistake in this book, we would be grateful if you would report this to us. Please visit `www.packtpub.com/support/errata` and fill in the form.

Piracy: If you come across any illegal copies of our works in any form on the internet, we would be grateful if you would provide us with the location address or website name. Please contact us at `copyright@packt.com` with a link to the material.

If you are interested in becoming an author: If there is a topic that you have expertise in and you are interested in either writing or contributing to a book, please visit `authors.packtpub.com`.

Share Your Thoughts

Once you've read *SLOs and SLIs Demystified*, we'd love to hear your thoughts! Scan the QR code below to go straight to the Amazon review page for this book and share your feedback.

`https://packt.link/r/1835889395`

Your review is important to us and the tech community and will help us make sure we're delivering excellent quality content.

Download a free PDF copy of this book

Thanks for purchasing this book!

Do you like to read on the go but are unable to carry your print books everywhere?

Is your eBook purchase not compatible with the device of your choice?

Don't worry, now with every Packt book you get a DRM-free PDF version of that book at no cost.

Read anywhere, any place, on any device. Search, copy, and paste code from your favorite technical books directly into your application.

The perks don't stop there, you can get exclusive access to discounts, newsletters, and great free content in your inbox daily

Follow these simple steps to get the benefits:

1. Scan the QR code or visit the link below

https://packt.link/free-ebook/9781835889381

2. Submit your proof of purchase
3. That's it! We'll send your free PDF and other benefits to your email directly

Part 1:
Reliability Engineering
Refresher

In this part of the book, you will receive a comprehensive overview of reliability engineering, emphasizing its significance, and recommendations on initiating and organizing discussions on the importance of the topic. This part will place emphasis on the hierarchy of reliability engineering and integrate the importance of observability within the hierarchy.

This part contains the following chapters:

1

SLIs and SLOs at the Heart of Reliability

Before developing and applying **Service Level Objectives (SLOs)**, it is essential to establish a shared understanding among all stakeholders of the components being measured and of what defines success. This chapter briefly introduces reliability engineering at a broad level, emphasizing the relationship between **Service Level Indicators (SLIs)** and SLOs, both within reliability engineering and as fundamental concepts. The chapter will outline the foundational principles of reliability engineering and guide you toward initiating workshops or discussions to gather the requirements and identify the necessary metrics to measure.

Each metric you identify for your application or platform will play a key role in determining its respective availability, performance, and reliability. We will guide you through examining various practices, principles, and implementations of SLIs and SLOs. This journey will cover concepts such as their definition, measurement, hierarchy, and relationship to observability and monitoring, as well as the consequences of not choosing the appropriate indicators.

Consider this chapter as a refresher for the practice of reliability engineering, as well as the definitions of core concepts and bringing the dependencies between each core concept to the forefront. This will ensure that before running your workshop, all participants have a clear understanding of the practice itself and the best practices surrounding structuring the workshop, and thus the team(s) for success.

In this chapter, we'll cover the following main topics:

- Reliability engineering principles and practices
- The hierarchy of reliability engineering
- The relationship between observability and monitoring
- The cost of not choosing SLIs

Let's get started!

Reliability engineering principles and practices

In today's technology industry, various standard and non-standard practices within sub-industries make up the core functions and processes within each organization. This can often lead to the development of several disciplines consisting of various opinions and different ways of doing things – that is, until a standard is created and unification happens. Further development then occurs from a cycle of implementation and formulating some hypotheses and strong opinions on how things should be done.

This is not said to shed a negative light but to emphasize how disciplines, despite their industry, begin with starting and vocalizing opinions. This is true whether people agree or disagree with them. Therefore, before diving into the complexities of reliability engineering, it's important to understand the various pillars, roles, responsibilities, and frameworks that create the practice as we know it today. From software development to infrastructure in distributed environments, and from storage networking to cybersecurity, each technical space presents its unique challenges and opportunities with performance tracking. By acknowledging this diversity within technology, organizations can better appreciate continuing to improve upon the breadth and depth of reliability engineering's applicability.

The importance of reliability in modern systems and services

In today's technical industry, there is an ongoing adoption of software, infrastructure, and platforms as services. This creates expectations of availability, high performance, and minimal latency, among other requirements. Along with provided services is a level of commitment that is made to external consumers. Within most organizations, you will see implemented **Service Level Agreements (SLAs)**, which inform the service user of the level or type of performance they can expect from your service, as well as how matters are handled in the event this commitment is not met.

SLIs and SLOs serve as linchpins in the pursuit of reliability excellence. SLIs are quantifiable metrics that represent the performance and health of systems, providing tangible measurements of reliability. SLOs, on the other hand, establish acceptable thresholds or targets for SLIs, aligning technical objectives with business requirements. The relationship between SLIs and SLOs is symbiotic, with SLOs guiding the establishment of meaningful SLIs and serving as the benchmark against which system performance is measured. Together, they form the foundation of a proactive and data-driven approach to reliability engineering.

Introduction to key reliability concepts

Reliability engineering is a multifaceted discipline that incorporates a range of methodologies, tools, and practices to ensure systems operate consistently and predictably under different conditions. At its core, reliability engineering seeks to minimize the occurrence and impact of failures, thereby enhancing system reliability and availability.

Key concepts as they relate to reducing failures within the scope of reliability engineering include topics such as the following:

- **Service level quantifiers**: SLIs, SLOs, and SLAs; the core topic of this book.

- **Error budgets**: A measurement of the allowable amount of downtime or outage of some component within the system.

- **Fault tolerance**: The ability of a system to operate without failure when a single or multiple components fail.

- **Redundancy**: The duplication of systems or components as a backup mechanism.

- **Failure analysis**: The process of collecting and analyzing data to determine the cause of a failure.

- **Incident response**: The set of processes in place for responding to and managing incidents.

- **Capacity planning**: The set practices in place to help determine the current and future demand(s).

- **Monitoring**: The set of processes and tooling used to monitor, and later alert, events within the system.

Each item in the list is central to the discipline, providing the foundation upon which reliability strategies are built. The proper implementation of each component enhances your services, platforms, and overall customer experience while structuring and shaping how you implement each of the pillars within your reliability engineering organization. We will discuss this topic via the pillars within the hierarchy of reliability engineering in a later section.

Reliability engineers ensure system reliability and resiliency

With the constant evolution of complexity and interconnection of software and technology, the role of reliability engineers has emerged as an indispensable part of ensuring the resiliency of critical infrastructure. This section focuses on the multifaceted responsibilities and key contributions of reliability engineers in safeguarding systems, while highlighting their role as architects of stability and champions of operational excellence. Within the industry, you will often hear about **Site Reliability Engineers (SREs)**, who are paired with DevOps engineers and occasionally compared to systems engineers. However, understanding the SREs' role is crucial to assigning them to the right initiatives that align with their specialties, and to clearly define collaboration within an organization for unified and efficient teamwork.

Reliability engineers are tasked with the following responsibilities:

- Designing, implementing, and maintaining systems and processes that meet stringent reliability requirements.

- SREs play a crucial role in ensuring that systems operate consistently and predictably under varying conditions, minimizing the occurrence and impact of failures; this can relate to enhancing processes through automation tooling.

- Reliability engineers leverage a combination of technical expertise, data-driven methodologies, and cross-functional collaboration to drive continuous improvement and enhance system resilience.

The various responsibilities of an SRE will often require them to maintain a broader scope of visibility within the organization. Thus, their responsibilities will sometimes span a wide range of activities aimed at promoting system reliability, as opposed to building it, to increase buy-in. They design and implement monitoring systems and alerting mechanisms to detect and address anomalies in real time. This will include conducting sessions such as retrospective analysis of incidents to identify root causes and implement preventive measures. Additionally, reliability engineers collaborate with cross-functional teams to design and implement reliability features and improvements, such as fault tolerance, redundancy, and disaster recovery, as mentioned earlier in this chapter.

Reliability engineers also make significant contributions to the organization through designing and implementing robust monitoring and alerting systems, which enable the proactive identification and resolution of issues before they impact users. Through continuous analysis and optimization of SLIs and SLOs, they can drive improvements in system performance and availability. By conducting thorough post-incident reviews, they identify systemic weaknesses and implement corrective measures to prevent future occurrences. Ultimately, reliability engineers are critical to fostering a culture of reliability excellence through software within the organization, where reliability is prioritized as a core value and marketed as a competitive advantage.

Challenges and opportunities of the reliability engineering role

Despite the critical importance of their role, reliability engineers face a myriad of challenges. Those include not only determining system reliability but sometimes also aligning their role and the work they do with the broader organization's goal. These challenges can include the following:

- Managing the complexity of modern systems as requirements change.
- Balancing reliability requirements with other competing priorities.
- Fostering collaboration across diverse teams and stakeholders.

These challenges also present opportunities for growth and innovation through service-level indicators and objectives. By embracing their responsibilities and rising to the challenges of modern technology, reliability engineers can use their technical skill sets to drive positive outcomes and foster a culture of reliability excellence within their organizations. Let's shift toward understanding the hierarchy of individual pillars that shape the practice of reliability to better understand the interworking and dependencies of each.

The hierarchy of reliability engineering

The hierarchy of reliability engineering provides the framework for which reliability goals are defined, implemented, and monitored across various layers. From infrastructure and application to business layers, each tier plays a crucial role in ensuring the overall reliability and resilience of systems and services. This section highlights the hierarchical structure of reliability engineering, delineating the responsibilities and objectives of different teams and stakeholders within each layer.

The term *hierarchy* was coined by *Mikey Dickerson*, a Google Engineer, to display the relationship between pillars within the practice. The hierarchy of SRE is based on Maslow's *Hierarchy of Needs framework*. Maslow's Hierarchy of Needs model categorizes human needs into two types, comprising various levels of necessity. The hierarchy of SRE functions in a similar manner. Within the practice of SRE, there are several "needs" that are required in a structured order, which you build upon to create a successful practice.

The hierarchy of reliability engineering lists the pillars of reliability engineering in the following order:

- **Product**: The product layer, as it relates to the hierarchy, represents the end goal, or packaged solution, that ships to the customers. It is the result of appropriately implementing each of the pillars.

- **Development**: Reaching the goal of a shippable product requires a seamless development process that includes the identification of a market need, researching industry competition, ideating the solution, developing a product roadmap, and building a **minimum viable product (MVP)**.

- **Capacity planning**: To run an efficient product and produce shippable products, we need to assess internal pipelines to determine the right amount of technical and human resources required to work sustainably.

- **Testing and release procedures**: Central to following up on the action items from retrospectives and root cause analysis is the process of implementing the appropriate test, test frameworks, and release procedures to ship the product most reliably to the target consumer.

- **Retrospectives and root cause analysis**: Retrospectives and root cause analysis are central to assessing and communicating what happened, where it happened, why it happened, and how to mitigate the occurrence moving forward, between the knowledgeable engineers and other staff. We will discuss this topic in more depth in later chapters.

- **Incident response**: This consists of the collective set of practices and tooling utilized to respond to critical events that occur in relation to your application, service, or platform.

- **Monitoring**: This consists of the set of processes and the tooling used to capture the events that occur within your application, service, or platform environment. Quality monitoring is important to better understand what's happening within your system, where it's happening, and why. As with most things in the field of technology, shifts, changes, and improvements happen.

During the process of implementing SLIs and SLOs, it was discovered that the hierarchy is not complete if the following conditions are met:

- Not ensuring that we are monitoring the right things.

- Lacking the visibility to ensure that we are monitoring the right things.

- Unclear regarding the boundaries within our systems that integrate to provide a unified piece of functionality to our end users.

The limitations previously mentioned result in the idea of observability serving as the foundation pillar in the hierarchy of reliability engineering. Observability provides us with the ability to monitor the "unknown" and "unknowns" utilizing what is considered the three pillars of observability: *metrics*, *traces*, and *logs*. The goal of this section is not to introduce or define observability but to paint a picture of its importance in the practice and at the foundation of the reliability engineering pillars. We can then view our updated hierarchy to appear as follows:

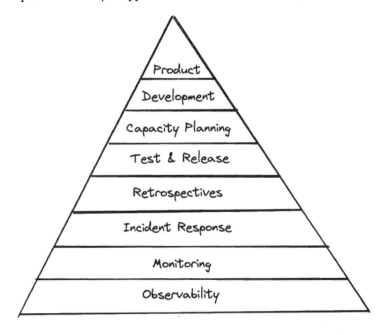

Figure 1.1 – The hierarchy of reliability engineering, which includes observability as the foundational building block

Figure 1.1 represents the updated hierarchy of reliability engineering, which includes the foundational layer of observability. You can also refer to Dickerson's original *Hierarchy of Reliability Engineering* and further information on it in *Part III* of *Site Reliability Engineering* (Google, Inc., 2017).

The next question you might have is, "What is the difference between observability and monitoring?". It happens often that the two are mentioned together, although they are not the same. Observability helps us monitor the known unknowns we are aware of, especially when considering aggregating data, while monitoring helps us identify the unknown unknowns. In simpler terms, one helps us monitor a problem we are aware of while the other helps us monitor and identify problems we are not aware of. We will investigate the two a bit more deeply in later chapters.

Responsibilities and objectives within each pillar

Within each pillar, various teams and stakeholders have distinct responsibilities and objectives geared toward ensuring reliability and resilience. The overarching goal of running successful workshops and thus ensuring successful implementation of your service level quantifiers aligns with your Reliability Engineering organization target goals. Those are as follows:

- Identify the overarching objectives of each pillar.
- Understand the required roles and responsibilities to accurately assign objectives to respective owners.
- Tie in the processes and overlaps for work within each pillar of another pillar. For incidents, retrospectives and incident response are separate pillars but contain several dependencies between them.

Although it's not the highlight of this chapter or book, it's important to understand the correlation between successful implementation and how aligned and structured the reliability engineering is within your organization. Even more important is how we communicate this information.

Effective communication and collaboration across layers are both essential for ensuring that reliability goals are aligned and achieved. This includes regular meetings, status updates, and progress reports shared between teams and stakeholders at different levels. Additionally, collaboration tools such as project management software, issue trackers, and documentation repositories can facilitate information sharing and coordination across teams. By fostering a culture of open communication and collaboration, organizations can break down silos and ensure that everyone is working toward common reliability objectives. As much as we may not want to admit it, how we communicate things and the amount of ease we provide regarding communication drastically affects the ability to consume information. This is an important soft skill for SREs working at various levels of an organization, as well as translating information to the target audience across several layers of the management pipeline.

Aligning reliability goals and objectives across the hierarchy

Alongside successfully communicating and collaborating at various levels of the management pipeline, being able to align reliability goals and objectives within the hierarchy is a further crucial skill. This is paramount for ensuring that efforts are focused on the most critical areas and that resources are allocated effectively. This is where setting clear performance metrics (SLIs), establishing SLOs, and defining escalation procedures across various SRE, engineering, and product teams provides support. By aligning on common objectives and metrics, teams and stakeholders can work together toward shared goals, fostering a culture of accountability and continuous improvement.

The hierarchical structure of reliability engineering is aimed at providing a framework within which reliability goals are defined, implemented, and monitored across infrastructure, application, and business layers. This is done through structuring various teams to collaborate through conversation, using processes developed and implemented within each pillar to foster alignment.

By delineating responsibilities, fostering collaboration, and aligning goals across the hierarchy, organizations can ensure the reliability and availability, within set performance thresholds (SLOs), of their systems and services, ultimately driving business success. In the section that follows, we will briefly discuss concepts within observability and monitoring that enable your technical teams to do just that.

The relationship between observability and monitoring

Observability and monitoring are indispensable components of reliability engineering, providing insights into system behaviors and performance. The simplified responsibility of this pillar is to ensure that the team can obtain the level of visibility into the system required to gather, aggregate, and synthesize data in a meaningful way. Observability specifically refers to the ability to understand and diagnose system behaviors through the collection and analysis of telemetry data. It encompasses the visibility, traceability, and understandability of system components, allowing engineers to gain insights into performance, latency, error rates, and other critical metrics. Observability is driven by telemetry, or the information and data that is used to produce insights for the respective consumers. You'll often hear logs mentioned in reference to telemetry data, which is not foreign if you are familiar with handling monitoring responsibilities. Metrics, system performance measurements and traces, and the journey of a request within the system are also forms of telemetry data. Despite not being the focus of the text, it's an important mention and thus covered a bit more in a later chapter.

Monitoring complements observability by providing capabilities for tracking SLIs and detecting deviations from expected behaviors in real time. It consists of the systematic collection processes used for the aggregation and analysis of observability data to detect anomalies, identify trends, and proactively address issues before they impact system reliability. We internally benefit from investing in both at the beginning stages, resulting in improvements in the quality of information available during later development stages and the incident management life cycle.

Together, observability and monitoring enable organizations to proactively identify and mitigate potential issues before they escalate, thereby enhancing system reliability. Each pillar serves as an indispensable practice for ensuring the reliability of systems and services in a structured manner, enabling your organization to maintain internal alignment and customer centricity. Both are critical to understand in relation to your SLI and SLO process to provide your team with additional insights into techniques and tools for gathering and analyzing observability data, as well as best practices for setting up effective monitoring systems and dashboards for later iteration phases.

How observability and monitoring contribute to SLIs and SLOs

Observability and monitoring play a pivotal role in the establishment of SLIs and SLOs, which serve as the foundation for measuring and maintaining system reliability. If we do not gather the right metadata within a system in a way that enables productive aggregation and synthesizing, then we will not be able to achieve insights that provide meaningful information regarding the customer experience. Let's go back to the earlier example of a person having a cold or high fever. We can monitor their temperature with a thermometer, or we can monitor whether they are hotter or cooler with the back of our hand. Both will tell us whether their temperature is worse or better but only one solution will provide us with a precise number that determines whether their temperature is within a specific threshold and requires additional care. This is how we want to think of observability and monitoring as it relates to acting as the foundation pieces for developing and feeding the appropriate metadata into our SLI and SLO metrics and thresholds.

By leveraging observability and its core data practices, organizations can define meaningful SLIs that accurately reflect system performance and health. We'll then shift toward our monitoring systems, which track these SLIs in real time, providing the data necessary to measure adherence to SLO thresholds and identify areas that require the team's attention prior to a live incident being logged. Although this is achieved through SLO dashboards, we can take advantage of alerting and monitoring capabilities within an observability or monitoring platform or tool of choice to aid in the following ways:

- Reducing the amount of downtime a service experiences through identifying issues before they occur.

- Improving KPI metrics for the customer experience such as NPS, customer churn rates, and customer acquisition rates through meeting SLOs.

- Improving internal **Mean Time to Detect** (MTTD), **Mean Time to Respond** (MTTR), and other metrics associated with the handling of live incidents as it relates to effectively detecting and quickly resolving issues.

In essence, the implementation of observability and monitoring provides the necessary insights to adequately create and build the feedback loops needed to iterate and refine SLIs and SLOs over time. This ensures that they remain relevant and aligned with overarching business goals and objectives.

Techniques and tools for gathering and analyzing observability data

The current state of your organization will determine the techniques and tooling of choice. It is best to always understand the fundamentals, even when procuring a third-party tool to understand your own user requirements, so you can ensure the tool can meet the current and future needs of your organization. Within the current market, at the time of writing this, there exist various techniques, frameworks, tools, and platforms for gathering and analyzing observability data. These range from tools for lightweight log aggregation and metric collection to ones for distributed tracing and performance profiling to commercially available platforms that support the creation and monitoring of SLIs and SLOs or provide a capability of another pillar within reliability engineering.

Commonly used tools for immediate use include Prometheus, Grafana, Jaeger, Elasticsearch, and Fluentd, which enable organizations to collect, store, visualize, and analyze observability data at scale. Additionally, techniques such as structured logging, distributed tracing, and application instrumentation can provide deeper insights into system behavior and performance, facilitating root cause analysis and troubleshooting. Regardless of the tooling, the underlying fundamentals as they relate to how you collect, aggregate, and use data will direct you toward the appropriate product.

Some best practices for setting up effective monitoring systems and dashboards

Setting up effective monitoring systems and dashboards requires careful planning, design, and implementation. If you are like me and only refer to certain chapters of certain books at the point in time when you need them, then you'll be glad to see that we'll cover some best practices within this section. If you are also like me and read through some books in their full entirety, then we will also cover this topic within a later chapter. In a nutshell, organizations should consider the following in order:

1. Start by defining clear objectives and requirements for monitoring, including the selection of relevant metrics for SLIs.
2. Identify key thresholds for each SLI, establishing meaningful targets that align with business goals and external commitments, possibly through an SLA.
3. Deploy monitoring agents, configure alerting rules, and design intuitive dashboards that provide real-time visibility into system performance.
4. Structure communication channels for regular reviews and updates to ensure tooling and processes remain effective and internal teams are responsive to changing requirements and conditions.

In a later chapter, we will cover this topic in a bit more depth. In addition, the previously mentioned steps depend heavily upon the current state of your organization and the implemented tooling of choice. However, both pillars provide the necessary visibility, insights, and feedback mechanisms needed to measure, maintain, and improve system performance over time. This makes both pillars, as well as their respective implementation practices, essential to the practice of reliability engineering and thus your SLIs' and SLOs' successful implementation. By leveraging observability data, organizations can define meaningful SLIs and SLOs, set up effective monitoring systems, and establish their own best practices for ensuring the reliability and resiliency of their systems and services.

The cost of not choosing SLIs

Beyond technical metrics, SLIs and SLOs have profound implications for business outcomes. My previous experience with SLIs and SLOs was specific to the services run by the team and internal product engineering teams. The introduction to both immediately reminded me of KPIs. I still firmly believe today that both are technical KPIs for platforms and services. Their implementations and target audiences just differ.

In a setting where your organization uses frameworks such as OKRs reporting the initiatives set to meet organizational strategies and business goals, you may run into instances where business groups and executives are using KPIs and your technical teams are using SLIs and SLOs to drive their SLAs. Understanding the similarities and differences of each, as well as their usages, will only set your organization up to have improved communication in collaborative environments where technical lingo is no longer a roadblock.

Writing this makes me hope that someone will publish evidence-based materials on their relationships and how executives can utilize each in their organization to more effectively achieve their goals. That's neither here nor there, just wishful thinking. By aligning SLIs and SLOs with key business objectives, organizations can quantitatively measure the impact of reliability on customer satisfaction, revenue generation, and brand reputation.

For instance, let's regress back to earlier mentions of **Net Promoter Score (NPS)** for customer satisfaction and customer churn rates. An NPS can inform your management team of the customer experience related to a company, product, or service. This metric might provide additional insight when assessing your overall customer churn rate, or the percentage of customers who discontinued business with your organization during some period using a specific formula. However, how do you then tie this into a specific piece of functionality that was due to poor technical implementation, a code patch, or simply a poor version of a release?

Within daily operations, it's very easy to focus on the metrics that fit within your silo. However, in my opinion, a more flexible organization will have a system in place to feed each of these metrics into the overall company objective to tell a clear story or sell a specific narrative.

The impact on business objectives, customer satisfaction, and brand reputation

The impact of inadequate SLI selection extends far beyond technical performance, affecting various aspects of business operations. Poor technical performance impacts the organization through inadequate performing systems. This can result in high incoming requests for customer support and success teams, as well as a high number of internal alerts to SRE and other product engineering teams to address various issues. An extensive period spent experiencing each issue can result in customers abandoning your product, employees leaving your organization, and a host of other problems. Each will also have an impact on financial implications. A product or service performing poorly will eventually result in revenue loss, penalties, and legal liabilities, undermining profitability and competitiveness. Furthermore, downtime and service interruptions can lead to dissatisfied customers, increased churn rates, and negative word-of-mouth, tarnishing the organization's reputation and hindering future growth opportunities.

In today's connected and distributed environment, where information is accessible with the click of a button (thereby making the customer experience increasingly critical), maintaining high levels of system reliability is essential for retaining loyal customers and attracting new ones. A single instance of downtime or poor performance can have far-reaching consequences in globally dispersed or startup organizations, driving customers to seek alternative solutions and damaging the organization's credibility in the marketplace.

Let's revert to earlier mentions of the NPS. It functions more as a survey mechanism where you receive a score from -100 to 100. Outside of direct responses, it does not truly assess the *why*, only that something was below average, average, or above average. This data can likely undergo synthesizing and aggregation to align with a period of high churn using the churn rate formula. We could then use this period to look at the performance of a specific technical product or service to provide an assessment of the following:

- Whether or not the poor metric was related to a poor-performing service or another mitigating factor.

- Whether the organization experienced poor service performance due to a period of high attrition, engineer burnout, or another human resource issue.

- Whether the degradation in customer success was due to a new feature or piece of functionality that did not meet the standards of the target customer base or merely did not perform as well as other market competitors.

- Whether internal engineering practices and a lack of a decision-making framework, as it relates to critical service availability and performance via error budget monitoring, prevented us from making go and no-go decisions.

Although this is a hypothetical scenario, SLIs and SLOs serve as critical tools for decision-making, enabling organizations to prioritize investments, allocate resources effectively, and drive continuous improvement initiatives that directly contribute to business success. This can either negatively or positively impact your KPIs or organizational goals.

A solid understanding of reliability engineering concepts, coupled with proficiency in SLIs, SLOs, observability, and monitoring, empowers individuals to navigate the complex area of system reliability with confidence and clarity. By recognizing the intrinsic relationship between technical metrics and business outcomes, individuals can drive meaningful change, enhance organizational resilience, and unlock new opportunities for innovation and further growth.

Accurately measuring system performance and reliability with case studies

To mitigate the risks associated with a lack of or inadequate practices for determining and maintaining system reliability, organizations must consider implementing processes for identifying and selecting appropriate SLIs that accurately measure system performance and reliability. Firstly, it is essential to align SLIs with key business objectives and customer expectations. By prioritizing indicators that directly impact business outcomes, organizations can ensure that monitoring efforts are focused on the most critical areas of concern.

Secondly, organizations should leverage a combination of quantitative and qualitative metrics to provide a comprehensive view of system performance. While quantitative metrics such as uptime, latency, and error rates are essential for measuring technical performance, qualitative metrics such as user satisfaction, response time, and usability provide valuable insights into the overall customer experience.

Finally, organizations should regularly review and refine their SLIs to ensure they remain relevant and meaningful in the evolving technological landscape. By staying agile and adaptable, organizations can respond quickly to changing business needs and market dynamics, ensuring that their monitoring efforts remain aligned with strategic objectives.

Additional examples and case studies

To illustrate the impact of SLIs and SLOs on system performance and thus your organization's key objectives, let's consider a few examples and case studies as selling points.

Gaming platform and services outage

In 2011 one of the largest brands, **Sony**, experienced a 24-day platform outage due to a security breach through illegal and unauthorized intrusion (https://www.gamesindustry.biz/playstation-networks-24-days-of-downtime-10-years-ago-this-month). This resulted in the leaking of approximately 77 million registered users' personal information and PlayStation credentials being obtained by an unauthorized individual. The PlayStation service being taken offline after not being sure whether financial information was leaked directly resulted in the network outage, with the restoration of certain services a week after the intrusion.

This scenario serves as an example of the need for reliability engineering, which is central to SLIs and SLOs. It also highlighted the need to understand the different system boundaries to identify key metrics to ensure extensive security coverage through implementing security features, as well as the need for a better understanding of points of vulnerability. In this case, the outage stemmed from a malicious attack via a user. However, files were identified on a server within the network, highlighting the need to include security engineers in your workshops. That's because security engineers can help to implement features such as the following:

- PCI compliance to improve how credit card information is secured and stored to provide additional reassurance to customers.
- Implementing vulnerability scans for additional vulnerability testing.
- Implementing penetration tests to replicate realistic potential attacks and identify security needs.
- Improve clarity surrounding areas such as e-commerce security to detect card skimming and other vulnerabilities to improve security for your customer base.

Through penetration testing and other testing mechanisms, organizations can create environments where they can produce relevant, albeit synthetic, data to report on the performance of their implemented security features.

The outage resulted in a class-action lawsuit that Sony settled for 15 million dollars in the form of free game downloads and additional identity theft protection services for impacted users (Sinclair, 2021). In this instance, the delay in implementing the correct authorization and authentication processes for internal servers and experiencing subsequent data breaches without mitigations highlighted the ongoing challenges, at the time, of ensuring that data is secure and reliable. This also highlights the importance of understanding each component that is implemented or integrated within your system to capture and monitor its performance and reliability.

Security is not often the first area considered when defining SLIs and objectives. However, implementing secure mechanisms and understanding the relevant touchpoints that create the boundaries for securing platforms and services is key to identifying the right metrics to monitor with SLIs. Evaluating security breaches includes various aspects of incident detection, response, and impact assessment. The number of incidents occurring within a defined timeframe can provide your team with an overview of the frequency and prevalence of security breaches, highlighting potential vulnerabilities requiring monitoring.

Severity metrics assess the impact of breaches on confidentiality, integrity, and availability of data and systems, aiding in prioritizing response efforts. **Time to Detection (TTD)** measures the efficiency of detection mechanisms by tracking the duration between breach occurrence and detection, with shorter TTD indicating more effective detection capabilities. Similarly, **Time to Respond (TTR)** gauges the efficacy of response processes, measuring the time taken to mitigate breaches after detection.

Assessing the scope of affected assets, including compromised systems and sensitive data, offers insight into the breadth of the breach's impact.

Further understanding the root causes of breaches enables organizations to address underlying vulnerabilities and strengthen security controls. Quantifying the financial costs through key security metrics and SLIs associated with breaches, including direct losses, regulatory fines, and reputational damage, aids in assessing the overall impact and justifying security investments. Analyzing attack vectors and incident response effectiveness provides valuable insights for enhancing security posture and resilience against future threats. Finally, monitoring compliance adherence ensures that security measures align with regulatory requirements and industry standards, mitigating the risk of non-compliance penalties.

These examples not only demonstrate the critical role of reliability engineering and SLIs/SLOs in ensuring stability, security, and long-term viability but also emphasize the importance of focusing on the user persona and user journey of the system to capture customer-centric workflows. We hope the workshop portion of the book helps your team collaborate and have the necessary discussions to further develop indicators and objectives to effectively monitor security-related features and performance.

Cloud service provider performance issues

In 2021, Google, a cloud service provider, experienced an extremely impactful networking issue due to a failure to monitor key SLIs related to network latency and availability, resulting in performance and reliability degradation (https://www.reuters.com/technology/google-amazon-several-other-websites-down-2021-11-16/). This led to customer dissatisfaction and increased churn rates, ultimately impacting the provider's market share and profitability.

In response to global outages, including disruptions in Snapchat, Spotify, and Google Cloud Networking services, several critical SLIs and SLOs could have been implemented alongside reliability engineering practices to mitigate incidents. In some instances, such as Google Cloud Networking Services, they likely were.

Key metrics for areas such as network uptime, measuring the availability of the network's internal infrastructure to ensure uninterrupted connectivity on an SLO dashboard, could have helped to identify a potential outage prior to the issue occurring. In addition to tracking response time metrics, measuring the responsiveness of cloud services such as Spotify and Google Cloud to end user requests, and error rate, capturing the occurrence of errors or disruption internal to the infrastructure, could have also helped.

By monitoring these metrics and aggregating their respective data to form queries that report on the user experience (SLIs), companies can work toward achieving uninterrupted connectivity and timely access to their platforms for users. Additionally, defining SLOs for service availability and incident response time sets clear targets for maintaining reliability and levels of operational excellence, as well as quickly addressing any disruptions that may occur, improving the overall customer experience.

To strengthen the reliability of their services, companies can implement various other reliability engineering practices. Some practices we'd like to highlight, although they're not the central focus of our discussion, include designing redundant architectures with failover mechanisms to ensure continuous service availability in the face of infrastructure failures. If we regress back to monitoring concepts, automating their processes and alerting systems, which play a crucial role in proactively identifying and addressing potential issues before they escalate, also helps to identify weaknesses in the system's resilience under controlled conditions.

Root cause analysis, which we will cover a bit more in a later chapter, following incidents allows organizations to identify underlying issues and implement corrective actions to prevent recurrence. Finally, capacity planning and scalability efforts ensure that cloud services can effectively handle fluctuations in their workload(s) without compromising performance or reliability. By implementing SLIs and SLOs, along with other reliability engineering pillars, companies can enhance the resilience of their distributed services and minimize the impact of service disruptions on users and clients.

Social media outage

In October 2021, a popular social media platform, **Facebook**, experienced a seven-hour outage that resulted in the loss of 79 million dollars in revenue (`https://engineering.fb.com/2021/10/05/networking-traffic/outage-details/`). The platform experienced a prolonged outage that could have possibly been mitigated sooner through SLI selection and SLO monitoring. This resulted in widespread user frustration and negative media coverage, damaging the platform's reputation and credibility in the eyes of both users and advertisers.

In this scenario, the implementation of SLIs and SLOs could have been used to monitor the network performance of components within the infrastructure. When considering network performance, it's important to measure the percentage of time the network remains operational and able to connect data centers to the internet, with an associated SLO ensuring a high uptime, perhaps targeting 99.9%. Additionally, monitoring DNS server reachability would be crucial, ensuring DNS servers can respond to user queries consistently, aiming for an availability determined by previous instances of throttling. Incident response time could also be tracked by setting an SLO on your agents to determine the detection time when SLO dashboards are implemented and configured to develop anomalies within the network.

If we consider the overall practice of reliability engineering, establishing a **Recovery Time Objective (RTO)** is also essential, defining the maximum acceptable duration for restoring network connectivity and service functionality post-outage, perhaps within a time frame that's ideal for the most critical use cases for your service or platform.

Earlier references were made to capacity planning practices; they are critical to the success of reliability. Proactively managing network capacity to accommodate traffic fluctuations without performance degradation, supported by specific SLOs, will ensure your organization is deploying and utilizing the appropriate amount of hardware and drive resource allocation decisions, ultimately improving profitability metrics over time.

Incorporate SLIs and SLOs that aggregate data on key components of the system such that reports on functionality and usability will enhance the reliability of their network infrastructure for customers.

Summary

In this chapter, we learned that SLIs and SLOs are essential components of reliability engineering and that they are implemented through observability and monitoring processes, as well as tooling. This helps to provide measurable targets for system reliability and performance as it relates to the customer versus engineering experience, as we explored in this chapter. By understanding the RE hierarchy, its relationship to observability and monitoring, and the long-term and domino effect resulting from not implementing the appropriate indicators, organizations can begin their journey toward system-related customer centricity. We covered this in this chapter as well. Internal engineers can also effectively monitor, measure, and improve the reliability of their systems and services as it relates to incident management and the impact of incidents on the customer, as this chapter explained. We further learned that through careful consideration and implementation of SLIs and SLOs, organizations can ensure they deliver and maintain high-quality, reliable, and resilient products for their customers.

Beginning the journey of defining and implementing SLIs and SLOs as a collaborative organization can seem challenging at first. With a solid understanding of reliability engineering concepts and methodologies, you can approach this with the necessary confidence to encourage your team and broader organization.

By leveraging the capabilities of SLIs, SLOs, observability, and monitoring, individuals can develop robust strategies for defining meaningful redefining system performance, establish relevant SLO thresholds for mitigating incidents before they occur, and implement effective monitoring solutions. Moreover, understanding the business impact of indicators can empower your organization to align technical metrics with organizational goals, driving tangible value and fostering a culture of reliability excellence.

By implementing robust monitoring strategies and regularly reviewing and refining SLIs and SLOs, organizations can mitigate the risks associated with inadequate SLI selection and maintain high levels of system reliability, customer satisfaction, and brand reputation. In the chapter that follows, we will cover the importance of having a team that is responsible for kickstarting this journey and key roles that you may want to include to ensure diverse perspectives.

Further reading

Here, you can find the referenced articles and books for additional reading about concepts mentioned in this chapter:

- Extensions Built Upon Ancient Foundations. *Perspectives on Psychological Science*, 292-314.

- Engineering at Meta. (2021, October 5). *More details about the October 4 Outage.* Retrieved from: `https://engineering.fb.com/2021/10/05/networking-traffic/outage-details/`.

- Google, Inc. (2017). *Site Reliability Engineering: How Google Runs Production Systems.* Sebastopol: O'Reilly Media.

- Reuters. (2021, November 16). *Google Cloud, Snap, Spotify back up after brief outage.* Retrieved from: `https://www.reuters.com/technology/google-amazon-several-other-websites-down-2021-11-16/`.

- Sinclair, B. (2021, April 14). *PlayStation Network's 24 days of downtime.* Retrieved from: `https://www.gamesindustry.biz/playstation-networks-24-days-of-downtime-10-years-ago-this-month`.

2

Establishing an SLI and SLO Team

In the previous chapter, we highlighted the hierarchy of pillars that make up what we know as the practice of reliability engineering. In addition, we were able to center the foundational principles around **Service Level Indicators** (**SLIs**), what they are, why we need them, and what they mean to reliability engineering. In this chapter, you can expect to explore many of the critical aspects of implementing SLIs and **Service Level Objectives** (**SLOs**) using a dedicated team. Your SLIs and SLOs play a crucial role in ensuring the reliability, availability, and performance of your systems and services. It is equally important to have the right mix of team members to bring your indicators to fruition.

We will first examine the significance of having a dedicated team for creating and managing your SLIs and SLOs, provide guidelines for assembling and tailoring the team, and discuss strategies for adapting the structure to organizational dynamics.

While this chapter of the book may seem straightforward, it is crucial to structure the right team members for the right tasks, just as it is to identify the correct metrics for the appropriate system components. In addition, increased organization and unification of a team can help to improve organizational buy-in and increase adoption rates and the ability to embed within the overall culture through more streamlined processes.

In this chapter, we'll cover the following main topics:

- The significance of a dedicated team
- Guidelines for team assembly
- Tailoring to team and organizational needs
- Adapting the structure to organizational dynamics

Let's get started!

The significance of a dedicated team

In the pursuit of system reliability and increased performance, having a dedicated team that is focused on managing SLIs and SLOs continuously proves to remain a priority. This section elaborates on the significance of such a team, highlighting its importance, and delineating the roles and responsibilities of team members. We will also discuss the benefits of centralizing SLI and SLO management through additional case studies and examples that showcase the impact of a dedicated team on reliability and performance improvement.

If SLIs are to be implemented within a business domain, group, or organization, it's essential to involve a mix of internal roles involved in the conversation. When initially discussing reliability engineering, we immediately shift to concepts such as availability, software, and systems engineers or developers. We need to shift this perspective toward including our program, product, and project managers, which are tied closely to the product as it relates to the customer experience and user requirements. It's not only important to create and implement objectives but also important that we think of the ongoing maintenance, reducing scope creep, and ensuring healthy channels are maintained between the technical team, the work being done, and the stakeholders invested in the initiative.

The importance of leveraging a dedicated team for SLI and SLO management

The importance of having a dedicated team for managing SLIs and SLOs cannot be overstated. Such a team is essential for ensuring that reliability goals are clearly defined, monitored, and maintained over time. By centralizing responsibility within a dedicated team for leading their SLI and SLO initiatives, organizations can ensure accountability, consistency, and alignment with business objectives.

If we take the approach of comparing it to a piece of internal infrastructure, think of the kernel in a Linux operating system, the control plane in a Kubernetes cluster, or the main branch in your production repository. There needs to be a single source of truth, and this source of truth needs to be managed in a way that is easily consumable by external customers, in some cases, and the broader organization.

Roles and responsibilities of team members, including SLI owners and stakeholders

Within a dedicated team for SLIs and SLOs, various roles and responsibilities are assigned to ensure effective management and oversight. This oversight alleviates many knowledge gaps and ensures an all-hands-on-deck approach from various perspectives within an organization. For the most part, when the need arises for SLIs, we want to ensure they are created in a way that enables the team to tie the data to internal metrics that are important to upper management. This can include metrics that contribute to internally holding technical teams accountable or support decision-making related to external commitments such as product **Service Level Agreements** (**SLAs**). In some instances, management may simply want quantifiable metrics in place to ensure nothing goes awry.

It can even consist of a team of individuals who simply want to implement these measurements to improve the work that they are completing, reduce technical toil and debt, or ensure they can report back to internal leaders regarding how their service is performing. Either way, none of the reasons are incorrect. We want to put our best foot forward to ensure that we can do these things in the most efficient way possible. Success greatly depends on the team composition, and ensuring that everyone contributes, owns, and develops the process to help capture the necessary voices and perspectives.

The following are roles that were central and key to the implementation of SLIs and SLOs within my team's organization:

- **SRE**: The group of SREs that are going to own the **end-to-end (E2E)** SRE process. This group is responsible for driving the definition, monitoring, and optimization practices for SLIs and SLOs to accurately measure system performance.

- **SLI owners**: They are also tasked with setting, monitoring, and ensuring that SLO targets are met. This group will include the SREs or other software developers who are familiar with the product or service being measured and will own the SLIs once they are handed off, if not maintained by the initial SRE team.

- **Program managers (PMs)**: PMs are tasked with the overarching responsibility of ensuring that the work that is being done can be tied back into the strategic goals of the broader organization. This reverts to the mention of scope creep within a program or project. This is something that is often downplayed but alleviates the responsibility of documentation and organization alignment from engineers who will need to focus mainly on the technical aspects of the initiatives.

- **Stakeholders**: This can include external customers, engineers, executives, or anyone else investing in or sponsoring the SLI and SLO initiatives. They will play a crucial role in providing input, feedback, and support to the team, ensuring that reliability goals are aligned with broader organizational objectives and consumer requirements.

- **Product engineers**: The engineers that are responsible for the design, development, and maintenance of the product and services requiring SLIs and SLOs. It's important to schedule your workshops surrounding this audience as they will have the most insights into the current state of the system and system boundaries.

Roles and responsibilities are mentioned to provide insight. This does not mean that you will have one from each category, or that you need to include all of them. It is to raise awareness of specific roles to internally identify, if required. Assigning the responsibilities of SLI and SLO management to a dedicated team offers numerous benefits for an organization. By consolidating responsibility within a single team, organizations can do the following:

- Streamline communication, coordination, and decision-making processes to improve communication throughout the SLO management journey.

- Facilitate a more cohesive and effective approach to reliability management improving internal buy-in and adoption rates.

- Leverage collective expertise, best practices, and lessons learned to drive continuous improvement and innovation in reliability engineering practices.

If your organization plans to package and sell reliability as a service, then it is even more important that the various roles work together to ensure customer success through individuals who own the external communication pipeline. Different experiences lead to different perspectives and voices contributing to innovation.

The goal of this book is not to reinvent the wheel but rather to guide you through solutions to challenges experienced throughout the SLO design, implementation, and management journey. Therefore, if you are interested in learning more regarding the various structures of SRE teams, then I suggest you review the blog text, *How SRE teams are organized, and how to get started* (details can be found in the *Further reading* section) by former Google SREs as a starting point. In a nutshell, you will learn how SRE teams have been structured within different organizations:

- **Kitchen sink SRE teams**: A single SRE team doing everything within a smaller scope, seen primarily in organizations where SRE is starting.

- **Infrastructure-based SRE teams**: Teams that are focused primarily on infrastructure-related tasks, typically clusters and CI/CD operations.

- **Tooling-focused SRE teams**: SRE teams that focus primarily on improving the developer experience through various types of tooling.

- **Product/application-specific SRE teams**: SRE teams that focus on business-critical or targeted applications and services.

- **Embedded SRE teams**: SRE teams that are placed within other development teams to ensure SRE alignment. This can be aligned with a product, service, or application team.

- **Consulting SRE teams**: Like embedded SRE teams, except consultants are not going to write or manage customers' application code and configurations.

So far, we understand the importance of having a dedicated team and what role each team member and stakeholder plays. Let's solidify this learning with the help of an example case study.

A case study to illustrate the impact of a dedicated team

There are several case studies and examples that highlight the tangible impact of a dedicated team on service reliability and performance improvement. We can also conclude that the main contributor to the success of your SRE organization is understanding the type of SRE team required and then staffing it with the right mix of individuals and skill sets to see the process through.

For instance, a leading bank, Standard Chartered Bank, embarked on its SRE journey, which included first creating a dedicated team. Let's take a look at this case study, which can also be viewed via the DevOps Institute as *From Pilot to Scale, The Successful SRE Journey at a Large Financial Institution*. To build their team, the bank took the following actions:

- Initiated an approved pilot within their organization by forming a team of five individual SRE "evangelists" that they felt would benefit from the model.

- Enabled/allowed the SREs to maintain continuous and iterative conversations with key stakeholders and individuals key to the practice of SRE.

- Trained everyone on the core and foundational principles of SRE.

- Assigned each SRE a single application that they were responsible for building the SRE journey for.

Richard Hall, the organization's Global Head of Transformation, Resilience, and Architecture for Functions T&I, coined it in *From Pilot to Scale*:

> "Continuous learning was a major factor in successfully changing the mindset within our team. We put education at the heart of our program, and we have gone from 'What is SRE?', to now being asked, when SRE can be deployed on their applications."

This statement is crucial for two reasons:

- It validates the importance of investing time upfront in your employees and understanding the need to allocate time for learning and communication during the process.

- The former validates these findings because they opted to hire individuals they felt would benefit from the model, not due to them already having had experience with a specific model.

This case highlights the importance of diverse perspectives and roles in guiding the SRE journey. It is also necessary to state that this team started with five SREs and can also be described as a research and innovation team. This means that your organization may initially start with a team of just five SRE engineers. And that, too, is okay.

A dedicated team for managing SLIs and SLOs plays a crucial role in ensuring improved system performance and availability. By delegating responsibility to a central team, defining clear roles and responsibilities, and leveraging collective expertise, organizations can drive improvements in reliability with improved efficiency in less time, enhance customer satisfaction, and, ultimately, achieve greater success in today's increasingly distributed environments.

Guidelines for team assembly

Assembling a dedicated SLI and SLO management team requires careful consideration of various factors. Organizations must assess the scope and complexity of their reliability objectives, as well as the resources available for team assembly. As previously mentioned, in some organizations, this task might begin as a single-member team. Additionally, factors such as organizational structure, culture, and existing processes need to be considered to ensure internal alignment with other teams and request support for the dedicated team.

With many organizations in the current workforce trying to increase the efficiency of remote and hybrid work styles, it is important to understand that when structuring your team, it is a must that you take inventory of the current culture and hierarchy of your organization to ensure the accuracy of identified candidates. This includes whether you are required to hire external SREs to join your organization. Having worked on globally distributed teams within the last year of writing this text, my team took the liberty of assessing management styles in remote environments. Some questions that you may want to ask before building your SRE team are as follows:

- **Does our organization have internal SRE engineers?**

  If the answer to this question is yes, then you will need to take inventory of whether it is a single team or many teams within an organization. If there are many teams, are there SRE teams that can invest in the process by allocating a few engineers to the initiative? If it's a single team, then are you able to reprioritize the work you do in a way that makes room to build out a more structured SRE team?

  If your organization does not have an SRE team, then it's important to understand why you want to adopt SRE to help identify the type of SRE team you want to build. That is not to say the trajectory will remain the same but as a friend once said, "*If you don't know where you are going, then any road is likely to get you there. Just start.*" It will prove helpful if you can assess the current workload and processes to guide your SRE process in a direction that supports the organization and the current work being done.

- **What type of SRE team do we assume we want?**

  If your organization is new to SRE, this question may not be immediately clear. Something like the previously mentioned Google blog regarding the types of SRE teams that exist can help you determine the answer to this question based on your current state.

Another audit those invested can take is assessing the type of tooling, platforms, or applications that are currently used to support service management. This should help guide you in the right direction. Often, speaking to or surveying internal development and product teams' pain points can act as another avenue of assessment.

Internal colleagues are going to want to invest in anything that solves a problem and improves workflow efficiency. If it results in economic or monetary gains while eliminating or reducing complex problems within the customer experience, then you're speaking the stakeholder's language. Improving the latter also reduces the workloads and requests submitted to internal support and customer success teams.

Identifying key stakeholders and subject matter experts within the organization

Identifying key stakeholders and subject matter experts within the organization is essential for ensuring the success of the dedicated team. These individuals bring valuable insights, domain knowledge, and organizational context to the conversation. They will also help the team to navigate facilitation and collaboration while ensuring alignment with broader business objectives is maintained. Key stakeholders may include internal engineers, external customers, operations personnel, and executives, among many others.

In the event your organization is newly adopting SRE, the task at hand may also include marketing or selling the idea of SRE to internal stakeholders. This relates to the earlier task of identifying internal pain points that SREs can solve and mapping monetary gains and losses. Does your organization have external SLAs that do not include internal mechanisms to ensure they are met? Marketing the idea of utilizing SLOs to the value of dollars lost if/when an SLA is breached will help drive the selling point.

My previous experience also includes working in development and technical support teams. An insight that I have developed is that there are customers who hold an organization to the SLA commitments that they make down to the dollar. What this means is that if a customer signs a contract with an expected SLA and continuously finds themselves submitting issues to the support team regarding downtime and outages, a good percentage of customers invest the time to do the calculations to request monetary reimbursement. This is also not limited to contracts and includes externally available SLA guidelines, too.

You can then market this to your organization as an opportunity to operate more efficiently in a way that notifies us before we breach, as well as enables the organization to forecast and make technical decisions before disrupting the customer's experience with our platform, products, and services.

Skills and expertise required for effective SLI and SLO management

Effective SLI and SLO management requires a diverse set of skills and expertise. It is not a requirement but can lighten the load on the team if team members possess skills such as technical proficiency in areas such as data analysis, monitoring tools, and system architecture, as well as strong communication and collaboration skills. It is commonly observed that some of the most technically skilled individuals may not excel in communication and collaboration. Even if they are the best, sometimes the focus needs to shift to the technical work required and utilize a program or project manager to handle much of the communication and collaboration external to the team, if needed. This also passively helps the team to maintain better control of documenting processes and implementation workflows. The same way we refer to engineer burnout in incident management is the same consideration we should have throughout the SLO journey.

Additionally, domain-specific knowledge related to the organization's products, services, and customer needs is crucial for defining meaningful SLIs and SLOs that align with business objectives. If your current SREs lack this knowledge, then collaborating among product staff can help fill in the necessary gaps.

Tailoring to team and organizational needs

While identifying individuals to create and structure your team or once you have created your team, it is going to be crucial to customize the SLI and SLO management practices to suit the unique requirements of both the team and organization to achieve success in reliability engineering. This section emphasizes the importance of tailoring SLIs and SLOs to align with specific organizational needs and objectives, reducing the occurrence of adding or increasing silos through consistent communication processes and feedback loops.

Incorporating feedback-friendly processes in this section is highlighted as a crucial aspect of effective SLI and SLO management if you want to increase proactive response. By taking a more structured approach to soliciting and analyzing feedback from stakeholders, product-centered engineers, and other required individuals, organizations can gain valuable insights into the effectiveness of their SLIs and SLOs and identify areas for improvement. This iterative process enables organizations to continuously refine and optimize their reliability practices to better meet the shifting needs of their users and stakeholders.

Ensuring alignment with organizational objectives and priorities is essential for maximizing the impact of SLI and SLO management efforts. When we align SLIs and SLOs with broader organizational goals, teams can ensure that their reliability initiatives contribute directly to the success of the business. This alignment fosters a cohesive approach to reliability engineering, where every effort is directed toward achieving strategic objectives and driving business value.

Tailoring SLI and SLO management practices to the specific needs of the team and organization is a foundational aspect of effective reliability engineering and will increase the acceptance of the shift in a new direction. This is also an important task when considering managing change. By creating SLIs and SLOs, incorporating feedback mechanisms, and aligning with organizational objectives, your team will optimize their reliability practices and achieve greater success in meeting the needs of their users and stakeholders at a much more rapid pace.

Incorporating feedback mechanisms

Incorporating feedback mechanisms is essential for continuously refining and improving SLI and SLO definitions. This may include soliciting input from stakeholders, gathering insights from monitoring data, and conducting regular reviews and retrospectives to assess the effectiveness of existing metrics and objectives. By embracing a culture of continuous improvement, organizations can adapt their SLIs and SLOs to evolving business needs and technological landscapes. To get your team started on the right track, you can consider and incorporate the following guidelines to start building out your process, as depicted in *Figure 2.1*.

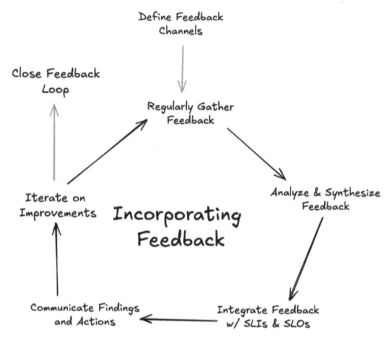

Figure 2.1 – Incorporating feedback into SLO feedback loops

Figure 2.1 shows the workflow for incorporating feedback mechanisms as a solution to meet the needs of your team and broader organization:

1. **Define feedback channels**: Establish clear channels for collecting feedback from various stakeholders, including users, customers, internal teams, and management. Typical methods include surveys, user interviews, support tickets, feedback forms, user forums, and social media platforms. Lean more toward channels that are accessible and convenient for your target audience during the beginning stages to ease the data collection process during the infant stages.

   The team can set aside time to solicit different internal channels that may already be in place internally and merely adopt the process that stakeholders and others are accustomed to, to decrease the amount of time required to ramp up on a new process.

2. **Regularly gather feedback**: Implement processes that support a healthy cadence for regularly gathering feedback at key touchpoints throughout the user journey. Establishing the right cadence for collecting feedback is just as important as selecting the appropriate method. It ensures that data is gathered at the most relevant points in the user journey. Too much or too little feedback can have a negative or positive impact on stakeholders and any other individuals you are attempting to win over during this process. Soliciting feedback from stakeholders, users, and customers after key interactions is important throughout the entire process to confirm that the team is on the right track. Feedback is not only necessary for stages such as product

launches, feature releases, service outages, or support interactions but is imperative during the beginning stages to ensure that "what" is being measured and "how" it is being measured remain in alignment with the overall goal. Ensure that feedback collection is ongoing and systematic to capture insights in real time.

3. **Analyze and synthesize feedback**: Once feedback has been collected, analyze and synthesize the data to identify common themes, trends, and patterns. During the initial stages, qualitative and quantitative analysis techniques can provide valuable insights into user preferences, though they may not be essential early on. During later stages when personas have been developed, user journeys outlined and defined, and SLIs and SLOs created, we may want to consider this a bit more. Moreover, take inventory of pain points and areas for improvement communicated by those you are interacting with or interviewing. Prioritize feedback based on its impact on SLIs, the SLO process, as well as organizational objectives.

4. **Integrate feedback into SLIs and SLOs**: During the later stages of SLI and SLO development, the team must understand how to use feedback insights to inform the definition and refinement of SLIs and SLOs. If we take inventory of requirements during the infant stages, we can and will create processes that do not require as much refinement later in the process. The team should proactively identify opportunities to adjust SLIs and SLOs based on user feedback to better align with user expectations and priorities. Ensure that SLIs and SLOs are aligned with user needs and contribute to improved reliability, performance, and user satisfaction.

5. **Communicate findings and actions**: Communicate feedback findings and actions taken to address feedback to relevant stakeholders across the organization. Share insights from feedback analysis, as well as any changes or improvements made to SLIs and SLOs because of feedback. Transparency and communication are essential for building trust and engagement with stakeholders. The sentiment here is like developing a healthy cadence; the method of communication used to communicate findings and actions is correlated to the customer experience for internal stakeholders and engineering teams, as well as externally facing customers if your service level journey includes them.

6. **Iterate and improve**: Use feedback as a catalyst for continuous improvement in SLI and SLO management processes. Iterate on SLIs and SLOs based on ongoing feedback and data-driven insights. Regularly review and update SLIs and SLOs to ensure that they remain relevant and effective in supporting organizational goals and meeting user expectations. We will dive more into this in the third part of this book, which will include practices for doing so.

7. **Close the feedback loop**: Close the feedback loop by following up with users and stakeholders to communicate how their feedback has been addressed and implemented. Acknowledge and thank users for their input and demonstrate how their feedback has influenced decision-making and improvements. Closing the feedback loop fosters trust and accountability with stakeholders and encourages ongoing engagement in the feedback process. It also showcases to other internal teams the impact of doing so. In some instances, it may require you to further engage with the team and continue through the cycle, shifting back toward regularly gathering feedback.

Much of software and technology development and maintenance is done through iterative approaches. The same philosophy is utilized for the SLO design, implementation, and management processes. As with most iterative approaches, success is achieved more efficiently when collaboration and alignment between different functions occurs.

Ensuring alignment with organizational objectives

Ensuring alignment between quantified performance and organizational objectives through service level measurements is critical for driving success in reliability engineering. SLIs and SLOs should be directly tied to business outcomes and priorities, such as customer satisfaction, revenue generation, and operational efficiency. By establishing clear alignment between technical metrics and organizational goals, teams can demonstrate the value of reliability engineering and garner support from key stakeholders, while providing internal accountability for meeting SLAs with external customers.

Tailoring SLI and SLO management practices to meet the specific needs of the team and organization is essential for achieving success in reliability engineering. By customizing SLIs and SLOs, incorporating feedback mechanisms, and ensuring alignment with organizational objectives, organizations can drive continuous improvement and deliver reliable and resilient systems and services that meet the needs of customers and stakeholders.

Adapting the structure to organizational dynamics

Adapting the structure of the SLI and SLO management team to organizational dynamics is essential for success in reliability engineering. This summary encapsulates key insights from the chapter, including strategies for adaptation, addressing challenges, implementing agile approaches, and building resilience into the management framework. Once your team is identified, establish clear guiding principles to maintain alignment with objectives and stay on course.

Strategies for adapting the structure

Organizational dynamics vary widely across different companies and industries. Therefore, it's crucial to adapt the structure of the SLI and SLO management team to fit the specific needs and dynamics of the organization. This may involve restructuring teams, reallocating resources, and adjusting processes to ensure alignment with broader organizational goals and objectives. To ensure internal alignment between your organization's indicators and objectives, your team will need to do the following:

- **Understand organizational goals**: Before beginning your service-level journey, you'll want to start by ensuring that you understand your organization's overarching goals and objectives. Ask yourself and your team, "*What are the key priorities for your organization?*" and "*How does your organization define success?*". These are questions that can be asked of the stakeholders involved with your SLO initiative and of any other teams or lines of management that you are required to interface with regarding the service or process you are to measure. Understanding these goals will help you tailor your SLIs and SLOs to directly support these objectives.

The way we adapt the implementation to fit the organizational culture and dynamics plays a crucial role in the success of adoption. It is imperative to understand what the broader organization or business groups are utilizing internally to better find alignment in the team that you are building and the SLIs and objectives your team will choose to measure.

- **Identify key performance metrics**: Upon understanding the overarching organizational goals, you'll want to then identify the critical performance metrics that directly impact your organization's success. These could include metrics related to system reliability, availability, performance, and user experience. Consult with stakeholders from various departments to ensure that you capture a comprehensive view of performance requirements. This step is crucial to gain visibility into what the organization is currently measuring and how each metric is being measured.

  The typical organization will likely maintain performance metrics surrounding operational, financial, and many other areas. The goal here is to understand what success looks like for your organization and possibly capture whether these metrics relate to or tie back to the customer experience, and how. We can think of this as an exploratory step that can act as an additional avenue to identify customer personas and customer sentiment and find alignment between organizational KPIs and future SLIs and SLOs.

You may also want to collaborate with customer-facing teams to help identify internal SLAs that can act as a starting point. It is also possible for an organization to have external commitments without developing the internal and necessary processes for technical accountability.

Addressing challenges

Organizational silos, conflicting priorities, and communication barriers are common challenges that can impede the effectiveness of SLI and SLO management efforts. To address these challenges, organizations must foster collaboration, break down silos, and establish clear lines of communication between teams and stakeholders. Additionally, creating a shared understanding of priorities and goals can help mitigate conflicts and ensure alignment across the organization. The previously mentioned challenges are difficult to resolve outside of SLI and SLO management.

To better support the process, let's outline ways to address and potentially resolve each respective challenge:

- **Foster collaboration**: Encourage collaboration across different teams and departments involved in SLI and SLO management. This is a must as the SRE teams managing the process will need to communicate with stakeholders and engineers who maintain the subject matter expertise necessary for the platform, application, or service they are measuring. Foster a culture of openness, trust, and knowledge-sharing to break down silos and promote teamwork. Silos are one of the top reasons for communication breakdowns within an organization. This issue often goes unnoticed until it becomes a significant challenge. We will discuss more of this in a later section when agile methodologies and processes are mentioned.

- **Break down silos**: Identify and address organizational silos that may hinder collaboration and communication. Encourage transparency and information-sharing between teams by promoting cross-departmental visibility and cooperation. Establish channels for sharing insights, best practices, and lessons learned across the organization to facilitate a more integrated approach to SLI and SLO management.

Silos tend to arise because of how we manage communication frequency and methods when compared to the overall need of specific teams or business groups within an organization. Silos tend to be caused by three main reasons:

- Emphasis placed on domain expertise versus general and cross-functional knowledge

- Processes are divided among multiple owners

- Geographic dispersion

In addition, silos can occur without realizing they are occurring. In the **Price Waterhouse Cooper (PwC)** text, *Dealing with Market Disruption: 7 Strategies for Breaking Down Silos*, a few strategies to avoid the shift toward silos or to break down existing silos are mentioned. Highlighted in the following list are actions/tasks to keep top of mind to reduce the chances of occurring or reoccurring silos:

- Align leaders and build governance

- Create cross-functional teams

- Create clear roles and responsibilities

- Create join incentives

- Co-locate teams during the transformation period

- Create a "two in a box" structure

- Clarify decision rights

- **Establish clear communication channels**: Improve communication channels and processes to ensure that information flows smoothly between teams and stakeholders. Use a combination of communication tools such as email, chat platforms, and project management software to facilitate communication and collaboration. Establish clear roles, responsibilities, and escalation paths to streamline communication and decision-making processes.

- **Create a shared understanding of priorities**: Align teams and stakeholders around common priorities and goals related to SLI and SLO management. Communicate the importance of reliability, performance, and user satisfaction as organizational priorities. Facilitate discussions and workshops to create a shared understanding of the significance of SLIs and SLOs in achieving these priorities and goals.

- **Mitigate conflicting priorities**: Address conflicting priorities by facilitating open dialogue and negotiation between stakeholders. Encourage teams to identify areas of overlap and potential conflicts early on and work together to find mutually beneficial solutions. Prioritize initiatives and projects based on their alignment with organizational goals and the potential impact on SLIs and SLOs.

- **Provide training and education**: Invest in training and education programs to enhance the skills and knowledge of teams involved in SLI and SLO management. Offer workshops, seminars, and online courses to help teams develop a deeper understanding of SLI and SLO concepts, best practices, and tools. Empower teams to take ownership of SLI and SLO management by providing them with the necessary resources and support. This can also be the output of the process developed by the initial SRE team, which is true for many organizations with reliability engineering organizations.

By implementing these strategies, organizations can overcome the challenges of organizational silos, conflicting priorities, and communication barriers in SLI and SLO management efforts. By fostering collaboration, breaking down silos, establishing clear communication channels, creating a shared understanding of priorities, and mitigating conflicting priorities, organizations can enhance the effectiveness and impact of their SLI and SLO management practices.

Implementing the best approach for your team

Agile and iterative approaches to SLI and SLO management enable organizations to adapt quickly to changing requirements and conditions. Embracing agile methodologies such as Scrum or Kanban will help teams prioritize tasks, respond to feedback, and deliver value incrementally. This iterative approach allows organizations to continuously refine and improve their SLIs and SLOs based on real-world data and feedback. It also improves the implementation process for the SRE team and other staff.

Many organizations tend to utilize an agile methodology or certain capabilities of the agile methodology to build software, processes, and run teams. Agile methodologies and their alternatives are utilized for the ability to iterate and work in short sprints at a faster cadence. It does not necessarily mean it is always the right approach but is utilized when development or an initiative requires a framework that enables them to respond quickly to change and release changes in an incremental manner.

Alternatives to agile approaches

As previously mentioned, the goal of this section is not to persuade you to adopt a specific methodology or to even advocate for or against one. It is to raise awareness of the things that, if considered during the beginning stages for your team and use case, will only simplify things in the long term. There are many alternatives available to utilize. Some teams may even find it best to simply isolate specific workflows from a methodology to use within the team. Let's have a look at other alternatives that our SRE or implementation team can benefit from:

- **Waterfall**: In contrast to agile's iterative approach, the waterfall methodology follows a sequential process where each phase of development is completed before moving on to the next. There is usually some dependency required before beginning the next phase. While less flexible than agile, waterfall may be suitable for projects with well-defined requirements and stable environments, and not ideal for SLO management.

- **Lean**: Lean methodology focuses on minimizing waste and maximizing value delivery. It emphasizes continuous improvement and customer-centricity, like agile. Lean principles can complement Agile practices and help streamline SLI and SLO management processes.

- **DevOps**: DevOps promotes collaboration and integration between development and operations teams to improve software delivery and reliability. While not a project management methodology like Agile, DevOps principles can influence how SLIs and SLOs are managed and monitored throughout the software development life cycle. Much of the later chapters will align with the DevOps focus.

- **Six Sigma**: Six Sigma is a data-driven approach to process improvement that aims to reduce defects and variability in business processes. While primarily used in manufacturing and quality management, Six Sigma principles can be applied to SLI and SLO management to identify and address performance issues systematically.

The methodologies and practices your team utilizes to implement SLIs and SLOs will play a pivotal role in the success of your SLO initiative. When considering structuring a team for SLI and SLO management, understanding the various processes and frameworks available will help you identify individuals with various skill sets in the early stages. Although it is not a requirement early on, it will only reduce later complications. In the event you are considering a small or single-person team, hopefully, this provides you with information that helps to improve the beginning stages of your journey.

Summary

Building resilience and flexibility into the SLI and SLO management framework is essential for accommodating change and uncertainty. This task is only achieved through investing in individuals and the processes they use to implement and manage the SLI and SLO processes. This helps to achieve the goal of designing processes and systems that can adapt to evolving business needs, technological advancements, and market dynamics. Building resiliency into the management framework will enhance sustainability for an organization and safeguard the longevity of reliability engineering efforts.

Adapting the structure of the SLI and SLO management team to organizational dynamics is crucial for achieving success in reliability engineering. By implementing strategies for adaptation, addressing challenges, embracing agile approaches, and building resilience into the management framework, organizations can navigate complexity, drive continuous improvement, and deliver reliable and high-performing systems and services that meet the needs of customers and stakeholders.

Implementing SLIs and SLOs requires careful planning, dedicated resources, and ongoing commitment from the organization. By establishing a dedicated team and following guidelines for team assembly, organizations can tailor practices to their specific needs. This approach helps to quickly implement seamless processes for SLO management and build internal reliability engineering organizations.

Now that we have a few guidelines for establishing our initial SRE team, in the next chapter, we will discuss a few things your team will need to consider before creating SLIs and SLOs, related to the end user (persona) and the persona journey.

Further reading

To learn more about reference articles and books mentioned in this chapter, review the following referenced artifacts:

- *Franco, G. and Brown, M. (2019, June 26). How SRE teams are organized, and how to get started.* Retrieved from: `https://cloud.google.com/blog/products/devops-sre/how-sre-teams-are-organized-and-how-to-get-started`.

- *Oehrlich, E. and Skiles, K. (2023, March). From Pilot to Scale: The Successful SRE Journey at a Large Financial Institution.* Retrieved from:

  - `https://www.devopsinstitute.com/case-studies/`.

  - `https://www.devopsinstitute.com/wp-content/uploads/2023/03/case-study-standard-chartered-bank.pdf`.

- Ribeiro, F., Giacoman, A., Thantham, and Maureen. (2016). *Dealing with Market Disruption.* New York: PricewaterhouseCoopers.

3
Things to Consider When Crafting Your SLIs and SLOs

In the previous chapter, we reviewed the reasoning behind establishing a dedicated team to build a formal SLI and SLO process. Although it is not required, it is important to consider how your SLIs and SLOs evolve as your organization scales its reliability engineering capabilities. In this chapter, you can expect to explore the integration of SLIs and SLOs with a customer-centric approach. Naturally, the utilization of SLOs and SLIs is an attempt to maintain customer centricity. By understanding the user journey and aligning your SLIs and SLOs with both customer needs and internal operational requirements, organizations can enhance the reliability, availability, and performance of their systems and services, as well as improve their ability to proactively remediate and mitigate any issues that arise.

In this chapter, we will dive into the concept of customer-centric measurement, navigate the user journey, explore the role of user journey mapping, and discuss strategies for integrating the user journey into engineering practices.

We'll cover the following main topics:

- Introduction to customer-centric measurement
- Navigating the user journey
- The role of user journey mapping
- Customer-centric focus throughout the process
- Integrating the user journey into engineering practices

Let's get started!

Introduction to customer-centric measurement

In today's rapidly evolving field of technology, customer-centric measurement has emerged as an important software development practice. This section provides an overview of what it means to be customer-centric, the significance of measuring customer-centricity, understanding and prioritizing customer needs, and an exploration of key metrics that will contribute to the success of SLIs and SLOs in measuring customer satisfaction. Additionally, case studies and examples are presented to demonstrate the tangible impact of customer-centric measurement on achieving positive business outcomes.

Customer-centric measurement in software development

Customer-centric measurement refers to the practice of evaluating the performance and effectiveness of software products and services based on their impact on the customer's experience with your platform, service, or application. It involves collecting and analyzing data related to customer interactions, preferences, and satisfaction levels to inform decision-making and prioritize efforts that enhance customer value.

In modern software development, customer-centric measurement holds significant importance for several reasons:

- **Focus on customer needs**: Customer-centric measurement complements internal metrics by incorporating customer-impacting SLIs, such as request latency, error rates, and availability, to address customer needs and expectations. By understanding how customers interact with software products and services, organizations can prioritize features and improvements that directly address customer pain points and preferences.

- **Enhanced user experience**: By measuring aspects of the user experience such as usability, responsiveness, and reliability, organizations can identify opportunities to enhance product usability and satisfaction. Customer-centric measurement allows teams to iterate on features and functionalities to ensure they align with user expectations and deliver a seamless experience.

- **Customer retention and loyalty**: Satisfying customer needs and delivering a positive user experience are essential for customer retention and loyalty. Customer-centric measurement helps organizations identify areas of improvement and address issues before they impact customer satisfaction, ultimately leading to higher retention rates and increased customer loyalty.

- **Competitive advantage**: Organizations that prioritize customer-centric measurement can gain a competitive advantage by delivering products and services that better meet customer needs. By continuously monitoring and improving the customer experience, organizations can differentiate themselves from competitors and attract and retain customers in a crowded market.

- **Data-driven decision-making**: Customer-centric measurement relies on data and analytics to inform decision-making. By collecting and analyzing customer feedback, usage patterns, and behavior data, organizations can make informed decisions about product development, feature prioritization, and resource allocation.

Customer-centric measurement is an essential feature within modern software development. It ensures organizations build products and services that resonate with their target audience, drive customer satisfaction and loyalty, and, ultimately, contribute to business success in a measurable way.

Understanding and prioritizing customer needs

To measure customer centricity or success, we need to first gather and analyze the customer's needs and expectations. Understanding and prioritizing customer expectations is crucial to the success of any organization, especially in today's competitive business-oriented industries. There are many key reasons that underscore this practice's importance that indirectly drives your organization to achieve specific business outcomes. *Figure 3.1* shows the relationship between customer needs, prioritization, and business outcomes, supported by identifying relevant SLIs that measure critical aspects of the customer experience such as latency, availability, and error rates. Needs and expectations are used interchangeably in this chapter.

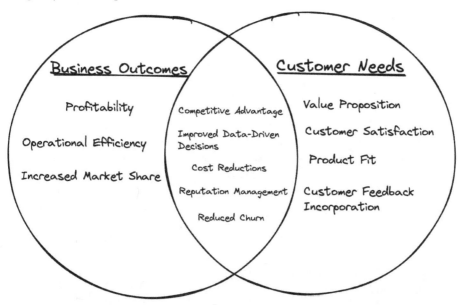

Figure 3.1 – The benefits of prioritizing meeting customers' needs

When successfully achieving items in both areas, the organization can improve or benefit in the following areas:

- **Competitive advantage**: Meeting your customer's needs and expectations is fundamental to ensuring customer satisfaction. When products and services align with what customers want and expect, they are more likely to have positive experiences, leading to increased satisfaction and loyalty.

- **Improved data-driven decisions**: Incorporating feedback through a formalized process enables the business to build datasets surrounding the customer's voice to ensure the technical services are meeting their needs. Services and SLOs built for the customer enable the organization to develop accurate trends and anomalies they can respond to, validating the decisions being made through live data.

- **Cost reductions**: Incorporating feedback from the customers to improve proactive data-driven decisions passively reduces the need to react to degraded service performance. With a decrease in downtime, system issues, and improved ability to release code changes, the organization experiences a reduction in cost. This also improves the internal engineering experience and will positively impact engineer burnout and attrition over the long term.

- **Reputation management**: An excessive number of outages and incidents that impact the customer experience can tarnish the brand's reputation.

- **Reduced churn**: When the customer experience is negatively impacted and the voice of the customer goes unheard, the business will eventually experience external and internal churn. When tailoring the process to include the customer at appropriate phases, the chances of "missing" the customer's voice are decreased.

Let's explore a few case studies to solidify this understanding.

Amazon's customer-centric approach to customer retention

Amazon is renowned for its customer-centric approach, prioritizing customer satisfaction above all else. By continuously gathering customer feedback and analyzing purchasing patterns, Amazon tailors its product recommendations and user experience to meet individual customer preferences. This focus on understanding and exceeding customer expectations has led to high levels of satisfaction and loyalty among Amazon's customer base. To maintain customer retention, they implement several approaches:

- **Customer-obsessed leadership**: Amazon's leadership principles, particularly the principle of "customer obsession," demonstrate a top-down commitment to prioritizing customer needs. Leaders focus on understanding and meeting customer expectations, which filters down through the organization's structure.

- **Continuous data collection and analysis**: Amazon's emphasis on customer engagement strategies, such as Amazon Dash and Amazon Mechanical Turk, enables the continuous collection of customer data. This data enables Amazon to establish actionable SLIs and monitor them against SLOs to gain insights into customer preferences, behaviors, and satisfaction levels. By leveraging these metrics, Amazon's reliability engineering teams can prioritize system reliability and performance improvements to effectively meet customer needs.

- **Incentive programs**: Amazon implements incentive programs such as referral bonuses and rewards for customer loyalty through programs such as Amazon Associates. These programs not only encourage customers to engage with Amazon but also reward them for their loyalty, thereby reinforcing the importance of meeting customer needs.

- **Adaptive business models**: Amazon adopts a competition business model, collaborating with competitors such as Apple to create mutually beneficial opportunities. This approach allows Amazon to expand its product offerings and improve customer experiences by partnering with other industry leaders.

- **Community engagement and sustainability**: Amazon's commitment to community welfare and environmental sustainability reflects its acknowledgment of broader societal needs. By investing in initiatives such as donation platforms and eco-friendly practices, Amazon demonstrates a holistic approach to meeting customer needs beyond just product offerings.

Amazon's customer-centric approach involves a combination of data-driven decision-making, leadership commitment, incentive structures, adaptive strategies, and social responsibility initiatives. These elements collectively prioritize understanding, meeting, and exceeding customer expectations, ensuring long-term customer satisfaction and loyalty.

Netflix's personalized recommendations for customer-centricity

Netflix leverages data analytics and machine learning algorithms to provide personalized recommendations to its subscribers. By analyzing viewing habits and preferences, Netflix identifies key SLIs such as recommendation accuracy, content engagement rates, and system response times. These SLIs help Netflix continuously measure and refine its recommendation system, enhancing the viewing experience and increasing customer retention. This personalized approach builds a stronger relationship with subscribers, reducing churn rates and improving customer lifetime value. Here's how they do it:

- **Transparency**: Netflix increased transparency by aligning its SLA commitments with detailed explanations of how its recommendation system works. This includes outlining algorithm categories, data collection methods, and how they meet defined SLOs for recommendation relevance and accuracy. This includes explaining the algorithms used, data collected (both explicit and implicit), and factors influencing the referenced recommendations.

- **User empowerment**: Netflix also offers its users greater control over their recommendation settings and preferences, such as allowing users to change or remove their rating for a title and remove a title from their watch history. Additionally, providing options for users to adjust recommendation settings based on their interests and privacy concerns empowers users to tailor their experience.

- **Feedback mechanism**: Netflix implemented a robust feedback process as part of its SLI monitoring strategy to gather user input on recommendation relevance and effectiveness. These insights drive iterative improvements to align the system with SLOs, such as maintaining a target recommendation accuracy. This contributes to improving the recommendation system and ensuring that it meets the evolving needs and preferences of users.

- **Ethical considerations**: Netflix addressed the concerns related to biased and discriminatory outcomes by implementing measures to mitigate biases in the recommendation algorithms. This includes ensuring diversity and fairness in the representation of content, as highlighted in the example of racially- and ethnically-driven thumbnail images.

- **Personalization and relevance**: Netflix focuses on delivering personalized recommendations that are relevant and valuable to individual users, such as leveraging data analytics and machine learning to tailor recommendations based on users' preferences and behaviors.

- **User education**: Netflix educates its users about the recommendation system and how they can make the most out of it, such as providing a high-level overview of the system in its online help center. This includes providing resources and guidelines to help users understand how recommendations are generated and how they can optimize their viewing experience on the platform.

By incorporating these examples, Netflix prioritized customer's needs and continues to ensure that its recommendation system remains customer-centric, ultimately enhancing user satisfaction and retention on the platform. Organizations that understand and prioritize customer needs gain a competitive edge by defining SLIs that measure key aspects of the customer journey (e.g., latency, engagement, and availability) and aligning them with SLOs that reflect business-critical goals such as 99.9% system uptime and low error rates in recommendations.

Apple's product innovation

Our next case study focuses on product innovation with Apple. Apple's ability to focus on understanding and anticipating customer needs has been key to its competitive advantage in the technology industry. By consistently delivering innovative products that seamlessly integrate with one another into users' personal lives, and the latest third-party software and technology, Apple has differentiated itself in the extremely competitive technology market. From the iPhone to the Apple Watch, Apple's products resonate with customers, driving brand loyalty and market leadership. Let's look at how Apple integrates the customer experience into product innovation and development:

- **Innovation and differentiation**: Apple's relentless focus on understanding customer needs drives its innovation efforts, leading to the development of groundbreaking products such as the Mac, iPod, iPhone, and iPad. These products not only meet but also exceed customer expectations, setting Apple apart in the highly competitive technology market.

- **Customer-centric innovation**: Apple's innovation strategy revolves around understanding and addressing customer needs rather than focusing solely on technological advancements. By designing products that resonate with users and create value for them, Apple ensures a high-quality user experience and strengthens customer loyalty.

- **Innovation leadership**: Steve Jobs played a pivotal role in fostering a culture of innovation at Apple. His vision and passion for creating "insanely great" products inspired employees to think differently and push the boundaries of what was possible. Jobs' leadership ensured that new ideas aligned with Apple's overarching vision and values, driving the company's innovation efforts forward.

- **Customer experience**: Apple's innovation strategy extends beyond product development to encompass the entire customer experience. By prioritizing simplicity, usability, and user-centric design, Apple ensures that its products not only meet but also exceed customer expectations. This focus on enhancing the customer experience reinforces Apple's reputation for delivering high-quality products and strengthens its competitive advantage in the market.

- **Continuous improvement**: Apple's commitment to innovation is evident in its continuous efforts to improve and refine its products and services. By listening to customer feedback and defining SLIs for product quality and user satisfaction, Apple ensures alignment with SLOs that reflect evolving customer needs. This approach, supported by SRE practices such as error budget monitoring, enables Apple to continuously adapt its offerings and maintain market leadership.

Apple's success in the technology market can be attributed to its relentless pursuit of understanding and meeting customer needs. By placing customers at the center of its innovation efforts, Apple continues to drive market leadership and maintain its competitive advantage in an ever-changing industry landscape.

Tesla's electric vehicles for customer centricity

Tesla revolutionized the automotive industry by prioritizing customer demand for sustainable transportation solutions. By including SLIs to measure the effectiveness of charging infrastructure and range anxiety mitigation, such as average charging station availability or average vehicle range per charge under real-world conditions, Tesla has become a leader in the electric car market. Its innovative approach to product design and technology integration has set it apart from traditional automakers, driving innovation and differentiation in the industry:

- **Customer-centric approach**: Tesla defines SLOs for customer-centric metrics, such as maintaining 99% uptime for the Tesla app's vehicle control features or ensuring a 90% success rate in resolving customer complaints within 24 hours. Despite facing challenges such as missed deadlines and supply chain issues, Tesla was able to remain focused on meeting customer demands and enhancing the overall customer experience. The disruptive impact on the automotive industry stems from its recognition of evolving customer preferences for electric and tech-savvy vehicles.

- **Commitment to safety**: The level of commitment to safety and customer satisfaction is evident through incorporating SLAs for Autopilot's availability and safety, such as specifying system availability during driving hours and a maximum response time for addressing safety-related bugs. While facing debates and challenges related to autonomous vehicles, Tesla's efforts to integrate AI-driven solutions reflect its dedication to enhancing customer safety and driving experience.

- **Easy accessibility**: Additionally, the distribution strategy utilized emphasizes accessibility and convenience for customers, with a strong online presence, social media engagement, and strategic partnerships with industry leaders. By introducing an SLO for transaction reliability, such as ensuring 99.5% uptime for the online purchasing platform and providing a response to transactional errors within four hours, Tesla ensures that its products are readily available and easily accessible to its target audience.

- **Survey and feedback**: Tesla's focus on community building and user-generated content reinforces its customer-centric approach by fostering a sense of belonging and engagement among its customers. By encouraging user participation and feedback, Tesla strengthens its relationship with customers and continuously iterates on its products and services to better meet their needs.

Overall, the organization's customer-centric initiatives, ranging from product innovation to distribution strategies and community engagement, highlight its commitment to prioritizing customer needs and expectations. Despite facing challenges inherent in a rapidly evolving industry, Tesla remains dedicated to delivering value to its customers and shaping the future of automotive transportation.

Airbnb's user feedback loop focusing on customer needs and expectations

Airbnb employs a robust user feedback loop by specifying SLIs for user feedback processing, such as tracking the percentage of feedback addressed within a designated time frame and the average resolution time for user-reported issues. By soliciting feedback from both guests and hosts, Airbnb identifies areas for improvement in its platform and service offerings, reducing the risk of negative experiences and costly disputes. This proactive approach to customer feedback minimizes risks associated with dissatisfied customers and contributes to overall cost savings for the company:

- **Enhancing end-to-end travel experience**: Airbnb focuses on enhancing the overall travel experience for its customers through establishing SLOs tied to the travel experience. SLOs such as ensuring a 95% positive rating for guest-host interactions or maintaining a 98% availability rate for the platform during peak travel times help to meet and exceed customer expectations, thus improving customer loyalty. The company trains hosts to provide the best possible experience and hires freelance photographers to showcase areas near the accommodation, aiming to attract more customers and encourage repeat business.

- **User-generated content**: Airbnb places significant emphasis on user-generated content to delight customers. One example is using data to define SLIs that measure the success of user-generated content, such as tracking engagement rates on user-generated posts or the number of successfully resolved content disputes within 48 hours. This approach saves costs on content creation while maintaining content safety and reliability SLAs, such as guaranteeing a 95% moderation success rate within 24 hours to maintain platform trust and prevent harmful content.

- **Multi-channel social media strategy**: Airbnb employs a multi-channel social media strategy to diversify content, leverage user-generated content, and attract, engage, and convert customers for perennial revenue streams. By utilizing platforms such as LinkedIn, X/Twitter, Facebook, Instagram, and YouTube, Airbnb reaches a wide audience, shares travel tips, promotes special deals, and connects with customers on various levels. This strategy allows Airbnb to maintain a strong online presence, engage with customers across different channels, and drive traffic and engagement effectively.

- **Community building and brand trust**: Airbnb has successfully built a strong community of passionate travelers who share their experiences with others. This community-driven approach enhances the quality of service and product offerings, leading to increased customer satisfaction and loyalty. By fostering a sense of community and trust among users, Airbnb differentiates itself from competitors and establishes itself as a trusted brand in the travel industry.

Overall, Airbnb's strategic focus on reliability engineering, including enhancing the travel experience, leveraging user-generated content, implementing a multi-channel social media strategy, and building a strong community, enables the company to meet and exceed customer needs and expectations. Prioritizing customer needs ensures that products and services are designed with the end user in mind. By focusing on usability, functionality, and other aspects of the user experience, organizations can create products that are intuitive, easy to use, and enjoyable for customers.

Understanding key metrics and their role in customer satisfaction

SLIs, SLOs, and SLAs are key components used to measure and maintain the performance, reliability, and overall quality of services provided by organizations. SLIs represent raw measurements, SLOs define internal performance targets, and SLAs formalize commitments to customers. They play a crucial role in assessing customer satisfaction and ensuring that services meet or exceed customer expectations.

SLIs are quantitative measurements that represent specific aspects of service performance, such as response time, throughput, error rates, or availability. These metrics are typically tied to customer-facing functionalities or features and provide insights into how well a service is performing from the customer's perspective.

SLOs, on the other hand, are specific targets or thresholds set for SLIs that define the level of service quality expected by customers. SLOs establish measurable goals for service performance and reliability, allowing organizations to track their progress and ensure that they are meeting customer expectations.

Together, SLIs and SLOs play a critical role in measuring customer satisfaction and reliability by providing actionable insights into service performance and quality. Here's how they contribute to this:

- **Monitoring customer experience**: SLIs track key performance indicators that directly impact the customer experience, such as response times for customer-facing applications or availability of critical services. By monitoring SLIs, such as response time or error rate, organizations can gain visibility into specific aspects of service performance. This monitoring may occur in real time for critical metrics such as uptime, or periodically for trend analysis and ensuring actionable insights to meet customer expectations:

  - **Example**: A company that provides an e-commerce platform monitors the SLI of page load time for its website. This SLI measures the time taken for web pages to load when users browse the site. By tracking this metric, the company gains insights into the performance of its website from the perspective of customer experience. If the average page load time exceeds the defined SLO threshold, it triggers an analysis of the error budget. This allows the team to allocate resources for system optimization or initiate an incident response plan to mitigate user dissatisfaction and improve reliability.

- **Setting performance targets**: SLOs establish clear performance targets based on customer requirements and business objectives. By defining specific thresholds for SLIs, organizations can ensure that they are delivering services at the level expected by customers. SLOs provide a tangible benchmark against which performance can be measured and evaluated:

  - **Example**: A **software-as-a-service (SaaS)** provider sets an SLO for system uptime, defining that the service should be available 99.9% of the time. This SLO establishes a clear target for reliability, ensuring that customers can access the service with minimal interruptions. The provider regularly monitors uptime SLIs and takes proactive measures to maintain uptime levels within the specified threshold, thereby meeting customer expectations.

- **Ensuring reliability and availability**: SLIs and SLOs are instrumental in measuring the reliability and availability of services. By monitoring SLIs related to uptime, error rates, and other reliability metrics, organizations can identify potential issues and proactively address them to minimize service disruptions and downtime:

  - **Example**: A cloud storage provider tracks the SLI of data replication latency, which measures the time taken to replicate data across multiple data centers. This SLI is critical for ensuring data reliability and availability. If replication latency exceeds the defined SLO, it could indicate potential data consistency issues or performance bottlenecks that may affect the reliability of the service. The provider takes immediate action to resolve these issues and ensure data integrity and availability for customers.

- **Driving continuous improvement**: SLIs and SLOs serve as key performance indicators that drive continuous improvement efforts. By tracking performance against SLO targets, organizations can identify areas for optimization and prioritize initiatives that enhance service quality and reliability, ultimately leading to improved customer satisfaction:

  - **Example**: A streaming media company monitors SLIs related to video buffering and playback errors for its streaming service. Based on user feedback and SLI performance data, the company identifies areas for improvement in streaming quality and reliability. It invests in infrastructure upgrades and software optimizations to reduce buffering and errors, ultimately enhancing the user experience and driving customer satisfaction.

SLIs and SLOs are essential metrics for measuring customer satisfaction and reliability. By monitoring key performance indicators and setting performance targets, organizations can ensure that their services meet or exceed customer expectations, driving enhanced customer satisfaction and loyalty. Additionally, SLIs and SLOs provide valuable insights that drive continuous improvement efforts, enabling organizations to deliver reliable and high-quality services that delight customers.

Customer-centric measurement is essential for modern software development practices. By understanding and prioritizing customer needs, leveraging key metrics such as SLIs and SLOs, and incorporating feedback from end users, organizations can deliver products and services that meet customer expectations and drive business success. Through case studies and examples, the tangible impact of customer-centric measurement on business outcomes becomes evident, highlighting its importance in today's competitive marketplace.

Navigating the user journey

Understanding the user journey and its various touchpoints across different stages of the customer lifecycle is integral to ensuring system reliability and resilience. The customer lifecycle can be defined as the process that a customer undergoes when considering, purchasing, using, or maintaining a product or service. If we consider the typical customer, not tied to a specific industry, the lifecycle happens in five continuous stages:

1. Awareness
2. Consideration
3. Purchase
4. Retention
5. Advocacy

The concept of the customer life cycle is out of the scope of this book. However, *Figure 3.2* provides a visual flow of the customer life cycle.

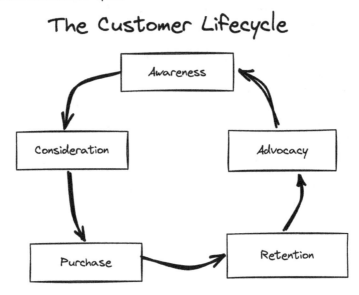

Figure 3.2 – The customer life cycle

This section highlights the user journey, which includes the identification of key moments of truth, techniques for analyzing and mapping the user journey, and strategies for identifying pain points and opportunities for improvement. However, during this process, we must understand the inner dependencies of what the customer experiences throughout their life cycle before we begin to dissect independently their experience utilizing the respective service offering. Let's discuss this relationship a bit more.

Understanding the user journey and customer life cycle relationship

Understanding the user journey is essential for organizations to deliver a seamless and satisfying customer experience. By mapping out the various touchpoints that customers encounter across different stages of the customer life cycle, organizations can gain insights into the customer's interactions with their products or services. For example, an e-commerce company may map out the user journey from initial product discovery to post-purchase support, identifying touchpoints such as browsing the website, adding items to the cart, completing the checkout process, and contacting customer service. By understanding these touchpoints, organizations can identify opportunities to streamline processes, remove friction points, and enhance the overall customer experience.

For instance, a ride-sharing company may analyze the user journey from requesting a ride to completing the trip, identifying touchpoints such as booking a ride, waiting for the driver, and rating the experience. By understanding each touchpoint and its impact on the customer experience, the company can optimize its app interface to provide real-time updates on driver location, minimize wait times, and solicit feedback after the ride. This holistic view of the user journey enables organizations to identify pain points and areas for improvement, ultimately leading to a more positive and satisfying customer experience.

Identifying critical interactions that shape customer satisfaction

Key moments of truth are pivotal interactions that significantly influence customer perception and satisfaction. These moments often occur at critical touchpoints along the user journey, where customers form lasting impressions of the brand based on their experiences. For example, in the hospitality industry, key moments of truth may include check-in at the hotel, the quality of the room, and interactions with staff during the stay. An event that might have a more lasting impact could be how a complaint is handled or what action is taken after a customer complaint. By identifying these key moments of truth, organizations can define SLIs to measure the performance of these critical interactions and establish corresponding SLOs to ensure they meet customer expectations.

Another example is a retail company that may identify key moments of truth such as product delivery and customer service interactions. By ensuring delivery on time and providing responsive customer support, the company can enhance customer satisfaction and loyalty. Additionally, organizations can leverage customer feedback and sentiment analysis to identify key moments of truth that are most impactful to their customers. By focusing on these critical interactions, organizations can optimize their processes and resources to deliver exceptional experiences and build strong customer relationships.

Techniques for analyzing and mapping the user journey

Analyzing and mapping the user journey involves employing various techniques to gain insights into customer behavior and preferences. Customer interviews allow organizations to directly engage with users to understand their motivations, pain points, and satisfaction levels at different stages of the journey. Surveys provide a scalable way to gather feedback from a broader audience, allowing organizations to collect quantitative data on user preferences and experiences. Analytics data, such as website traffic and user interactions, offers valuable insights into user behavior, allowing organizations to identify patterns and trends in how users engage with their products or services. By combining these techniques, organizations can create comprehensive user journey maps that provide a holistic view of the customer experience.

A software company may conduct user interviews to help further understand how customers navigate their applications and identify areas of frustration or confusion. Surveys can then be used to gather feedback from a larger user base, confirming or expanding on the insights gained from interviews. Analytics data, such as heatmaps and user session recordings, can further validate findings from interviews and surveys, providing quantitative evidence of user behavior. By triangulating insights from multiple sources, organizations can create robust user journey maps that accurately reflect the needs and preferences of their customers, guiding efforts to improve the overall user experience.

Identifying pain points and improvement opportunities

Identifying pain points and opportunities for improvement along the user journey is essential for enhancing the overall customer experience. By pinpointing areas where users encounter obstacles or frustrations, organizations can adjust SLAs to reflect realistic performance guarantees and ensure accountability for optimizing the user journey. Strategies for identifying pain points may include conducting usability testing to observe how users interact with products or services in real-world scenarios, analyzing customer support tickets to identify recurring issues, and monitoring social media and online reviews for customer feedback. Additionally, organizations can leverage journey mapping exercises to visually map out the user experience and identify moments of friction or delight.

For instance, an e-commerce company may identify pain points such as a cumbersome checkout process or difficulty finding product information. By analyzing user behavior and feedback, the company can streamline the checkout flow and improve product navigation to enhance the overall shopping experience. Similarly, a SaaS company may identify opportunities for improvement in onboarding and user training processes. By addressing these pain points, guided by performance insights from SLIs and SLO adherence, organizations can systematically improve reliability, enhance customer satisfaction, reduce churn, and, ultimately, drive business growth.

Mapping the user journey is integral to aligning system design with reliability objectives, ensuring that SLOs are met at critical touchpoints that directly influence the user experience. By understanding the user journey, identifying key moments of truth, leveraging techniques for analyzing and mapping the user journey, and implementing strategies for identifying pain points and opportunities for improvement, organizations can deliver a superior user experience that drives customer satisfaction and business success.

The role of user journey mapping

Understanding the user journey through effective mapping techniques is instrumental in refining SLIs and SLOs to ensure customer-centric measurement. This section encapsulates key insights from the chapter, including the definition and purpose of user journey mapping, the process for creating user journey maps, the tools and templates available for visualization, and how user journey mapping informs the selection and definition of SLIs and SLOs.

Definition and purpose of user journey mapping

User journey mapping is a methodical approach to understanding the customer experience by visualizing and documenting the various touchpoints and interactions across different stages of the customer life cycle. Its purpose lies in gaining insights into customer emotions, behaviors, pain points, and preferences, allowing organizations to identify opportunities for improvement and deliver a more seamless and satisfying user experience.

Process for creating user journey maps

Creating user journey maps involves several components, including defining personas, identifying touchpoints, and mapping customer emotions and behaviors. Personas represent fictional characters that embody different user segments, while touchpoints are the points of interaction between the customer and the product or service. Mapping customer emotions and behaviors helps to contextualize the user journey and highlight areas for optimization. Let's review each component at a lower level for further understanding.

For clarity, we can think of a journey map as a high-level description of the process a customer goes through to achieve some goal. That goal could be retrieving information from an application, database, platform, and so on. It could also be placing an order on an e-commerce website. In most scenarios, you'd see this information outlined in a similar format to *Figure 3.3*.

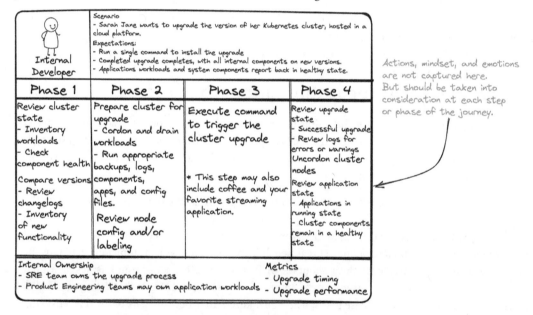

Figure 3.3 – Example of customer journey information collection

Each individual journey map should consist of the following at a bare minimum:

- An actor or persona
- The scenario and persona expectations
- Journey phases or steps

- Actions, mindsets, and emotions
- Internal ownership and metrics

Informing SLIs and SLOs through user journey mapping

User journey mapping plays a crucial role in informing the selection and definition of SLIs and SLOs. By gaining insights into customer pain points, preferences, and expectations, organizations can define SLIs that measure the system's performance from the customer's perspective, ensuring that reliability aligns with customer expectations. For example, SLIs may include metrics related to page load times, transaction success rates, or customer support response times, SLOs establish specific targets or thresholds for these metrics, and SLAs formalize these targets into contractual commitments to ensure service reliability aligns with user expectations.

User journey mapping is a powerful tool for refining SLIs and SLOs to ensure customer-centric measurement. By understanding the user journey, organizations can identify opportunities for improvement, optimize the user experience, and, ultimately, drive customer satisfaction and loyalty. Through the process outlined in this chapter, organizations can create comprehensive user journey maps that guide the continuous refinement of SLIs and SLOs, enabling the delivery of reliable and resilient products and services that consistently meet evolving customer expectations.

Customer-centric focus throughout the process

When building anything to market and selling to a customer base, it's important to centralize focus on the customer. The same applies to your SLI and SLO process, to ensure that what we are measuring is based on the customer versus our internal assumptions. We will highlight this more in *Part 2* of the book when we discuss system boundaries.

Customer expectations are continuously changing and growing. We have already discussed the importance of adopting a customer-centric approach in all facets of business operations, including developing SLOs. SLIs act as critical metrics for measuring specific aspects of service quality and performance, which are used to define SLOs as benchmarks that align with customer expectations. By infusing a customer-centric focus throughout the SLO development process, your business can align your reliability objectives with customer expectations, establishing clear SLOs that define the level of service customers can expect. These SLOs, when formalized, may become part of an SLA, ensuring that both parties have a shared understanding of service performance and customer expectations. Let's discuss a bit further how understanding and prioritizing customer needs and preferences can inform the establishment of meaningful SLOs that truly reflect the value customers derive from the services provided.

Conducting cross-functional reviews with teams and stakeholders

Regular reviews and updates of SLIs and SLOs are necessary to accommodate changing customer needs and market conditions. In *Chapter 12*, we will discuss SLO performance reviews. By soliciting customer feedback and monitoring user satisfaction metrics, organizations can identify areas for improvement and refine SLIs and SLOs accordingly. This approach ensures that reliability objectives remain aligned with customer expectations and business goals over time.

Involving cross-functional teams and stakeholders in the SLI and SLO review process is essential for ensuring alignment with customer needs. By bringing together representatives from product management, engineering, design, and customer support, organizations can maintain diverse perspectives and insights throughout the SLO management life cycle. This collaboration fosters a shared understanding of customer needs and ensures that SLIs and SLOs are consistently relevant and meaningful across the functional areas they were designed for.

This is not to be confused with sending and receiving status updates. Truly engage in meaningful connections for validating how things are being done, where they are being measured, and ongoing relevant processes to continuously validate the team is on the right track.

Incorporating customer satisfaction metrics

Incorporating customer satisfaction metrics such as **Net Promoter Score (NPS)**, **Customer Satisfaction (CSAT)**, and **Customer Effort Score (CES)** into SLI and SLO monitoring provides valuable qualitative and quantitative insights into the user experience. This helps organizations measure how well their services align with the customer experience. NPS and CSAT ratings offer quantitative measures of customer sentiment, while feedback forms such as surveys and user interviews provide qualitative insights into user perceptions and preferences. By incorporating these metrics into SLI and SLO monitoring, organizations can track customer satisfaction levels and proactively address any issues or concerns that arise.

Maintaining a customer-centric focus throughout the process of customer journey mapping in reliability engineering is essential for delivering products and services that meet the needs and expectations of users. By integrating customer-focused practices into SLI and SLO development, involving cross-functional teams and stakeholders, conducting regular reviews and updates based on customer feedback, and incorporating customer satisfaction metrics into monitoring and reporting, organizations can drive continuous improvement and ensure customer satisfaction and loyalty.

Incorporating usability testing

By gathering feedback directly from users and conducting usability tests, teams can easily do the following:

- Identify usability issues
- Uncover areas for improvement
- Validate design decisions

Integrating findings from test outcomes into iterative development processes enables teams to iteratively refine and enhance products and services based on real user insights. This ultimately leads to achieving a higher level of customer satisfaction and engagement through an evidence-based process.

Summary

By adopting a customer-centric approach through SLI and SLO implementation, organizations will better understand and address customer needs by ensuring business solutions meet their expectations. In the long term, this will improve the reliability and performance of their systems and services and drive business success.

By integrating the user journey into engineering practices, the organization enforces internal alignment of SLIs and SLOs with customer expectations. This helps the organization to create more meaningful and impactful experiences for their customers that can be aligned with data-driven business decisions, thus improving business outcomes.

With continuous measurement, analysis, and iteration, organizations can build a customer-centric culture and deliver value that resonates with their customers due to improved observability of the systems and processes being used to drive decisions. In the following chapter, we will discuss the fundamentals of observable systems, which provide the organization with the level of visibility needed to build SLIs. Through observing the right components and processes, we can set a solid foundation for measuring the right metrics in the most accurate and sensible way, improving the thresholds we follow to measure system performance.

Further reading

You can review the following referenced articles and books for additional reading about concepts mentioned in this chapter:

- Agius, A. (2024, November 20). *Customer Journey Maps: How to Create Really Good Ones*. Retrieved from: `https://blog.hubspot.com/service/customer-journey-map`.

- Kumari, P. (2022, Nov 22). *Airbnb Business Case Study: What Makes Airbnb So Successful*. Retrieved from: `https://hackernoon.com/airbnb-business-case-study-what-makes-airbnb-so-successful`.

- Lorincz, N. (2024, June 24). *Ecommerce Customer Lifecycle Management: Everything You Need to Know*. Retrieved from: `https://www.optimonk.com/customer-lifecycle-management/`.

- Macri, K. P. (2018, Feb 20). *Case Study: How Tesla Changed the Auto Industry*. Retrieved from: `https://www.supplychaindive.com/news/case-study-how-tesla-changed-the-auto-industry/517251/`.

- Podolny, J. M., & Hansen, M. T. (2020, November). *How Apple Is Organized for Innovation*. Retrieved from: `https://hbr.org/2020/11/how-apple-is-organized-for-innovation`.

- Singh, S. (2020, March 25). *Why Am I Seeing This? Case Study: Netflix*. Retrieved from: `https://www.newamerica.org/oti/reports/why-am-i-seeing-this/case-study-netflix/`.

4

Observability and Monitoring Are a Necessity and a Must

In previous chapters, we discussed the hierarchy of reliability engineering and the importance of incorporating observability as its own practice. Developing robust **Service Level Indicators** (**SLIs**) requires deep comprehension of your application, system, or platform, enabling precise measurement of its components. This necessitates establishing suitable mechanisms in advance to ensure the requisite level of observability and monitoring of key aspects.

This chapter provides an overview of both observability and monitoring, to highlight their integral connection with SLIs and **Service Level Objectives** (**SLOs**). Its aim is to cultivate this mindset throughout your journey with SLIs and SLOs and embed a solid understanding of not only the importance of both but also the differences between them. The goal of this chapter is not to suggest a specific product or solution or even a way of working. It is, rather, to highlight processes and solutions to support improved monitoring and observability to drive SLIs.

We'll be covering the following main topics:

- Observability and monitoring at its core
- The pillars of observability
- Integrating observability thinking into the SLI and SLO journey
- Strategic monitoring for effective measurement

Now, let's get started!

Observability and monitoring at its core

Observability and monitoring serve as the foundational pillars of modern **site reliability engineering (SRE)** practices. In essence, observability refers to the ability to infer the internal state of a system based on its external outputs. This involves collecting and analyzing data from various sources within the system to gain insights into its behavior, performance, and health. Monitoring, on the other hand, involves the continuous observation of key metrics and indicators to detect and respond to anomalies or issues in real time. Together, observability and monitoring provide SRE teams with the visibility and insights needed to ensure the reliability and performance of their systems.

It is often the case that the two concepts are mistaken for one another, used interchangeably, or not clearly defined in the context of their usage. While the goal is not to focus on observability and monitoring as a practice, I hope to provide additional insight as to why it is important to include observability as a pillar of reliability engineering, differentiate it from monitoring, and showcase its relationship and dependency to creating quality SLIs that meet their SLOs. Let's go!

The significance of observability and monitoring in reliability engineering

Observability and monitoring play a crucial role in reliability engineering by enabling teams to gain a deep understanding of system behavior and performance. Before we begin the discussion, it is important to understand that behavior can be described as an event that occurs and leads to the triggering of another event internally or within another system. On the other hand, performance can be described as a measurement of the amount of useful work or output of a system, for instance, its speed, throughput, or response times to some requests.

Through comprehensive observability practices, SRE teams can collect and analyze these sorts of data types from across the entire system stack, including infrastructure, applications, and user interactions. This allows for the ability to identify patterns, diagnose issues, and optimize performance to meet SLOs. Additionally, effective monitoring ensures that SRE teams can quickly detect and respond to incidents, minimizing downtime and ensuring a seamless user experience.

The two concepts work together to enhance the amount of data availability for increased accuracy when measuring and quantifying internal events. According to AWS, *"Monitoring is the process of collecting data and generating the reports on different metrics that define the system's health"* (AWS, 2024). Observability is the aggregation of the data being monitored in a more investigative manner. Observability takes the lead when looking at distributed system components' interactions and utilizing data collected through the process of monitoring to find the root cause of an issue. If we are not observing the right things in the right places, then how do we accurately move up the hierarchy of reliability engineering?

It is easy to misconstrue or use interchangeably the observability and monitoring concepts. Therefore, it is important to highlight the differences between the two. As previously mentioned, monitoring answers the following questions:

- **What happened?** Resource utilization (CPU, network, etc.) spike?
- **Is this a known issue?** Does incident management data support a recurring issue?
- **How did we previously resolve it?** Do we have an internal knowledge base or some documentation regarding the temporary fix?

Monitoring informs both internal engineers and business stakeholders about the system's health. While end users might not directly monitor internal metrics such as CPU usage, the impact of such metrics on user experience, such as response times or error rates, should align with defined SLIs and SLOs that reflect user expectations. A customer securing a plane ticket through an airline's web or mobile application is not going to relate to "CPU usage is nearing maximum capacity." This representation of monitoring is more important to the engineers looking to mitigate and potentially root cause an issue within **Service Level Agreement (SLA)** guidelines.

On the other hand, observability takes a more investigative approach to better understand how to prevent an issue from happening again:

- **Why did it happen?** Did we experience exhaustive resource consumption due to increased use due to performance testing or data center outages?
- **Is the system performant?** Is the system able to perform according to "defined customer expectations" under the current conditions?
- **How do we improve resiliency?** Was the previous fix a temporary patch, incorrect pushed code, inaccurate understanding of user requirements, etc.?

Although the two are different conceptually, they work together to achieve a level of observability that supports high standards for metric definition and creating SLIs, especially in distributed environments. See *Figure 4.1* for further reference.

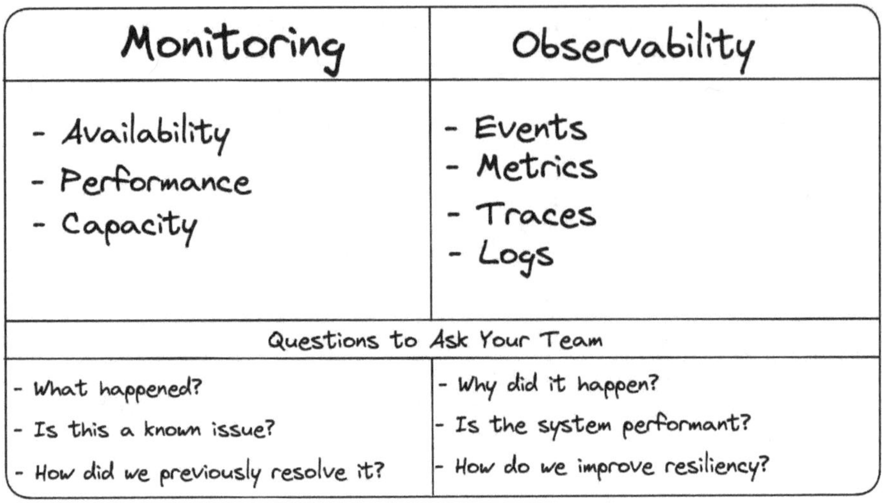

Monitoring	Observability
- Availability - Performance - Capacity	- Events - Metrics - Traces - Logs
Questions to Ask Your Team	
- What happened? - Is this a known issue? - How did we previously resolve it?	- Why did it happen? - Is the system performant? - How do we improve resiliency?

Figure 4.1 – Observability versus monitoring question-based concepts

Observability and monitoring are integral to the definition and management of SLIs and SLOs. SLIs are metrics that measure the performance and reliability of a system, such as latency, error rates, and throughput. These indicators provide the data needed to assess whether the system is meeting SLOs. SLOs define the targets for acceptable performance, based on those SLIs, and help to align system behavior with business objectives and user expectations. By leveraging observability tools, SRE teams can continuously track SLIs and ensure SLOs are met within the defined SLA. This will further allow organizations to set realistic targets for system reliability and performance, while also providing a framework for continuous improvement.

Proactive SLO management is essential for effective SLI and SLA alignment in SRE. SRE teams must define clear SLOs that reflect user expectations and monitor SLIs to ensure these objectives are consistently met. This involves continuous measurement, regular reviews, and adjustments to keep the system aligned with business goals while meeting SLA requirements. This involves setting up alerts and triggers based on predefined thresholds, conducting regular performance reviews, and performing proactive capacity planning to ensure that systems can handle expected loads. By adopting a proactive approach to observability and monitoring, organizations can minimize the impact of incidents, improve system reliability, and enhance the overall user experience.

Data-driven decision-making for SLI and SLO optimization

Observability and monitoring empower SRE teams to make data-driven decisions when optimizing SLIs and SLOs. By collecting and analyzing large volumes of data from diverse sources, teams can gain valuable insights into system performance trends, identify areas for improvement, and prioritize efforts accordingly. This data-driven approach enables teams to continuously monitor and adjust SLIs to ensure they align with SLOs, based on real system performance data and evolving user expectations. Regular reviews of SLOs, discussed in *Chapter 12*, should ensure they are realistic and meet business objectives, with defined error budgets to assess performance against SLAs. Ultimately, data-driven decision-making ensures that SRE teams can continuously improve system reliability and performance to deliver exceptional user experiences.

Observability and monitoring together enable continuous improvement through feedback loops in SRE practices. By collecting data on system performance and user interactions, teams can identify opportunities for optimization and innovation. This feedback loop allows teams to adjust SLIs based on real-time data and monitor how those changes impact SLOs. This continuous iteration helps to refine service levels and improve overall system performance while ensuring SLAs are consistently met within the defined error budget. Additionally, feedback loops facilitate collaboration and knowledge sharing across teams, enabling organizations to leverage collective insights and expertise to drive continuous improvement initiatives. By embracing feedback loops, organizations can foster a culture of learning and innovation that accelerates their journey toward greater reliability and performance.

Challenges and opportunities in observability and monitoring

While observability and monitoring offer significant benefits to SRE practices, they also present unique challenges and opportunities. An organization can experience various challenges due to the complexity of modern distributed systems, such as the following:

- The inability to collect, analyze, and interpret data effectively.
- Increased data overload.
- Increased needs for navigating issues related to data privacy, security, and compliance when implementing observability solutions.

However, it is important to highlight that these challenges also present the following opportunities for innovation and growth:

- Improved reliability of organizational data.
- Increased accessibility of accurate data.
- Internal organizational alignment resulting from a broader visibility of internal infrastructure.

By investing in advanced observability tools and techniques, organizations can overcome these challenges and unlock new possibilities for optimizing system reliability and performance. Ultimately, by embracing the power of observability and monitoring, organizations can achieve greater agility, resilience, and competitiveness in today's digital landscape.

The pillars of observability

Observability is central to maintaining and improving the performance, reliability, and overall health of any system. At its core, observability relies on four fundamental components: **logs**, **metrics**, **traces**, and **events**. Each component plays a crucial role in providing insights into the inner workings of a system, helping engineers and operators understand its behavior and diagnose issues effectively. Remember, when we can observe the correct components at the right log level, we are able to productively monitor and create quality SLIs and SLOs.

Figure 4.2 depicts the four pillars of observability, including "events" on which the other three pillars rely heavily. We can also think of the pillars of observability as passive sequential tasks that include other observability tasks. As it relates to observability, we can think of each pillar within the following context as independent concepts that also occur in a sequential order.

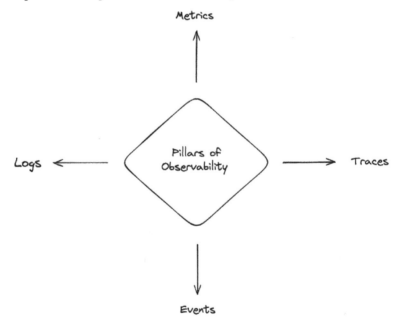

Figure 4.2 – Pillars of observability

Let's take a moment to review what each pillar means according to industry standards, and its role within observability.

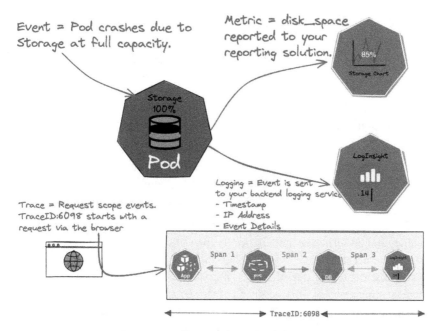

Figure 4.3 – Observability pillar definitions

As depicted in *Figure 4.3*, for the logging process to be invoked, we must first experience some event within our application, platform, or system that occurs. An event can include errors or warnings regarding changes in your system. These changes can include a pod within your cluster crashing due to disk storage being at full capacity or your organization's website being down due to network throttling or a server outage in the associated data center. Logs provide a narrative of what transpired within your distributed environment, helping to identify the root causes of issues and track down anomalies. By analyzing logs, engineers can gain context around specific incidents and trace the sequence of events leading up to them.

The events that occur within your system provide an overall measurement via its associated metric regarding the health or performance of your system. Traces, although tied to events, are specific to requests within an end-to-end workflow where each touchpoint within a trace is assigned a span ID, while the collective spans make up the trace, which is assigned a trace ID. We can think of each in the following contexts:

- **Metrics**: Metrics are quantitative measurements that provide a snapshot of the current state of a system. They can collectively make up **key performance indicators** (**KPIs**) and are typically aggregated over time intervals. Metrics serve as the foundation for defining SLIs, which are used to measure how well a system is meeting its SLOs. These metrics can be aggregated over time intervals to determine whether the SLOs are being met and whether the system is performing with acceptable thresholds. Common metrics include CPU utilization, memory usage, request latency, and error rates.

- **Events:** Events are discrete occurrences or notifications that signify significant changes or milestones within a system. They can range from user actions and system state transitions to infrastructure events and external integrations. Events trigger real-time monitoring and alerting, allowing SRE teams to respond promptly to potential SLA breaches or issues that may consume the error budget. These events can represent failures, warnings, or other significant state changes that impact the service's ability to meet its SLOs. Event-driven architectures leverage events to decouple components and enable asynchronous communication.

- **Logs:** Logs are textual records generated by a system that capture events, actions, and state changes over time. They provide a detailed chronological account of what has happened within a system, including errors, warnings, and informational messages. Logs are invaluable for troubleshooting issues, auditing system activity, and analyzing historical data.

- **Traces:** Traces offer end-to-end visibility into the flow of requests, providing detailed insights into latency and performance bottlenecks. By correlating traces with defined SLIs, SRE teams can assess whether the system meets its SLOs for response times, error rates, and throughput across services, identifying areas that could impact the SLA. Traces consist of individual spans, each representing a unit of work within a request. By correlating spans across services, traces enable engineers to diagnose performance bottlenecks, identify dependencies, and understand the overall request flow. Tracing is particularly valuable in microservices architectures and complex distributed systems.

Each observability pillar contributes a unique type and level of visibility of the overall performance and events within the organization. This collectively forms a comprehensive picture of its behavior and performance to further understand SLIs and SLOs. By leveraging each of the four observability pillars in tandem, organizations can achieve a holistic understanding of their systems, empowering teams to make informed decisions and troubleshoot effectively, while continuously improving system reliability and performance.

Integrating observability thinking into the SLI and SLO journey

Now that we have covered a few concepts within observability, let's focus on the practice as it relates to reliability engineering and the journey toward defining and achieving organization SLIs and SLOs. Observability is not merely about setting metrics. It's a strategic approach to ensuring systems perform as expected and meet user needs, by capturing the right data and information in the right places and in alignment with customer expectations.

Observability is the ability to infer the internal state of a system based on its external outputs, so it's important that we understand how this process maps to customer expectations without confusing it with the practice of monitoring.

Integrating observability thinking into the SLI and SLO journey involves a fundamental shift in mindset. It's about recognizing that understanding system behavior requires more than just monitoring predefined metrics. Instead, it necessitates a holistic approach that encompasses not only what can be measured but also how it's measured and interpreted. Observability encourages a proactive stance toward reliability. It prompts teams to proactively define and measure SLIs that accurately reflect user experience and system reliability, enabling them to anticipate potential SLO violations before they occur, rather than just reacting to incidents after the fact. By embedding observability into the fabric of SLI and SLO definitions, organizations can foster a culture of resilience and continuous improvement.

Building observability into the process

Defining meaningful SLIs and SLOs is the cornerstone of any reliability engineering initiative. However, traditional approaches often fall short of capturing the full spectrum of system behavior and user experience. This is where observability steps in, offering a more opinionated and dynamic lens through which to assess system performance. Building observability into the process of defining SLIs and SLOs entails a shift from static, predefined metrics to a more adaptive and responsive framework. It involves asking not only what we want to measure but also how we can best observe and interpret the signals emitted by our systems.

Strategic monitoring for effective measurement

With the fast-paced development of modern technology, strategic monitoring is indispensable for ensuring the seamless operation of complex systems. At its core, strategic monitoring is centered around the measurement of SLIs that are used to define and assess SLOs. These SLOs reflect the commitments made to users regarding system reliability, performance, and availability. To achieve strategic monitoring excellence, it's imperative to establish clear, actionable SLOs that align with business objectives.

Effective strategic monitoring begins with a deep understanding of the user experience and the critical aspects of the system that impact it. By identifying key user journeys and critical system components, organizations can define meaningful SLOs that reflect user expectations. For instance, an e-commerce platform may set SLOs for page load times, checkout success rates, and uptime during peak shopping hours.

Strategic monitoring involves continuously assessing SLIs to ensure they are accurate and reflective of user needs. SLOs should be reviewed and refined periodically, in collaboration with stakeholders, to ensure they remain aligned with evolving user demands, technological advancements, and business objectives. Regular review sessions with stakeholders ensure that SLOs remain relevant and achievable. Additionally, leveraging historical data and user feedback enables organizations to refine SLO targets for optimal performance.

In essence, strategic monitoring is not just about collecting data—it's about leveraging that data to drive actionable insights and improvements. By prioritizing SLO measurement and aligning it with business objectives, organizations can enhance user satisfaction, mitigate risks, and stay ahead in today's competitive landscape.

Implementing strategic monitoring systems

Implementing strategic monitoring systems requires a combination of robust processes, cutting-edge technologies, and organizational alignment. Kickstarting this initiative in the right way can only enhance the SLO journey and experience for your organization. It is also important to reiterate the importance of establishing a cross-functional team comprising individuals contributing various skillsets from engineering, operations, and business organizational domains, as mentioned in *Chapter 3*. This team will drive the strategic monitoring initiative from inception to execution. The process can be described in the following simple tasks, similarly outlined in the publication *7 Steps for Setting Up a Monitoring and Evaluation System (2022)*:

1. Define clear objectives and scope:

   - Identify systems and services to be monitored.

   - Define the purpose and scope of the system you are monitoring.

   - Agree on outcomes and objectives—theory of change (including indicators).

2. Organize your data:

   - Plan data collection and analysis (including development of tools).

   - Plan the organization of the data.

   - Plan the information flow and reporting requirements (how and for whom?).

3. Identify suitable monitoring tools and platforms:

   - Includes the capability for managing reliability engineering data, for example, SRE incident management platforms or SLO platforms.

   - Ensure scalability, flexibility, and integration capabilities are included.

4. Monitor workflows and processes:

   - Develop an internal reflection process. This aligns with the retrospectives mentioned in previous chapters.

   - Plan the necessary resources and skills. Hire or train staff to support ongoing maintenance.

5. Transition into an iteration phase:

- Implement dashboards and other mechanisms to visualize the state of monitored systems.

- Implement processes to review and make changes to SLIs or SLOs as needed.

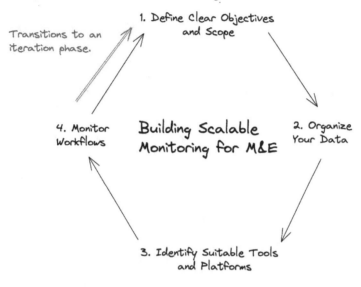

Figure 4.4 – Process for building scalable monitoring systems

Before beginning any initial tasks regarding implementing strategic monitoring systems for enhanced observability, it is key to first define clear objectives and scope. This involves identifying the systems and services to be monitored, along with the corresponding SLOs. SLOs for your monitoring system can and will likely fall under the **Monitoring** column depicted in *Figure 4.1*. Collaboration between development and operations teams is crucial at this stage to ensure that SLOs are realistic and achievable, as both groups will understand best what the expectations are regarding system performance and availability.

Once objectives have been defined and data has been organized, organizations can proceed to select suitable monitoring tools and platforms. It is essential that monitoring tools can collect and report on SLIs that directly measure the performance relative to the defined SLOs. These tools should provide the necessary visibility into how well the system is meeting its reliability targets and allow teams to track progress toward SLO compliance. Additionally, the selected tools should offer scalability, flexibility, and integration capabilities to accommodate future or potential growth and changes in the technology environment.

With the appropriate tools in place, organizations can then establish monitoring workflows and processes. This includes defining escalation policies, setting up automated alerts, and creating dashboards for real-time visualization of observability data. Regular training sessions and knowledge-sharing initiatives ensure team members can effectively use the monitoring systems.

Continuous iteration and improvement are key principles in the implementation of strategic monitoring systems. Regular reviews and retrospectives help identify areas for optimization and refinement. By embracing a culture of learning and adaptation, organizations can maximize the value derived from their strategic monitoring efforts.

Observability platforms and tooling for SLI and SLO monitoring

Observability platforms and tools play a pivotal role in enabling organizations to measure and manage their SLOs effectively. These platforms provide the necessary infrastructure for collecting, processing, and analyzing SLIs in real time. Let's explore some of the key features and capabilities of observability platforms and tools for SLI and SLO monitoring.

Observability platforms offer comprehensive data collection capabilities, allowing organizations to monitor a wide range of metrics across their systems and services. These metrics may include the following:

- Response times
- Error rates
- Throughput
- Resource utilization

By aggregating and correlating these metrics, organizations gain valuable insights into the health and performance of their systems.

Moreover, observability platforms provide advanced analytics and visualization features that enable teams to derive actionable insights from the collected data. Interactive dashboards, customizable charts, and trend analysis tools empower users to identify patterns, anomalies, and performance bottlenecks quickly. This real-time visibility into system behavior is essential for proactively addressing issues and optimizing performance.

Observability platforms often integrate with other tools and systems within the organization's ecosystem, such as incident management platforms and CI/CD pipelines. This seamless integration streamlines workflows and enables automated responses to detected issues, thereby reducing the mean time to resolution and minimizing downtime.

In addition to these features, observability platforms prioritize scalability, reliability, and security to meet the needs of modern enterprises. Cloud-native architectures, distributed data processing, and robust access controls are some of the hallmarks of leading observability platforms.

By harnessing the power of these platforms, organizations can ensure the reliability, performance, and availability of their systems, thereby enhancing the user experience and driving business success.

Techniques for real-time alerting, visualization, and reporting

As a reminder, the goal of this chapter is not to suggest a specific product, solution, or way of managing your internal infrastructure and logistics. It is, rather, to raise awareness of the processes and solutions available to support improved monitoring and observability and build more accurate SLIs. Real-time alerting, visualization, and reporting are essential components of any observability strategy, enabling organizations to detect and respond to issues swiftly while providing stakeholders with actionable insights.

Clear alerting thresholds, defined based on the SLO targets derived from SLIs, are essential for ensuring that the system meets its reliability objectives. Automated alerting mechanisms, such as PagerDuty integrations or email notifications, should be configured to notify stakeholders when SLIs exceed predefined thresholds that indicate a failure to meet the SLOs.

Furthermore, visualization plays a crucial role in enabling teams to make sense of complex observability data. Interactive dashboards and customizable charts allow users to visualize key SLIs and track SLO performance in real time, enabling teams to proactively address potential breaches before they affect service reliability. In addition, scheduled reports, executive summaries, and ad hoc queries empower stakeholders to stay informed about the health and performance of the systems.

Additionally, integrating reporting tools with collaboration platforms will help to facilitate seamless communication and collaboration among teams. The right tool is always the tool that the governing organization needs or is best suited to get the job done. You'll see SRE-related tools highlighted throughout many chapters of this book; these are not recommendations but are mentioned to give you somewhere to start if you decide to look into it today.

Let's further discuss important characteristics of observability and monitoring platforms:

- **Metrics collection**: Processes should focus on gathering metrics from various sources within the system, including application logs, infrastructure metrics (CPU usage, memory usage, and network traffic), and user interactions. Specialized tools such as Prometheus, StatsD, or custom instrumentation can aid with collecting these metrics efficiently.

- **Alerting rules**: Define alerting rules based on predefined thresholds or anomaly detection algorithms. These rules trigger alerts when certain conditions are met, such as a sudden increase in error rates, high latency, or resource saturation.

- **Real-time monitoring**: Implement real-time monitoring systems that continuously ingest and process metrics data to provide insights into the health and performance of the system. Tools such as Grafana, Kibana, or custom dashboards can visualize this data in real time, enabling operators to detect issues promptly.

- **Anomaly detection**: Employ machine learning algorithms or statistical techniques to detect anomalies in the system behavior. These anomalies could indicate potential issues or unusual user activity that requires investigation.

- **Automated remediation**: Integrate alerting systems with automated remediation workflows to respond to alerts quickly—for example, automatically scaling up resources in response to increased demand or restarting failed services.

- **Distributed tracing**: Implement distributed tracing to understand the flow of requests across various components of the system. Specialized solution offerings such as Jaeger or Zipkin can enable the visualization of request traces and identify performance bottlenecks or errors.

- **SLOs and SLIs**: Define SLOs and SLIs to measure the reliability and performance of the system from a user's perspective. Monitor these SLIs in real time and trigger alerts when they deviate from the defined objectives.

- **Historical analysis**: Store historical metrics data for trend analysis and capacity planning. By analyzing historical SLI data, you can identify trends, forecast potential SLO violations, and optimize resources to ensure continued alignment with SLOs.

- **Integration with incident management**: Integrate alerting systems with incident management platforms such as PagerDuty or Opsgenie to streamline the incident response process. Automatically create and escalate incidents based on incoming alerts, ensuring the timely resolution of issues. This can help to improve your organization's ability to integrate incident management data into the metric collection step previously mentioned.

- **Continuous improvement**: Continuously review and refine your observability practices based on feedback and lessons learned from past incidents. Regularly update alerting rules, visualization dashboards, and monitoring configurations to adapt to changes in the system architecture and user requirements.

In addition to these techniques, organizations can and should prioritize usability, scalability, and reliability when selecting alerting, visualization, and reporting tools. Often, incident management is missing as a part of the metric collection process, as opposed to merely managing and responding to alerts. We will highlight this in *Chapter 14*, later in the book. User-friendly interfaces, scalability to handle large volumes of data, and robustness to withstand failures are critical considerations in ensuring the effectiveness of these capabilities.

Summary

Although real-time alerting, visualization, and reporting are indispensable components of observability strategies, it's important to understand that each enables observability, and understanding how to utilize events, metrics, traces, and logs is the goal. The fundamental components work together to enable organizations to detect, analyze, and respond to issues swiftly while providing stakeholders with actionable insights, thus better aligning the product to achieve success with the customer.

By leveraging these techniques effectively, organizations can enhance the reliability, performance, and availability of their systems, thereby driving business success. If observability acts as the foundational layer of SRE, setting the reliability engineering practice up for success through increased observations and transparency, then it is necessary to make mention of its capabilities here. It is even more important to ensure you incorporate it into your reliability journey to build a solid foundation for long-term SLO management.

In the next chapter, we will focus on some of the economic benefits of integrating reliability with SLIs and SLOs into your organization. We'll also cover a few examples of issues that can arise if you decide not to, before we move on to the workshop chapters.

Further reading

You can review the articles and books referenced here for additional information about the concepts mentioned in this chapter:

- *AWS. (2024). The Differences Between Monitoring and Observability.* Retrieved from: `https://aws.amazon.com/compare/the-difference-between-monitoring-and-observability/`.

- *EvalCommunity: Jobs & Experts. (2023, Sept 10). Smart Indicators in Monitoring and Evaluation.* Retrieved from: `https://www.evalcommunity.com/career-center/smart-indicators/`.

- *Neymeyer, S. (2022, Jan 6). 7 Steps for Setting Up a Monitoring and Evaluation System.* Retrieved from: `https://www.activityinfo.org/blog/posts/2022-01-06-seven-steps-for-setting-up-a-monitoring-and-evaluation-system.html#:~:text=Step%201%3A%20Define%20the%20purpose,the%20organization%20of%20the%20data`.

- *Practical Mel. (2023, December 19). How to Set M&E Objectives.* Retrieved from: `https://practicalmel.com/how-to-set-me-objectives/`.

5

The Financial Impact of Not Adopting Indicators

In the previous chapters, we were able to highlight the hierarchy of reliability and observability concepts as they relate to SLIs and the importance of building a dedicated team to manage each component of the process. This chapter highlights the economic benefits of doing so and the financial impact associated with the adoption or lack thereof regarding SLIs. We will begin by taking some time to explore the core concepts of reliability engineering as they relate to the economic benefits. With the rapid development of modern businesses via technology, reliability isn't just a luxury; it's a necessity. You can expect to learn more about the tangible costs associated with unreliable systems and explore how prioritizing reliability can lead to significant cost efficiencies.

Without a strong focus on reliability measured through SLIs, systems are more prone to numerous negative impacts, including the extreme case of system downtime. SLIs provide actionable insights to ensure the system meets reliability targets and avoid economic losses associated with outages. This downtime can result in significant economic losses due to missed opportunities, decreased productivity, and potential damage to the business's reputation.

Let's consider the case of a major e-commerce platform. Any downtime, even for a few minutes, can translate into substantial economic losses. If, during peak shopping seasons such as Black Friday, the business experiences downtime, every second can result in millions of dollars in missed opportunities. By investing in robust reliability measures, such as implementing **site reliability engineering (SRE)**, with well-defined SLIs, SLOs, and error budgets, this platform can remain proactive and minimize downtime. SLOs set clear reliability targets, while error budgets allow for controlled experimentation without risking SLA violations, safeguarding revenue and customer trust.

In this chapter, we will cover the following main topics:

- The unintended consequences of not investing in reliability
- Communicating economic implications within your organizations

Let's get started!

The unintended consequences of not investing in reliability

Although we primarily discuss investing in reliability engineering from a systems and platform perspective, it's important to understand the intrinsic value increases that occur due to the intangible benefits that are not as immediate. This includes the various concepts previously mentioned in prior chapters, such as customer centricity, impact on the organization's brand, and the customer relationship, all of which impact the business's bottom line. We need a way to conceptually tie intangible aspects into service-level measurements to tie and align the value into strategic direction and decision-making.

Although this book does not extensively discuss the topic, error budgets contribute to the decision-making aspects by providing the team and broader organization with increased visibility of technical outage limits allowed before impacting the customer experience. They are equally as important to any reliability engineering organization. Although we mention them in a later section and discuss the concept later in the book in *Chapter 15*, when discussing financial investments and the economics of reliability engineering, it is important to at least introduce them so that we understand the correlation and take concepts such as the error burn rate into consideration.

In simplest terms, your error budget is the maximum allowable amount of time or room for errors or failures for a system or process to occur in a specific period. You can refer to Google's SRE Workbook for an example of an error budget policy (`https://sre.google/workbook/error-budget-policy/`).

According to the latest report prepared for Salesforce by IT & Data Management Research of EMA (`https://www.servicenow.com/lpebk/enterprise-sre.html`), "*Reliability, because features that aren't available don't count.*" If we are not implementing processes that ensure maximum availability, then we are not performing at our best. When approaching the SRE function from an economic benefit perspective, it's beneficial to consider questions such as the following:

- What is the minimum level of service that a user will find acceptable for any given task, at a not-to-exceed cost that makes sense from a business point of view?
- How can a specific level of service reliability be quantified, monitored, and enforced?
- What are the earliest and best indicators of any possible service degradation?
- How can automation eradicate repetitive, manual tasks that waste time and add no value?

At first glance, the previous questions appear as if they may be negligible, but underneath the surface, there is a ripple effect that begins to emerge. The goal of SRE is typically thought of as finding an issue, fixing the issue, and automating where it makes sense, as depicted in *Figure 5.1*. However, an additional component is being able to quantify the metric in a way that you can financially tie it back to organizational value and the bottom line by improving upon SLA commitments.

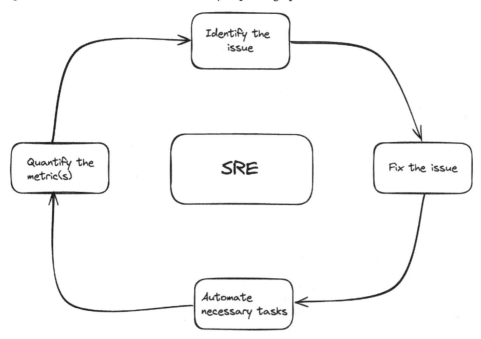

Figure 5.1 – The cyclic task/responsibilities of SRE engineers at a high level

Let's explore the impact of the ripple effect, depicted in *Figure 5.1*, that can occur when SRE is not prioritized or implemented as needed.

A business's success is often referred to and measured by its profits and losses, overlooking the importance of how not incorporating a framework for accountability can prove to be a costly oversight. Regarding this book, SRE is the recommended framework or tool for doing just that. SRE is fundamentally a set of core principles to measure how your systems are performing according to your customer's expectations.

When implemented correctly, the selected metrics, often regarded as the pulse of service performance, provide many invaluable insights into the health and performance of the respective operations. Yet, despite their significance, many organizations continue to operate in the dark, oblivious to the potential financial repercussions of neglecting SLIs.

Now, let's imagine an e-commerce giant, by the name of **Technology Insights**, who plans to disregard SLIs altogether in pursuit of rapid expansion. This negligence can lead to SLA breaches, damaging customer satisfaction and trust. Monitoring SLIs ensures that the business meets SLA commitments, thereby preserving customer relationships and reducing financial risks. With their focus solely on acquiring new customers and scaling operations, **Technology Insights**, or **Tech Insights** as we will refer to it, fails to monitor critical indicators such as website uptime, response time, and customer satisfaction levels regarding their application and platform performance, missing out on the opportunity to improve through the customer experience and feedback. Some of the disadvantages of ignoring this opportunity are as follows:

- Increased engineer burnout. This can also creep into burnout of other staff outside of your engineering and support domains.

- Burnout of your employees can also result in high turnover rates within your organization.

- Decreased ability to mitigate risks such as security vulnerabilities and compliance failures, resulting in increased downtime and a more negative customer experience.

- The previously mentioned reasons can incur additional financial losses by increased opportunities for data breaches and financial fraud.

Although it's important to highlight the disadvantages, we also want to mention the advantages, especially when considering platforms and applications within the financial industry, warehouse management, human resource information systems, and many other platforms and applications that support various levels of government services within the public sector. Some of the advantages that directly improve your organization's bottom line are as follows:

- Being able to proactively monitor and manage your incident lifecycle management processes and systems.

- Improving the software and development process through increased and efficient automation practices.

- Efficient scalability and capacity planning capabilities through identifying bottlenecks and improved performance testing.

- As mentioned earlier, improving security vulnerabilities.

- Providing an opportunity for your organization and team to learn together through iteration and implementing processes such as retrospectives.

There are likely many other benefits that we can list here, but let's take a minute to continue exploring the disadvantages of not investing in reliability. To further explore disadvantages, we can align each one with a concept implemented in the practice of reliability engineering. Each concept is there to help reduce the negative impacts. Before we go further into the discussion, let's learn about the concept of error budgets and how they fit into the bigger picture.

Error budgets as a defense mechanism

This chapter is written under the assumption that you, the reader, maintain some level of familiarity with the concept of error budgets as they relate to your indicators and objectives. Your error budget represents the maximum allowable amount of time or errors a system can tolerate without breaching the defined SLO. It is derived directly from SLIs that measure critical metrics such as latency, availability, and error rates. Without accurate SLIs, the calculation of error budgets and their alignment with SLOs is incomplete. Let's refer to *Figure 5.2* as a refresher of what this means in numerical form.

Availability SLO	Error Budget Per Year	Error Budget Per Month
90%	36.5 days	72 Hours
95%	18.25 Days	36 Hours
98%	7.30 Days	14.4 Hours
99%	3.65 Days	7.20 Hours
99.5%	1.83 Days	3.60 Hours
99.8%	17.52 Hours	86.23 Minutes
99.9%	8.76 Hours	43.2 Minutes
99.95%	4.38 Hours	21.56 Minutes
99.99%	52.6 Minutes	4.32 Minutes
99.999%	5.26 Minutes	5.9 Seconds
99.9999%	31.5 Seconds	2.59 Seconds

Figure 5.2 – Error budget in comparison to SLO based on a 28-day period

Figure 5.2 provides the relationship between the SLO you would like to achieve and the allowable length of time of outage per year or month. Earlier in this chapter, we mentioned *Tech Insights*, an e-commerce organization, disregarding the need to measure the response times for certain customer workflows in the system. However, they have implemented external facing SLAs providing the customer with performance-level commitments. Let's pretend this commitment is three 9s or 99.9% of availability for some workflow focused on the customer experience or some application. The expectation internally is that SLOs are defined as measurable targets that encompass the components necessary to maintain service reliability. Internal SLOs should be set slightly more stringent than the external SLA to provide a buffer and ensure SLA commitments are not breached.

Internally, we'd want to implement an objective that was a bit more aggressive to ensure we do not breach the agreement. Therefore, we might decide to implement an internal SLO of 99.95%. This affords the team 4.38 hours per year or 21.56 minutes per month of downtime for the respective services. In some organizations, this can seem a bit aggressive. As a rule, achieving higher levels of reliability (9s) requires exponential increases in operational effort, monitoring, and infrastructure investments. This is due to the diminishing returns of reliability improvement as systems approach perfection. For instance, moving from 99.9% to 99.99% availability necessitates significantly more stringent monitoring, fault-tolerance mechanisms, and operational readiness. Monitoring, on-call scheduling, and the scope of disaster recovery and other processes need to be taken into consideration. This is beyond the scope of this discussion, but it is important to mention.

To achieve a specific level of 9s, Tech Insights would want to perform some assessment to determine what processes are currently in place and what processes they need to implement to achieve the level of desired performance. As the number of 9s your organization wants to achieve increases, the amount of time available for any issues and outages (error budget) will decrease. This will also result in an increase in costs and the effort to remain in compliance with the error budget. In *Figure 5.3*, we can picture this relationship and correlation in the following manner:

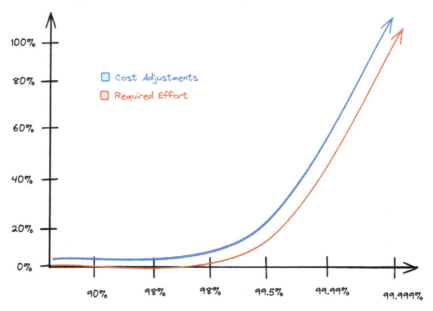

Figure 5.3 – A positive correlation between cost adjustment and required effort to achieve some level of 9s of reliability

Now, let's consider an instance where you've deployed a multi-region application into a cloud-hosted and multi-node container-orchestrated cluster (we will discuss it in detail in later chapters).

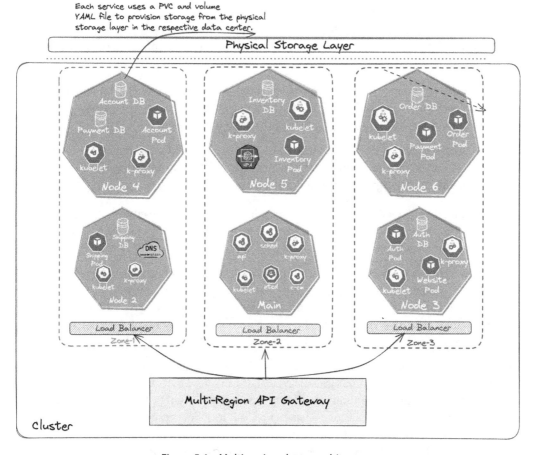

Figure 5.4 – Multi-region cluster architecture

Your commitment to the customer should explicitly define SLIs that measure the real-time performance of your service, such as latency, errors, and saturation. These indicators should inform SLOs, which are measurable performance targets aligned with customer expectations.

As a refresher, the four golden signals are metric categorizations that should be used during the monitoring process at a bare minimum, to ensure standard details are captured. The standard signals are latency, traffic, errors, and saturation. What does each of these mean to you?

- **Latency**: Captures the time it takes to serve a request between the identified endpoints.

- **Traffic**: Captures the total number of requests across the network.

- **Errors**: Captures the number of requests that fail.

- **Saturation**: Captures the load on your network and servers.

Capturing the four golden signals (latency, traffic, errors, and saturation) as SLIs provides visibility into your service's health and directly supports meeting SLOs. This helps align operational efforts to fulfill SLAs and improve reliability, enabling on-call engineers to make informed decisions during live incidents.

As a result, at a bare minimum, your organization could consider each when developing your indicators to begin to experience the benefits of reliability as regards service levels. This does not include the many other practices of reliability that are not mentioned in this chapter.

Now, you might be asking yourself, *"How does this relate back to the disadvantages of not adopting reliability?"*. Let's discuss the disadvantages that you can experience due to the earlier-mentioned ripple effect. An organization can experience the following negative effects:

- **Customer dissatisfaction and churn**: Unreliable systems can lead to customer dissatisfaction and churn. Losing customers due to poor reliability can have a direct impact on revenue and profitability, resulting in customers seeking out improved products from a competitor.

  Tech Insights' SLIs, such as response time and error rate, indicate poor performance during holidays and peak shopping hours, breaching established SLOs. This degradation leads to abandoned shopping carts, missed sales opportunities, and increased customer churn. By leveraging SRE practices to monitor SLIs and adjust thresholds dynamically during peak times, the organization can prevent downtime and ensure consistent customer experience.

- **Damage to brand reputation**: With many organizations continuing to shift business processes toward digital transformation, a tarnished reputation can spread faster than in previous times, due to the numerous digital platforms available to provide followers of that brand with information regarding the product and customer experience. This includes negative feedback as, according to a study conducted by Zendesk, customers are more likely to leave reviews for negative experiences than positive experiences (*2013, Customer Service and Business Results, Zendesk*).

  Tech Insights was once revered for its innovation and reliability. Due to a reduction in performance and availability, it now finds itself at the mercy of scathing reviews and negative publicity. Prospective customers eventually become wary of engaging with a brand plagued by service issues, which tends to result in turning to competitors offering a more seamless experience that meets their targeted needs.

  A study conducted by Colorado State University reported that negative reviews can have more of an impact on some of a business's most important customers.

- **Escalating support costs**: Unreliable systems often require more frequent maintenance and support interventions. If we refer to *Figure 5.1* earlier in this chapter, SRE tasks are thought of as a cyclic set of tasks surrounding technical support. Instead, it should be thought of as incorporating theoretical principles into practice to guardrail issues from reoccurring and report also on performance. This mindset can lead to increased labor costs and the need for additional resources to resolve or mitigate an issue, which impacts organizational culture and the customer experience.

As incoming customer complaints flood in, Tech Insights' support teams become overwhelmed by support tickets and customer inquiries, resulting in stretched resources. With every minute spent addressing service-related issues, the cost of support escalates, further denting the company's bottom line. Meanwhile, skilled engineers are diverted from strategic projects into firefighting mode, stunting innovation and hindering growth.

With the stunt of innovation and growth hindered, organizations are also likely to experience increased engineer burnout and high rates of attrition.

- **Scalability challenges**: Systems that are not designed for reliability may struggle to scale effectively. This can result in additional costs associated with over-provisioning resources or retrofitting systems to handle increased loads.

Consider Tech Insights during peak hours or holidays struggling to handle surges in user traffic due to system architecture. Without reliability practices in place to capture the time periods and components associated with bottlenecks, the engineering team could scale up application resources or add additional nodes to the cluster, which can result in over-provisioning and additional operational expenses.

- **Security vulnerabilities and regulatory compliance costs**: Unreliable systems are often more susceptible to security vulnerabilities and breaches. The economic costs of security incidents can include fines, legal fees, and remediation costs, while also resulting in damage to brand reputation. This is especially important when considering the handling of customer personal data with increased regulations, such as GDPR, in specific countries.

A financial institution that experiences a data breach faces not only financial losses but also regulatory fines and reputational damage. Weaknesses in system reliability often result in security breaches, underscoring the importance of integrating security into every layer of infrastructure design. By implementing robust security measures alongside reliability practices, organizations can mitigate the economic impact of security incidents.

In regulated industries such as healthcare, non-compliance with reliability standards can result in hefty penalties and legal expenses. A healthcare provider experiencing frequent system outages risks violating patient data privacy laws, inviting regulatory scrutiny and financial repercussions. By integrating reliability best practices and compliance standards, organizations can mitigate the risk of regulatory fines and safeguard their financial interests.

- **Long-term technical debt**: Neglecting reliability to benefit from short-term gains can result in the accumulation of technical debt over time. Addressing technical debt can become extremely costly, requiring significant investments in refactoring code and system architecture improvements, among other tasks.

Tech Insights neglects to refactor legacy systems over time due to a lack of time and internal staff begins to face mounting maintenance costs and diminished agility. By proactively managing technical debt through SLOs, organizations can reduce long-term costs and future-proof their systems.

- **Lost revenue opportunities:** With the advancement of technology and the increase in digitization, every second counts. Tech Insights' failure to meet SLA conditions, driven by unmet SLOs for availability and latency, results in immediate revenue losses due to transaction abandonment and long-term reputational damage. Establishing precise SLIs to measure transaction success rates and latency during high traffic periods can enable proactive remediation before breaching SLA agreements, safeguarding revenue and future opportunities. Potential partnerships and collaborations evaporate as industry peers view the company as unreliable and unstable. Unreliable systems may limit the ability of an organization to pursue new business opportunities or expand into new markets. This can result in missed revenue opportunities and potential competitive disadvantages. Coupling SLIs and SLOs to support SLAs helps organizations mitigate loss of revenue and opportunities.

  Imagine that Tech Insights is unable to launch a new product in a timely manner due to system instability with critical system components. Competitors can seize the opportunity, capturing market share and leaving the company at a competitive disadvantage. By investing in reliability engineering, organizations can seize business opportunities swiftly and stay ahead of the curve in dynamic markets.

- **Quantifying the costs:** While the financial impact of neglecting SLOs may vary depending on the scale and nature of the business, the cumulative effect is undeniable. Lost sales, increased support costs, damage to brand reputation, and missed growth opportunities all contribute to a significant dent in profitability. What initially seemed like minor deviations from service standards transitioned into a full-blown financial crisis. Lack of reliability can lead to inefficiencies in operations, such as manual intervention to address issues, firefighting, and ad hoc workarounds or short-term patching. These inefficiencies can increase operational costs and reduce overall productivity.

Tech Insights was previously plagued by unreliable inventory management systems and resorted to manual interventions and workarounds to fulfill orders on time. These inefficiencies incurred additional labor costs and eroded customer trust due to delayed shipments. Streamlining operations through reliable systems and automation backed by SLIs and SLOs, operations and fulfillment center teams can reduce costs and enhance customer satisfaction.

Each of these sections underscores the critical role of reliability in driving cost efficiencies and sustaining business success. By prioritizing reliability as a strategic imperative, organizations can minimize economic risks, unlock new opportunities, and cultivate a culture of resilience in an ever-changing digital landscape.

Communicating economic implications within your organizations

For Tech Insights, the road to redemption begins with a fundamental shift in mindset. Recognizing the pivotal role of reliability engineering in defining SLIs, which form the basis of measurable SLOs, and ensuring that these SLOs align with externally committed SLAs is the start. The company agrees and commits to a holistic approach to service excellence. By investing in robust monitoring tools, implementing proactive maintenance strategies, and fostering a culture of continuous improvement, Tech Insights begins to embark on a journey toward reclaiming its position as a market leader.

Apart from getting started within an organization experiencing various levels of turmoil throughout, it is imperative that the key stakeholders can communicate the importance, benefits, and next steps to internal staff to create buy-in. Based on the previous sections, we might conclude that Tech Insights should consider the following actions, in the respective order:

1. Formulate the "why" behind service-level metric implementation:

    -   For Tech Insights, these might be the various reasons mentioned previously packaged in a formal proposal document.

2. Communicate the "why" to internal stakeholders. This can also include a **proof of concept** (**POC**) of an end-to-end POC against an internal service or platform. Internal stakeholders might include the following:

    -   The engineering teams and their respective management chain of a specific internal product or platform solution.

    -   An internal SRE business group.

    -   Internal customer support team managing customer support tickets.

    -   External customer accounts identified through internal professional services groups.

3. Implement or begin your data-gathering process by first defining relevant SLIs for each system or service. SLIs should reflect critical user journeys and measure key aspects of reliability such as latency, availability, and error rates. This data will then inform the establishment of SLOs:

    -   This step is dependent on the respective stakeholders:

        -   Customer support might include internal support tickets and other methods of communication with customer accounts established by the support team's process.

        -   SRE business group or engineering teams' data would include technical artifacts such as logs, design documents, and various other artifacts established around the product or product line.

- For each group, the team should investigate whether the organization or group has externally published SLAs. If so, these commitments can guide the reliability targets. However, the team should first establish achievable SLOs using SLIs to determine realistic goals that align with both customer expectations and system capabilities.

4. Start your process on the targeted stakeholders using the outline provided in *Chapter 6*:

   - This could be the initial POC step if not implemented in *step 2*.

You'll also need to emphasize how this information is communicated to the right staff members in a consumable way to drive internal agreement. The manner and method by which the team communicates with the engineering organization for buy-in differs from the method used with upper management responsible for sign-off, allocating resources, and budgeting.

As much as we discuss reliable applications and systems, it is equally important to ensure the methods and practices we use to communicate are equally reliable. Expect to see many of the topics mentioned in this chapter utilized in the workshop chapters that follow.

Summary

Reliability is often a key differentiator for businesses but is reviewed in hindsight rather than thought of at the forefront. Failure to embrace SRE and deliver reliable services can result in a loss of competitive advantage and market share.

Equipped with a newfound appreciation for the importance of service-level measurements, Tech Insights, as well as your organization, can emerge from the shadows of uncertainty stronger and more resilient than ever before. By prioritizing service excellence and embracing a data-driven approach for service-level performance, the company not only safeguards its financial health but also lays the foundation for sustained growth and prosperity in an ever-evolving marketplace.

In today's competitive and demanding technology industry, where success hangs in the balance, the significance of SLIs in conjunction with SLOs and SLAs cannot be overstated. Neglecting these interdependent metrics not only jeopardizes financial stability but also undermines the trust and confidence of customers and stakeholders alike. Organizations must prioritize defining SLIs that align with SLOs and support SLA commitments to ensure reliability and sustained trust. By taking advantage of the warning signs and proactively addressing service issues, organizations can unlock untapped potential and chart a course toward a brighter, more prosperous future.

In the next chapter, we will direct attention toward the steps following receiving buy-in within your organization. In more simplified terms, "I am ready to implement SLIs and SLOs in my organization and need to establish a process or method for kicking off the implementation conversation." You can expect to navigate through the process using relatable examples across various aspects of an internal system.

Further reading

Here, you can review the referenced articles and books for additional reading about concepts mentioned in this chapter:

- Barnhill, P., & McDonald, J. (2022, Dec 15). *Effective Site Reliability Engineering (SRE) Requires an Observability Strategy*. Retrieved from `https://www2.deloitte.com/us/en/blog/deloitte-on-cloud-blog/2022/effective-site-reliability-engineering-requires-an-observability-strategy.html`.

- Dimensional Research. (2013, April). *Zendesk Whitepapers*. Retrieved from `http://cdn.zendesk.com/resources/whitepapers/Zendesk_WP_Customer_Service_and_Business_Results.pdf`.

- EMA Research. (2021, June). *Enterprise SRE: Service Reliability Ebook*. Retrieved from `https://www.servicenow.com/lpebk/enterprise-sre.html`.

- Ewaschuk, R., & Beyer, B. (2017). *Monitoring Distributed Systems*. Newton: O'Reilly Media, Inc. Retrieved from `https://sre.google/sre-book/monitoring-distributed-systems/#xref_monitoring_golden-signals`.

- MoldStud. (2024, Feb 14). *Understanding the Economics of Site Reliability Engineering*. Retrieved from `https://moldstud.com/articles/p-understanding-the-economics-of-site-reliability-engineering`.

- Sylte, A. (2022, March 21). *Why Negative Reviews Could Have More of AN Impact on Some of the Most Important Customers*. Retrieved from `https://biz.source.colostate.edu/negative-online-reviews-impact-study/`.

- Vierling, A. (2024, February 20). *Measuring the Impact of Site Reliability Engineering: Strategic Value and KPIs*. Retrieved from `https://www.connectria.com/resources/measuring-the-impact-of-site-reliability-engineering-strategic-value-and-kpis/`.

Part 2:
The Tough Stuff – Kickstarting the SLI and SLO Conversation

In this part, you will find examples used to delineate the process of identifying and implementing your SLIs. You can anticipate hands-on chapters with illustrative examples to provide practical references and enhance comprehension of the process for developing SLIs and SLOs in distributed environments.

This part contains the following chapters:

6

Workshop Preparation: Structuring the SLI and SLO Conversation

In this chapter, we migrate toward the fun stuff. In *Chapter 2*, we explored the organizational and team aspects of implementing SLIs and SLOs within your organization. In *Chapter 3*, we defined and outlined personas and the customer journey as it relates to SLIs and SLOs. By understanding this process in its totality, we provide ourselves with an opportunity to ensure that our engineering teams clearly capture and understand our customers' needs.

In doing so, we can accurately establish application boundaries to identify, implement, and prioritize SLIs, which, in turn, help define SLOs and monitor performance against SLAs to ensure stable reliability through appropriate metrics. This chapter's goal is to outline the workshop's structure before applying it. In the chapters that follow, we will apply these learnings to different applications and architectural settings to further demonstrate the previous chapters.

This chapter also highlights the significance of establishing application boundaries and will provide insights into identifying and categorizing critical applications and components.

We'll be covering the following main topics:

- Developing customer-centric SLIs
- Defining system components for customer journey visibility
- Focusing SLIs on customer journey metrics
- Setting SLO targets and performance thresholds

Now, let's get started!

Developing customer-centric SLIs

Using a formalized process or framework will help structure your conversation with invested stakeholders, the engineering team, product managers, and other parties invested in SLIs and SLOs. This also helps to ensure that specific information and requirements are captured in a way that is easily translated into SLIs. At a high level, the previous chapters are condensed into a set of steps that will enable you to build your SLIs. It can be identified as follows:

1. Define and map personas and their journeys.
2. Identify your system boundaries.
3. Implement your SLIs.
4. Set SLO thresholds.

Before we actualize the process, let's dive a bit deeper into what each step entails as well as a few things to consider that help to ensure we capture information in a way that resonates with you, the reader. In hindsight, the process was structured as a conversational workshop to ensure the requirements were captured in a consumable way. The goal of this chapter is not to guide you on the tooling to use; however, it is imperative to consider it initially, which will help facilitators and other staff capture the data in a consumable manner.

Just to ensure the correct context is considered, the following section outlines minimal terminology in the context that is used in this book. Much of the information that is gathered to formulate each category is collected during market and/or organization research and surveying.

Let's take a moment to briefly review terminology to ensure there is an understanding as we discuss various topics throughout this chapter and the chapters to follow:

- **Persona**: Personas represent users or customers of your product or service, and are used to understand how SLIs and SLOs impact different user journeys and the overall user experience. The characteristics that describe a persona typically include a persona name, their role, and any other qualitative or quantitative information that helps to describe their role in interacting with your product or service.

- **User journey**: The user journey, or persona journey, is the series of steps the persona takes to achieve a specific outcome during interactions with your product or service. Typically, you will experience a one-to-one ratio between the journey and the series of steps to achieve a specific outcome.

- **Journey mapping**: Your journey map is the process of visualizing the steps a persona takes to achieve a specific outcome. A journey map, just like any other data visualization process, is depicted in various forms. Journey mapping, like personas, also comes in different types. This can also include the emotions and feelings of a persona regarding the journey or step(s) along the journey. It can be segregated in two ways:

  - **Multi-persona journey map**: A multi-persona journey map is just that – a journey that includes multiple personas on the same journey. This can happen if the emotions felt heavily influence the outcome and vary according to specific personas.

  - **Single persona map**: Single persona maps consist of a one-to-one ratio for a persona to a specific journey and outcome. This is what you will typically see or experience when using the process with an organization or business.

- **Scenarios**: A scenario is a brief description or story that provides additional insight as to why the persona is using the product or service to achieve an outcome, with a specific context. It also describes how the persona is doing it.

- **Touchpoints**: Touchpoints are important to the process as they showcase where the interaction with your product or service occurs. If we consider a single product that is sold in a storefront and online, the product could have been suggested through an employee, from another loyal customer brand, or a marketing ad. This initial method of interaction can greatly impact the customer experience. Touchpoints can have an impact on the persona's emotions during a journey. This is important to consider during your research.

Now that we understand referenceable terminology as it relates to the text within this book, let's start the conversation with starting points for defining a persona and persona journey.

Defining and mapping personas and journeys

This section provides a comprehensive overview of the following:

- Defining personas

- Defining the user journey

- Outlining the process for mapping personas to their journey

Leverage the insights developed during the process, which will help define your SLIs and establish SLOs to align with user needs and expectations.

Developing personas and the user journey mapping process are both fundamental techniques used to understand the needs, motivations, and behaviors of users. Personas represent fictional characters that embody different user segments, while user journey mapping visualizes the end-to-end experience of users as they interact with your product or service. Both tools help organizations empathize with users, identify pain points, and design solutions that address their needs effectively.

Process for defining personas

Defining personas involves conducting research, interviews, surveys, and analysis of available user data to create profiles that represent your target users. This process includes gathering demographic information, understanding user goals and challenges, and identifying common behaviors and preferences at different phases of their experience. By synthesizing insights from qualitative and quantitative research, organizations can develop personas that accurately reflect the diverse needs and characteristics of their user base. When probing your users or developing personas, you want to ask questions that help you to understand their needs, goals, and motivations. This should also include questions that help you understand why they behave or make a specific decision at a given touchpoint.

Let's reference a simple cosmetics website that supplies different beauty brands to its male and female customer base. The customer success organization may want to not only evaluate the technical performance and availability of the website through SLIs but also set SLO targets to define acceptable levels of performance and availability that align with SLAs, to ensure contractual commitments to customers are met. The customer experience or interactions with the website might look something a bit like the depictions in *Figure 6.1* at a high level.

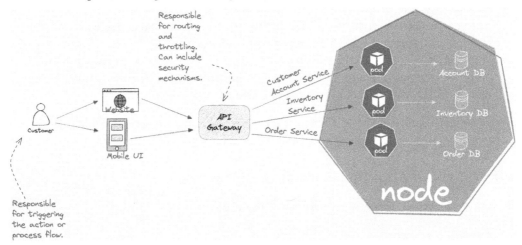

Figure 6.1 – A high-level display of a cosmetics website for various customer personas to place orders

You might take the following steps to develop your data, identify personas, and then build out their journey:

1.   Submit a request to your customer support team to solicit product-related data:

   •   Are we receiving customer inquiries regarding a specific product, brand, and so on?

   •   Are customer requests/tickets related to products being sold or website performance and availability?

2. Reach out to your marketing team and retrieve data regarding products frequently and infrequently purchased, as well as information on industry-related products and competitors:

    - What are the top-selling products (makeup, hair, body, etc.)?

    - Who are the organization's market/industry competitors?

3. Reach out to your customer success team and retrieve customer **Net Promoter Score** (**NPS**) data related to the customer experience:

    - What is the NPS for your customer support organization?

    - How does your organization's NPS compare to identified market competitors?

    - Are there focus areas triggering a decrease in NPS?

      - Poor customer support?

      - Poor performing products?

    - Do we even have NPS or some other mechanism to measure the customer experience setup?

    - Are there internal mechanisms, such as surveys, in place to highlight loyal customers leaving or coming from a competitor?

4. Reach out to internal engineering teams to understand any technical implications that could impact product availability and sales:

    - What incidents are related to website uptime and availability?

      - What is the impact on products being available?

    - Are purchase orders being abandoned due to latency on specific web pages?

These references are merely hypothetical questions you'd want to consider as well as different channels you'd want to leverage to begin your data gathering process. Much of the information is typically gathered during facilitation sessions, internal or external surveying mechanisms, and data storage repositories that might already be in place internally. By utilizing the feedback provided, you might conclude that you want to focus on the following personas categories:

- B2B buyers
- User personas
- Customer personas

Persona categories are identified based on the ability of different personas to fall into the following categories to provide further characteristics or context surrounding the persona as it relates to your product or service. Persona categories are described as follows:

- **Proto personas**: These are personas based on market research that help businesses understand what the target market wants and needs.

- **Customer personas**: These are realistic representations of the target customer, which include additional information about the customer's demographic, behaviors, and needs.

- **User personas**: These focus on the typical user of a product or service to help a business understand how the user interacts with their product or service.

- **Buyer personas**: These represent a target market for a product or service and help the business understand the needs and wants of a target market who both use and buy their products or service.

For demo purposes, let's select the following personas, each from one of the persona categories and identified using the previous questions asked. Our list of personas to begin is as follows:

- B2B salesperson
- Loyal customer
- New customer
- CRM integration

We'll include an integration for **customer relationship management** (**CRM**) to represent the customer experience and ensure we focus on the technical aspects of the website from a different consumer perspective. Just to ensure we are on the same page, a CRM system is simply a technical solution leveraged by a business, organization, or team to manage various customer relationships. It's typical to hear the acronym associated with sales, customer support, and IT teams within an organization.

In this instance, you'd typically use a brainstorming tool to map this process out. Experience has acclimated me with virtual tools such as Miro and the standard whiteboard. In *Figure 6.2*, you'll find a sample of what a virtual board might look like, which can be replicated on any whiteboard within an office.

Figure 6.2 – SLI/SLO virtual template using Miro

Whiteboarding or brainstorming aids to facilitate the conversation with more control while still providing a collaborative, communicative, and flexible environment. In our dashboard, we have the following categories:

- **Personas**: Fictional characters that represent a user or customer of your product or service.

- **Persona journey**: The journey, or series of interactions, a persona takes to achieve some outcome related to your product or service.

- **Expectations**: The expectations a persona has for a specific step or outcome. It is important the expectations are tied to some form of historical data.

- **SLI specification**: The specification describes what you want to measure without technical details.

- **SLI implementation**: SLI implementation incorporates the technical details surrounding how you are going to measure your SLI.

- **SLI prioritization**: SLI prioritization aids in prioritizing your SLIs for physical implementation according to business impact and feasibility.

We'll use the preceding steps to work through a few SLI and SLO examples. SLO thresholds should be defined as part of the persona mapping process to ensure that expectations are measurable. By collaborating with historical data, the team should explicitly identify and document SLO thresholds during this phase to set clear performance objectives for each persona, which will guide the development of SLIs.

Based on our persona categories and prior data gathering, we have identified the personas in *Figure 6.3*.

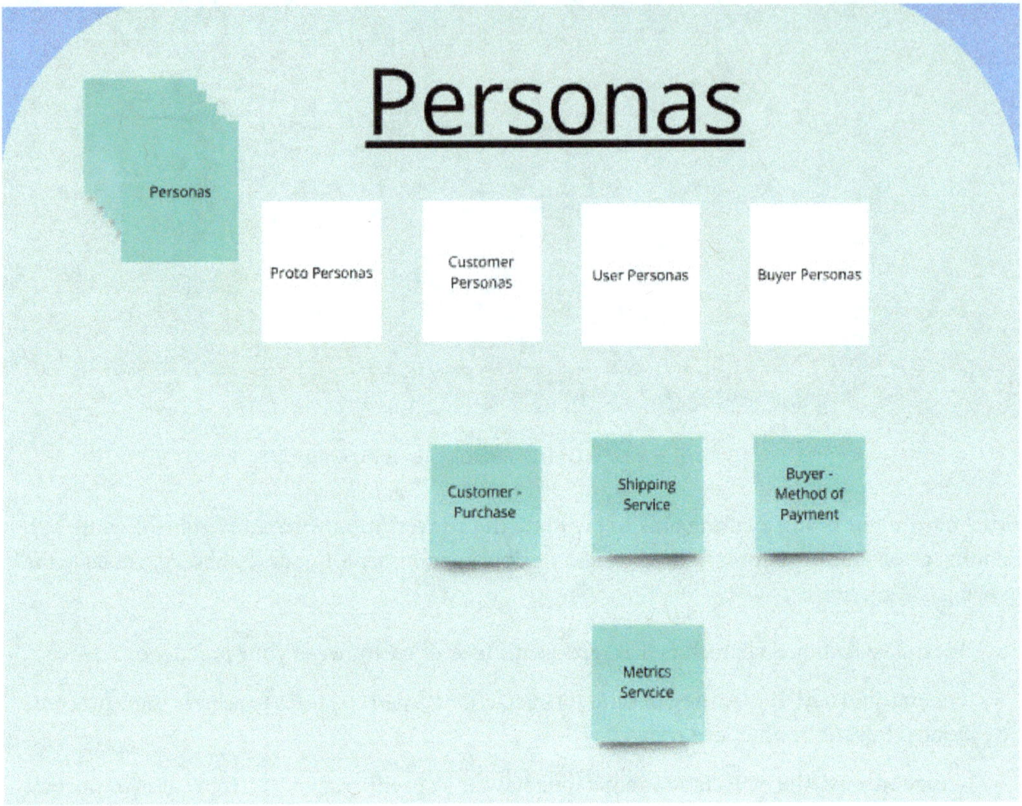

Figure 6.3 – Identified personas

As a team, it is best to use a ranking system that is understandable and fair to you all to rank each persona according to criticality. The goal of this step is to identify and prioritize personas based on their impact on business-critical SLIs. The team should align personas with specific SLIs that directly affect the user experience and business outcomes, helping to prioritize personas that are most critical to meeting SLOs. Depending on the time allocated, a team might also want to work through all personas and develop an iteration process at a later stage.

Mapping the user journey

Mapping the user journey is simply the process of visualizing the series of steps and touchpoints that users encounter when interacting with a product or service. This process helps organizations understand the context in which each persona engages with their offerings. It also helps to identify pain points and uncover opportunities for improvement. By mapping out the user journey, organizations can gain a holistic view of the user experience and prioritize initiatives that enhance usability, efficiency, and satisfaction accurately. This also raises awareness of the importance of including the tooling and different integrations as personas as well.

Under each sticky note (*Figure 6.5*), you will find a white dot. This dot reflects the personas we are going to move forward with. In an actual workshop, you'd want to set up some timing mechanism to allow for discussion as well as a voting process for the team to identify which personas are critical. It's also important to note that this does not mean the remaining personas are complete. In fact, it is encouraged that the team stores this information in some repository that is accessible for a period. This allows the team to reflect on previous decisions made and iterate on any identified gaps or improvements.

In the context of SRE, decisions on persona prioritization and the journeys should be based on SLOs and SLIs rather than just historical data. For example, historical data can guide the team to identify critical personas based on the impact on user experience, but specific thresholds and indicators should be tied to measurable service levels. This only helps to solidify why the team made the decision and map any future issues to the decision. It's easier to correct if we understand the "why." With our persona journey and the next step in the process, we will update our virtual whiteboard with the personas in *Figure 6.4*.

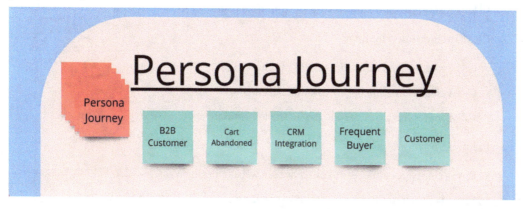

Figure 6.4 – Selected personas

The goal of the persona journey, as previously mentioned, is to outline the series of steps that a person takes to achieve some outcome related to your product or service. It's imperative that the team communicates and collaborates regarding the possible outcomes that a persona takes. Each outcome or workflow should be broken down with minimal dependencies on other outcomes and workflows to ensure better accuracy.

Hypothetically speaking, we have already migrated the prioritized personas we want to initially focus on. Remember, the remaining items are not being ruled out; we are merely starting with the personas that the team agrees, based on some historical data, are most critical to the business. Therefore, we identify that the following journeys that each persona attempts to achieve in our system are business critical, and if unavailable, the customer would notice. In other words, the following characteristics were taken into consideration to determine criticality:

- Importance to the business
- Importance to the customer
- Measurement or comparison of emotions

Our **Persona Journey** board would appear with the following personas and journeys:

- **B2B Customer:**
  - Successful bulk purchase of product "x"

- **Customer – Cart Abandoned:**
  - Successful purchase after leaving the purchase page

- **CRM Integration** – tooling:
  - CRM tooling sends confirmation of purchase
  - CRM creates an issue upon customer submission
  - CRM routes the customer inquiry to the appropriate team

- **Frequent Buyer:**
  - Buyer completes a successful purchase via website notification
  - Persona purchases items via marketing advertisement

- **Customer** – standard:
  - The website is available
  - The customer account is accessible
  - The product inventory is available

In *Figure 6.5*, the persona journeys are listed with the most critical journeys being marked with a white dot. This is the mechanism used to serve as a reminder of where the initial focus should remain. As mentioned previously, developing a ranking system and iteration process that works best for your team is extremely beneficial.

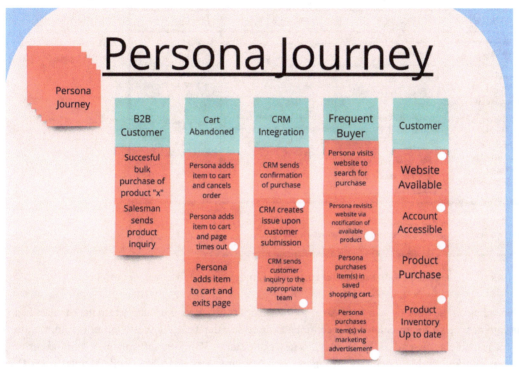

Figure 6.5 – Identified personas

Upon identification of our personas and their respective journeys, we need to focus on the expectations that the respective persona would have for a journey or specific touchpoints during the journey. It is also possible at this point that the team realizes that a journey needs to isolate some parts of the journey. That is okay and the purpose of communication and collaboration during the process. If we remember *Chapter 3*, *Figure 3.3*, a customer journey card might look something like *Figure 6.6*.

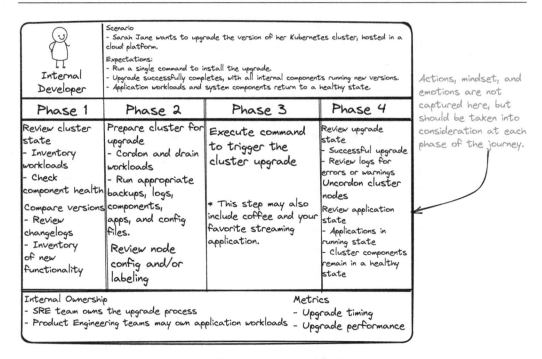

Figure 6.6 – An example of customer journey chart for an customer persona

Depending on the working style or needs of your team or organization, the journey card may be classified as comprehensive documentation. I recommend you review the Agile Manifesto for more information (link available at the end of the chapter). A key value states, "*Working software over comprehensive documentation*" and "*Individuals and interactions over processes and tools*" (*Agile Manifesto, 2001*). This may or may not fit the culture of your organization but aligns with the workshop style outlined within this book. For this book and chapter, we will not focus as much on the map but will include a single example.

If we use the *Customer* persona for *Product Purchase* as an example, the customer journey would appear as depicted in *Figure 6.7*:

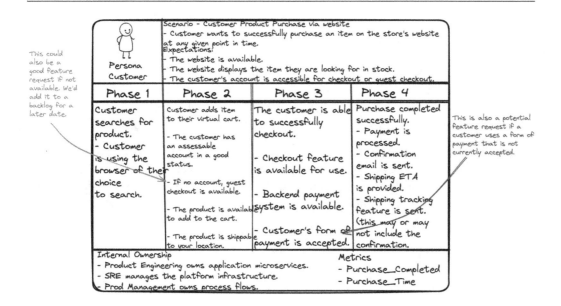

This could also be a good feature request if not available. We'd add it to a backlog for a later date.

Scenario - Customer Product Purchase via website
- Customer wants to successfully purchase an item on the store's website at any given point in time.
Expectations!
- The website is available.
- The website displays the item they are looking for in stock.
- The customer's account is accessible for checkout or guest checkout.

Persona Customer

Phase 1	Phase 2	Phase 3	Phase 4
Customer searches for product. - Customer is using the browser of their choice to search.	Customer adds item to their virtual cart. - The customer has an assessable account in a good status. - If no account, guest checkout is available. - The product is available to add to the cart. - The product is shippable to your location.	The customer is able to successfully checkout. - Checkout feature is available for use. - Backend payment system is available. - Customer's form of payment is accepted.	Purchase completed successfully. - Payment is processed. - Confirmation email is sent. - Shipping ETA is provided. - Shipping tracking feature is sent. (this may or may not include the confirmation.

This is also a potential feature request if a customer uses a form of payment that is not currently accepted.

Internal Ownership
- Product Engineering owns application microservices.
- SRE manages the platform infrastructure.
- Prod Management owns process flows.

Metrics
- Purchase_Completed
- Purchase_Time

Figure 6.7 – Customer journey mapping for the Customer Product Purchase persona

Within both **Phase 2** and **Phase 4**, there are steps within the phase that can be utilized as a feature request if requested by the customer or internal data shows there is a necessity for it. In this instance, the journey map is helpful in visualizing potential gaps within the system that might need to be reported back to the product management teams or added to some backlog managed by the appropriate individuals in your SRE enablement team.

Occasionally, you'll find other steps within a phase that are good candidates for SLIs if they are measurable and directly impact the SLOs. For example, the shipping ETA and tracking IDs could help us determine whether shipping partners are meeting their SLAs (e.g., delivery time promises) and whether the integration between the shipping feature and our website meets the required SLOs, such as returning the tracking number within a specific timeframe. In both instances, depending on the architecture of the system, there may be external dependencies if the SLAs of the shipping provider do not align with your process or discrepancies are on the shipping partner's side. These are gaps that are easily identifiable through communication via the right individuals during the workshop.

Let's stick with this example and move on to the next step in the process.

Identifying your system's boundaries

As it relates to reliability engineering, defining clear boundaries for applications and services is extremely important to support effective monitoring, maintenance, and optimization of your systems and services. In other scenarios and workflows, more people-oriented processes might take place, as they relate to personas. We'll try to reflect that within this section as well. Therefore, it's possible that the service you are providing involves a system but focuses solely on the behaviors of the persona.

You might be asking yourself what we mean by identifying a system's boundaries. It's the cumulative methods that are used to define where one system ends and another begins. This aids with the management process for validating, maintaining, and change management for systems or components. When doing so, we want to do the following:

1.   Identify, define, and categorize critical components and dependencies.

2.   Define clear boundaries.

3.   Categorize or prioritize components as needed.

Let's review what each of these means to our process in more depth.

Identifying critical components and dependencies

Understanding the intricate architecture of applications involves identifying critical components and dependencies that contribute to overall system performance and reliability. By conducting thorough analyses and assessments, teams can pinpoint components that are essential for maintaining service availability, functionality, and performance, thereby guiding monitoring and optimization efforts.

In the *Figure 6.1* example, we will hypothetically consider the account service as a critical component since a user is unable to complete tasks outside of viewing products without the appropriate account access.

Defining clear boundaries

Defining clear boundaries in the context of SRE involves understanding the interactions between components, services, and dependencies that contribute to service availability. It is crucial to set boundaries based on the SLOs for each component or service, ensuring that performance and reliability metrics are measured at each boundary to align with business goals. In other words, how does a set of components work together to achieve a desired outcome for the customer? We can refer to it as the touchpoints of components that expose a specific functionality to the customer.

We've concluded that the accounts service is one of our critical components in the previous section. The application website consists of an account service and account database that work together to provide a user's account functionality on our website. We can conclude that an account system boundary exists and consists of each of the services related to functions that involve interacting with the user's account. This includes services that enable the user to update their profile avatar, manage personal information, and various other tasks that are essential to account management.

We might then infer that our service includes the Java application and other binaries that make up the account management service and the backend MySQL database. Each of the services or components works together to create a workflow for a user to create, view, update, or delete their account profile. We should define a specific SLI for account creation, measure the success rate or latency of account creation requests, and establish a corresponding SLO that sets an acceptable threshold for the percentage of successful account creations within a defined time window (compliance period). This will help ensure the reliability of this critical functionality and track whether it meets the expected customer experience.

Clear application boundaries delineate the scope of monitoring and management efforts, enabling teams to focus resources efficiently. By defining boundaries, organizations can establish ownership, accountability, and responsibility for each application or service, facilitating streamlined operations and ensuring effective incident response.

Categorizing and prioritizing applications

Categorizing applications based on business impact, customer needs, and technical complexity is essential for resource allocation and prioritization. By classifying applications into tiers or categories, organizations can tailor monitoring strategies, allocate resources efficiently, and prioritize incident response efforts based on the criticality of each application.

Let's revisit our earlier example, which includes measuring the performance of creating, updating, or viewing the account profile. In the real world, where an organization is managing thousands and sometimes millions of microservices or applications on top of infrastructure, this can end up being the least of concern to the organization. However, degradation of specific functionality within the account can have a substantial negative impact on the business, such as:

- Backend payment management and security

- Measuring the availability of the infrastructure hosting the applications and services

- Security, as it relates to the reduction of security and data breaches

The preceding can play a more integral role in the organization's reputation, as the lack of concern can have a much larger consequence when things go awry. Therefore, it is important for teams to understand what critical means to the team and business groups as it relates to the broader organization's strategy and mission regarding meeting customer expectations.

Clarifying the role of each component and the responsibilities each has in meeting the expectations of the customer through some workflow within the system, the next step should naturally move the team toward the discussion of what we want to measure. Let's continue to the next section to explore this concept a bit further.

Defining system components for customer journey visibility

We already understand that our SLIs are the vital metrics we use to gauge the reliability, availability, and performance of our systems and services. Understanding the key metrics and indicators used to measure system reliability is fundamental for effective SLI identification. Metrics such as latency, error rates, throughput, and availability serve as essential indicators of system performance and user experience. It's important to understand that the specification step should focus on defining the SLO for the critical workflows within the system, ensuring that these objectives are measurable and achievable. This step sets the baseline for what success looks like from the customer's perspective and how it will be tracked through specific SLIs.

If we refer to our earlier example related to actions a customer can take against the account service, we'll need to gauge what performance and success look like to the customer. Do they have issues with the speed of the page loading? Is data within the account consistently outdated or incorrect? Have they received external alerts from their security provider referencing their email, password, or payment method being made available through a breach? Ultimately, what "things" do we need to measure, and at what "cadence" do we need to measure them? This is the goal of the specification step.

In addition, if your team is not sure where to start, it is always a good idea to consider the four golden signals that are typically used for monitoring distributed systems. According to Google's SRE Book, *"If you can only measure four metrics of your user-facing system, focus on these four."* (SRE Book, 2017). The signals are as follows:

- **Latency**: The duration of time when a request is waiting to be handled.

- **Traffic**: A measurement of the demand or workload(s) placed on your system.

- **Errors**: The measurement of failed requests.

- **Saturation**: The capacity measurement of your system – how "full" it is.

Your SLIs can encompass a variety of metrics that reflect different aspects of system behavior and performance. Other types of SLIs include the following:

- **Throughput**: The measurement of the amount of information a system can process within a given period.

- **Availability**: The measurement of a system's ability to perform its intended functions for users when needed. Availability includes the operation state of services that directly impact end user experience, and a system is considered unavailable if the user-facing services are down, even if other internal services are operational.

- **Uptime**: The percentage of time a system is operational and available to meet its SLA commitments. Uptime specifically refers to the system's overall ability to be online but does not guarantee that all individual services within the system are available.

- **Response time**: The measurement of the total time it takes from a client request to the system and the return response.

- **Durability**: The level of protection data is from being corrupted or lost over a given period.

Each type offers unique insights into system reliability and user experience. Understanding the relevance of each type of SLI to different types of applications is essential for selecting indicators that accurately reflect system performance and user satisfaction. It's also important to remember the process of identifying and defining SLIs involves aligning metrics with application boundaries and user needs.

Considerations for selecting meaningful SLIs

Selecting meaningful SLIs requires careful consideration of factors such as relevance, actionability, and alignment with business objectives. SLIs should be selected based on their ability to provide actionable insights into system health, facilitate timely decision-making, and support organizational goals. By choosing SLIs that are meaningful, relevant, and aligned with business objectives, organizations can effectively monitor and optimize system performance to meet user expectations and drive business success.

To achieve the goals previously mentioned, we need to understand how what we are trying to measure and at what cadence can be mapped to the current technical architecture. Is the current logging system providing sufficient data insights in logging for us to measure what we need? Is the current logging system subpar and in need of improvement? Is there an opportunity to probe for synthetic data or even innovate and build into the product some feature that helps to achieve the expectation of the customer? Let's continue to the implementation step to better understand how we can achieve this goal.

Focusing SLIs on customer journey metrics

Implementation, as it relates to SLIs, focuses on understanding the technical grouping of the underlying components and how they work together to meet the expectations of the customer, through a workflow or piece of functionality. This is a crucial step in the process, enabling organizations to monitor, measure, and optimize system performance with increased efficiency as it relates to the customer experience. The implementation portion shifts the focus of the conversation toward how we measure the outcome we have identified.

If we refer to the example in the previous specification sections, we might want to begin the conversation with an understanding of where we can retrieve the information to answer and address the hypothesis of the information in the specification step. In other words, is the current system architected in a way that provides us with the information we need to measure performance? Do we currently have a metric system that provides the level of observability through monitoring, to create the algorithms needed to measure customer experience? Do we need to build upon what is currently in place to provide more robust capabilities?

Based on the outcome of the previous questions, how do we then determine the threshold of decreased performance before the customer notices? Before the customer submits a ticket? Before chaos ensues? The implementation stage should help the team establish clear SLOs and set thresholds that reflect acceptable levels of performance. These thresholds should define what "normal" system behavior looks like in terms of user experience and guide the team in identifying when the system is at risk of violating these objectives, triggering alerts for actions based on predefined SLOs.

Establishing baseline values and thresholds

Establishing baseline values and thresholds for SLIs is essential for tracking performance and detecting anomalies within the context of SLA. Baseline values serve as benchmarks for normal system behavior, while thresholds define the acceptable ranges of performance aligned with the SLA's commitment to the customer. These thresholds trigger actions when the system's performance is outside the acceptable SLA range. Organizations must set realistic thresholds based on historical data, user expectations, and business objectives to ensure effective SLI monitoring and alerting.

Setting SLO targets and performance thresholds

Setting SLOs based on SLIs is crucial for ensuring the team or organization captures performance from the customer's perspective. SLO thresholds can be gauged through the following:

- Researching through historical data to understand past performance.
- Creating synthetic data to gauge current normal system performance.
- Utilizing internal engineering and support team data, including support tickets and incident management systems.
- Configuring SLIs and monitoring them over some period to establish a baseline value.

Your SLO thresholds can be configured via two methods. The two main methods at the time of writing this are as follows:

- **Request-based**: SLOs that focus on successful requests within a period calculated via a percentage.
- **Windows-based**: SLOs that measure based on a window of time or a time interval.

Which timing method is utilized is heavily dependent on the goal of the indicators the team is trying to create and the ultimate customer experience story you want to tell. Upon doing so, there should exist a baseline for understanding how each impacts the bottom line of the business and the ability to prioritize accordingly, which leads us into our next section.

Importance of prioritizing SLIs

Prioritizing SLIs ensures that organizations focus on monitoring the metrics that are most critical to user satisfaction and business success. It helps to shift the focus of resources and efforts on the metrics that have the most significant impact on user experience and business objectives.

By identifying and prioritizing SLIs based on their impact on user experience, organizations can allocate resources effectively, prioritize improvement initiatives, and mitigate risks that could affect service reliability and performance.

Customer feedback provides valuable insights into the metrics that are most important to users, while business priorities help align SLIs with organizational goals and objectives. Risk assessment involves evaluating the potential impact of SLIs on service reliability, performance, and reputation.

Establishing SLOs based on prioritized SLIs

Once SLIs have been prioritized, the organization is able to establish SLOs to set measurable targets for reliability and performance. Often, these can stem from or be used to reference external SLAs in an **anything-as-a-service (XaaS)** environment, ensuring that SLOs align with contractual commitments made to customers. SLOs will enable the team to define acceptable levels of performance for each prioritized SLI, providing clear goals and benchmarks for monitoring and optimization efforts. Acceptable SLO thresholds define the point at which service degradation becomes noticeable to customers, leading to potential dissatisfaction or operational issues.

By aligning SLOs with prioritized SLIs, which drives meeting SLA goals, organizations can effectively measure and track progress toward meeting user expectations and business objectives. Through diligent SLI prioritization practices, organizations can enhance service reliability, optimize performance, and drive business success.

SLI prioritization is an iterative process that constantly evolves based on the changing business needs, user feedback, and market dynamics. Organizations must continuously review and adjust SLI prioritization to ensure alignment with evolving priorities and objectives. By soliciting feedback from invested stakeholders, monitoring changes in user behavior, and reassessing various risk factors, organizations can refine SLI prioritization to reflect current realities and future opportunities.

Summary

Implementing SLIs and SLOs requires careful planning, collaboration, and alignment with user needs and business objectives. By defining personas and understanding the user journey, establishing clear application boundaries, and identifying, implementing, and prioritizing SLIs, organizations can effectively measure and ensure the reliability, availability, and performance of their systems and services. Through continuous monitoring, analysis, and iteration, organizations can drive improvements in reliability and deliver exceptional experiences to their users.

In the chapters that follow, we will dive deeper into and utilize the learnings and processes from this chapter in a more robust manner. We will reference the same architecture but expand on the infrastructure and workload deployments a bit more to provide an improved scope.

Further reading

Here, you can review and read the referenced articles and books for additional reading about concepts mentioned in this chapter:

- Cunningham, W. (2001). *Manifesto for Agile Software Development*. Retrieved from: `https://agilemanifesto.org/`.

- Ewaschuk, R., and Beyer, B. (2017). *Monitoring Distributed Systems*. In R. Ewaschuk, and B. Beyer, *SRE Book*.

- Indiana University School of Informatics and Computing at IUPUI. (2017). Personas and Scenarios. In J. Lyst, & M. Frontz, *CxD Principles & Practices*. Indiana University School of Informatics and Computing at IUPUI. Retrieved from: `https://docs.idew.org/principles-and-practices/practices/design-practices/personas`.

- Schebrova, A. (2021, September 30). *Multiple Personas on One Customer Journey Map*. Retrieved from: `https://uxpressia.com/blog/multiple-personas-on-one-customer-journey-map`.

7
Scenario 1: SLIs and SLOs for Web Applications

In this chapter, we will implement, in more depth, the previous learnings from *Chapter 6*, with the focus shifted toward building SLIs and SLOs for the web application architecture referenced in the section to follow. When considering the application and build process, we are accustomed to measuring specific metrics to determine what went wrong when an issue occurs. However, it is imperative to understand that SLIs for applications are used to measure the performance and reliability of the system, helping to ensure that the system's performance aligns with user expectations and impacts customer experience. These metrics reflect critical aspects such as availability, latency, and error rates.

Customer-centric performance measurements also help to direct your engineers toward the components involved in an incident, during the incident's life cycle. It's important to clearly understand the goal to communicate the added organizational value.

In this chapter, along with the chapters that follow, we will utilize the same outlined process, working with different components of the previously referenced application and infrastructure architecture. This will help to highlight the SLI and SLO build process for different components of your system.

We'll be covering the following main topics:

- Understanding the application architecture
- Identifying personas and the persona journey
- Establishing application (system) boundaries
- Specifying SLI types based on the identified system boundaries
- Implementing SLIs with accurate touchpoints based on the system specifications
- Understanding required considerations when prioritizing SLIs and SLOs

Let's get started!

> **Important note**
>
> In this chapter, we will reference the application architecture depicted in *Figure 7.1* throughout each step. *Chapter 6* elaborated on the SLI and SLO process with a bit more detail. Expect this chapter and those that follow in this part of the book to place emphasis on how the process works with minimal detail. If additional detail is needed, please review *Chapter 6*.

Understanding the application architecture

In the previous chapter, we introduced our simple website, which offers cosmetic products to individual customers and businesses looking to purchase in bulk. We'll continue with this example and scale it to include infrastructure and additional zones, ensuring that our SLOs for availability, latency, and error rates are met across regions. Scaling could be done with a focus on maintaining the system's reliability, aligning with the defined SLOs. The referenceable architecture is depicted in *Figure 7.1*.

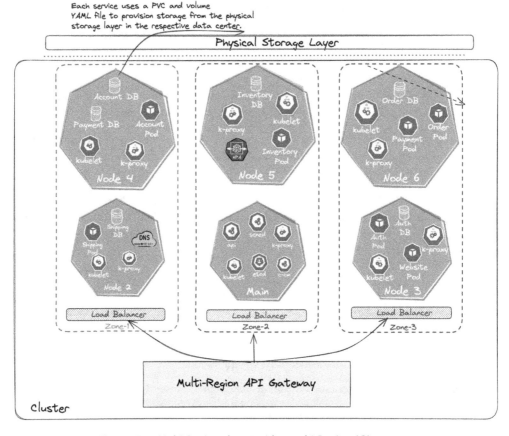

Figure 7.1 – Multi-Region cluster with a multi-Region API gateway

Let's discuss the architecture a bit further; to gain a better understanding of the individual components and functionality they provide to the larger system.

Our application and its infrastructure are hosted across three Availability Zones, which we will refer to as **Zone-1**, **Zone-2**, and **Zone-3**. Each zone is fronted by a load balancer and hosts some microservice in our application layer. We use an API gateway for a single point of entry for calls from client applications and backend services for API calls and interfaces. In a real-world scenario, we'd consider multi-Regions with multiple Availability Zones, as needed, and implement the services to run replicas within the necessary Regions and zones. In this scenario, we are not focused on additional replicas or instances, only that we have a single instance microservice to reference that resides in some assigned zone.

Within our multi-zones, we have a seven-node cluster running Kubernetes orchestration. The main node runs the applications and services required to ensure the cluster is in a good state. This includes the following:

- **API-server**: Exposes the container orchestrator of choice and acts as the frontend for the cluster. All client requests route through the API server before routing to other cluster components.

- **Scheduler**: Assigns new pods to a node with available resources and aligned configurations (if labeled).

- **Kubelet**: Node agent, which monitors servers and routes requests to servers.

- **Kubeproxy**: Maintains network connectivity between services and pods.

- **Controller Manager**: Single binary deploying various controllers to a cluster. Controllers call the API server to make updates to an object's current state to the desired state.

- **Etcd**: Key value store deployment that stores all cluster data.

We also have three additional workload nodes that are running two critical services to the application workloads deployed to the scheduled zone running in a healthy state. The main cluster components are hosted only on the control plane nodes. The following components are deployed to all nodes within a cluster and are reiterated in this section to place emphasis on them:

- **Kubelet**: Node agent that monitors servers and routes requests to servers.

- **Kubeproxy**: Maintains network connectivity between services and pods.

In addition to those services, each node is running the respective containers that contribute to our website's availability and functionality:

Zone-1 Node	Zone-2 Node	Zone-3 Node
• Account	• Inventory	• Order
• Account DB	• Inventory DB	• Order DB
• DNS (system)	• HPA	• Auth
• Shipping	• Payment	• Auth DB
• Shipping DB	• PaymentDB	• Website

Table 7.1 – List of services and the respective zone of the node they are hosted on

The diagramed cluster also includes a load balancer within each Region to route traffic to the appropriate service. External storage is our storage provider for persistent volumes and volume claims, which are attached to the respective application pod. Each application consists of a microservice or pod deployment containing the application code and other app libraries and dependencies. Each application also has its own database deployed, which includes the code and logic regarding the database configuration and necessary data.

As for the individual functionality of each deployed application, each listed application has its own role and responsibilities. This will be discussed in more depth in the *Establishing application (system) boundaries* section of this chapter.

Now that we have a better understanding of the workflows, applications, and infrastructure, we can shift the conversation toward identifying critical personas and defining the persona (user) journey within the system.

Identifying personas and the persona journey

For this chapter, our focus targets the web applications deployed in the cluster versus the actual infrastructure or platform they are deployed to. Therefore, the personas established for this scenario are going to focus on the web application. If we reflect on *Chapter 6*, we understand that we want to utilize data repositories likely owned by teams internal to the organization, such as the following:

- Internal incident management teams
- Customer success teams
- Technical support teams
- Product management teams

…and any other internal teams your organization might have that are responsible for managing the customer experience. Utilizing data from customer surveys, incident tickets, and other customer support workflows helps the team identify SLIs that measure the customer experience. By tracking these SLIs, the team can gain insights into performance issues and understand how they impact SLOs, which in turn ensures that the system's behavior aligns with user expectations. It also aids in understanding which workflows, or functionality, are of importance to your critical customers.

We can then assume that our team is able to generate data and formulate the following personas and their respective journey, from the previous chapter:

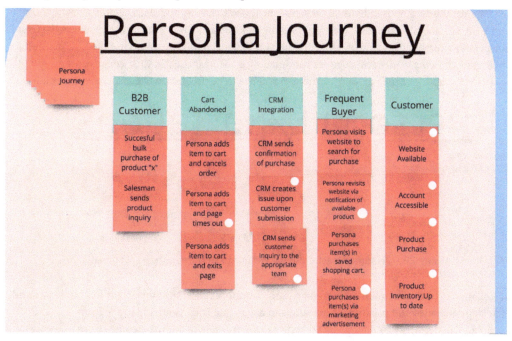

Figure 7.2 – Personas and persona journeys identified in Chapter 6

Before moving further, it's important to highlight sticky notes are color-coded to better organize and visualize focus areas as we move through each step of the process:

- Green note: Represents the persona
- Pink note: Represents the journey
- Purple note: Represents an expectation
- Yellow note: Represents a dependency
- Orange note: Represents a hypothetical question raised by a participant

For the purposes of this chapter, we will focus on the following personas and their respective journey on our updated board:

- Product purchase journey

- Product shipped journey

- CRM issue creation and assignment journey

- Website availability journey

Each column heading is an individual person's journey, which is a good starting point for the team to begin their SLI and SLO process. See *Figure 7.3* for an example of how this might appear on a virtual or in-person whiteboard. In a workshop setting, it is beneficial to the team to use the best method to indicate which items from each stage are candidates for the next step. In this scenario, a single white dot is used to represent the persona journey we will use to begin identifying associated expectations.

Figure 7.3 – Persona expectations we will use to shift through the SLI process

In a collaborative environment centered around communication, it's important to emphasize and notate dependencies and parking lot questions in a way that is consumable to the team, especially if done in a virtual setting. In *Figure 7.4*, you will see an example of a few outcomes from a discussion surrounding the expectations a consumer has for each of the associated persona journeys.

When having a discussion, it is important to document any dependencies that one item might have on another. For example, in *Figure 7.4*, the success of fulfilling a customer order, including shipping and delivery, involves dependencies that might fall outside the scope of the application, such as external third-party services (e.g., shipping companies). These dependencies should be captured as external SLIs or accounted for in the SLOs to ensure that service targets remain realistic and reflect the entire customer experience. Often, when approaching these instances in discussion, it is beneficial to utilize a process that uses a step-by-step approach to list and visualize them to provide additional clarity and understanding when iterating in later stages.

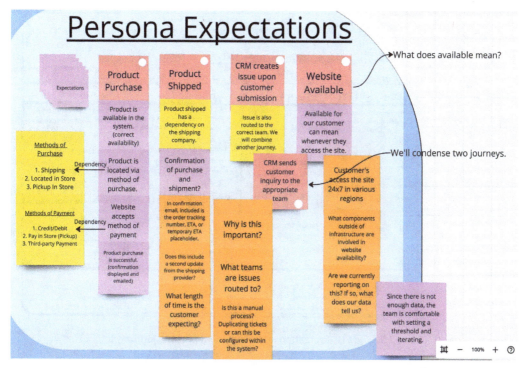

Figure 7.4 – An example of dependencies, expectations, and questions for each journey

Before we dive into each of the personas and their respective expectations, it's important to remember that you can use other tooling and processes to visualize or document your persona journey. This is out of the scope for the book and the selected tooling is utilized out of convenience and choice.

However, if we use CRM integration as an example, based on the persona journey depicted in *Figure 7.4*, the customer journey visual would consist of the information depicted in *Figure 7.5*, utilizing a phased approach to working through the steps within the persona journey.

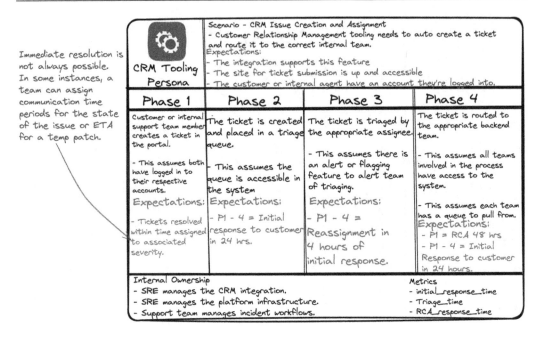

Immediate resolution is not always possible. In some instances, a team can assign communication time periods for the state of the issue or ETA for a temp patch.

Figure 7.5 – CRM issue creation and assignment persona journey

We'd then use the preceding information to either diagram the technical process between the systems or flesh out the details through group discussion to begin documenting the process workflows in preparation for SLI specification. It is also beneficial to use the visual depicted to help the team map out the functional processes and improve the ability to map the underlying application components that work together to create the journey. The charted visualization is not necessary but helpful to ensure all phases are captured in a consumable manner for the teams involved.

In this instance, we are going to shift our focus toward the product purchase persona. If we visualized the phases within our journey chart and diagrammed them, the phases required to achieve an outcome would appear as follows for the team:

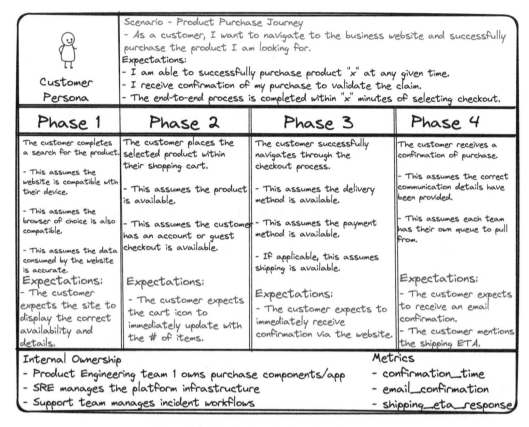

Customer Persona

Scenario – Product Purchase Journey
- As a customer, I want to navigate to the business website and successfully purchase the product I am looking for.
Expectations:
- I am able to successfully purchase product "x" at any given time.
- I receive confirmation of my purchase to validate the claim.
- The end-to-end process is completed within "x" minutes of selecting checkout.

Phase 1	Phase 2	Phase 3	Phase 4
The customer completes a search for the product.	The customer places the selected product within their shopping cart.	The customer successfully navigates through the checkout process.	The customer receives a confirmation of purchase.
- This assumes the website is compatible with their device.	- This assumes the product is available.	- This assumes the delivery method is available.	- This assumes the correct communication details have been provided.
- This assumes the browser of choice is also compatible.	- This assumes the customer has an account or guest checkout is available.	- This assumes the payment method is available.	- This assumes each team has their own queue to pull from.
- This assumes the data consumed by the website is accurate.		- If applicable, this assumes shipping is available.	
Expectations: - The customer expects the site to display the correct availability and details.	Expectations: - The customer expects the cart icon to immediately update with the # of items.	Expectations: - The customer expects to immediately receive confirmation via the website.	Expectations: - The customer expects to receive an email confirmation. - The customer mentions the shipping ETA.

Internal Ownership
- Product Engineering team 1 owns purchase components/app
- SRE manages the platform infrastructure
- Support team manages incident workflows

Metrics
- confirmation_time
- email_confirmation
- shipping_eta_response

Figure 7.6 – Product purchase persona journey

An important requirement during this phase is to gather the metrics currently configured within your system. It is even more helpful to understand what each metric means to the customer relationship and the components that emit the associated data. For our example, here, we have identified the following metrics that will help to guide the SLI specification and implementation processes:

- **Confirmation time:** This should be tracked as an SLI to measure the latency from the successful payment submission to the display of the purchase confirmation. The target for this SLI should be defined in the SLO, indicating the acceptable time range for customers to receive confirmation (e.g., 95% of requests should be completed within 2 seconds).

- **Email_confirmation:** The length of time it takes for the email to send the purchase confirmation to the email address associated with the customer account. (It's important to note the time calculated is how long it took for the system to send the email as opposed to how long it took for the customer to receive it, as calculating the latter can have additional blockers and dependencies outside of what the business can control.)

- **Shipping_eta_response:** The length of time it takes for the customer to receive an ETA for their product after a successful purchase. (It's important to understand that in certain architectures and depending on the business's shipping logistics, there can be dependencies that are outside of the business's control.)

A better understanding of what metrics currently exist, and their respective configurations, improves the ability to gauge user expectations regarding when an issue is noticeable and when complaints or tickets become of concern. The data, through event logging, can also provide better visibility into how components work together, which leads us to the next section.

Establishing application (system) boundaries

Based on the previous steps, depicted in *Figure 7.6* of the previous section, we outlined for the product purchase journey, we want to understand and possibly visualize what this means from a technical perspective. If we refer to our application and system architecture from earlier in the chapter, then we already know there are a few application services that are involved with the product purchase workflow. We can assume the following services contribute to a successful customer experience:

- Website microservice

- Inventory microservice

- Account microservice

- Order microservice

- Payment microservice

It's important to note that microservice, in the context of each scenario, refers to the containers that support the application and the database components together.

At first glance, a team member can assume that we want to measure a single metric for a single service. The concept of SLIs should be tied to specific, measurable aspects of service reliability at each touchpoint, not just the workflow. Instead of focusing on all components collectively, it's important to measure the reliability of each individual service, especially when it influences the user experience. For example, the latency of the website microservice or the error rate in the payment microservice should be the focus of individual SLIs. The workflow can then be modeled as a sequence of SLIs that align with SLOs across each service.

It's possible to have a discussion during the workshop with the technical teams that are experts on application architecture. The technical teams may also have design documentation accessible for the group to review together. Based on our architecture, the flow of touchpoints appears as follows:

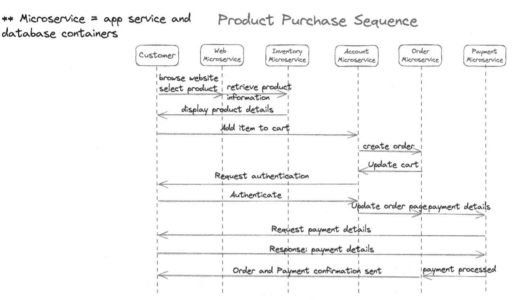

Figure 7.7 – Product purchase sequence diagram for purchase workflow

Based on the sequence chart depicted in *Figure 7.7*, we can conclude the interaction or workflow is triggered by the customer and includes interactions between five microservices hosted on our platform. Each microservice depicted in the figure includes the application service and the database service as well. Therefore, a good starting point for measuring the length of time would be the client interaction, continuing through each phase of communication between each service. The touchpoint that ends the workflow would involve the payment microservice's response to the customer, which concludes with an order and payment confirmation communication being provided.

We can take this information and move on to the next step within our SLI and SLO build process.

Specifying SLI types based on the identified system boundaries

Let's reflect on the discussion in *Chapter 6* about how building the right SLIs and SLOs requires the team to determine the appropriate specifications for what they are measuring. In that, we also mentioned the four golden signals of monitoring (Google, Inc., 2017) being a good starting point if there is not enough data available to develop an SLI or if you are unable to determine a good SLI type. In addition, if your organization or team already has a monitoring system in place, as a reminder, it is good to work backward.

Let's first revisit the various SLI types, depicted in *Figure 7.8*.

SLI Type	Definition	Example
Latency	Duration of time a request is waiting to be handled.	The time it takes a system to load a customer's info when they select "account".
Traffic	Measure of the demand or workloads placed on your system.	The amount of data used when downloading an email or software update.
Errors	The measurement of failed requests.	Failed attempts in your system, out of memory, failed to download, storage full.
Saturation	The capacity measurement of your system. How "full" is it?	CPU, memory, or network bandwidth being utilized to the point of not functioning
Throughput	The measurement of the amount of information a system can process in a period of time.	How many "bits" or units are processed in x min? Can be read and write transactions.
Availability	The measure of a system's ability to perform responsibilities when needed.	The business apps hosted on a server are up and operational for customers.
Uptime	The percentage of time a system is available for the end user.	My server is up and running, but a hosted app is not accessible.
Response Time	The total time it takes for a system to return a response to a client request.	I searched for a product on a website and it took 30 seconds for details to load.
Durability	The period of time that data is available for consumption.	The product metadata associated with the website is available for 'x' months/years.

(Marginal annotation, left: "4 Golden Signals" bracketing Latency, Traffic, Errors, Saturation)
(Marginal annotation, right: "It's important to not confuse the two!" pointing to Availability and Uptime)

Figure 7.8 – SLI types that are good starting points when building your SLIs

The types are not limited to what is listed here and you should also feel free to think of or create your own SLI types as needed by your team or organization. Some other types that are not depicted here but can be taken into consideration are the following:

- **Quality**: The percentage of requests that are processed and correct without the service experiencing degradation.

- **Coverage**: This type captures the percentage or amount of data processed that is also valid.

- **Correctness**: This type captures the rate at which retrieved data is populated in the correct format, type, and various other configuration options available.

- **Freshness**: This type captures the recency rate of data. In many environments, this may be measurable through timestamps.

Some types will also perform better when coupled with the correct functionality. For example, request and response measurements will likely pair better with availability and latency SLI types. Another example is, when measuring storage, durability and throughput might stick out more than others. That's not to say this is a one-size-fits-all scenario, but it is important to understand what your data is informing you of and what your organization needs you to measure.

Based on our sequence diagram and our SLI-type chart, let's say the team identifies three SLIs they want to focus on. When starting out, the recommendation is to use a three-by-three mindset. Select three user journeys to start and then attempt to build three SLIs per journey. When working, it is common for ideas and communication to flow; we can utilize the parking lot method to revisit the item later.

For this scenario, we are going to continue to focus on the product purchase user journey and refer to the sequence diagram to identify the areas that we want to focus on. The team decides to break the product purchase user journey into the following three focus areas for SLIs, based on internal incidents, customer support tickets, and application and server-side logs:

- **Display product details**: A client-side request to the website, which interacts with the web microservice API to retrieve information from the inventory microservice, which includes a backend database.

- **Authentication**: Authentication implemented with an auth SDK and sidecar container using gRPC for event-driven communication between services.

- **Payment details**: Implemented by using a token system for the payment process via the payment API.

We might then decide that, based on our data, we want to focus on response time, errors, and latency for the selected SLIs, respectively. In a workshop setting, it's important to understand these decisions are made through communication in a collaborative setting. The one thing that remains consistent is we want our decisions to reflect the narrative of what our customers are experiencing, as well as what the data from the requirement-gathering process has informed us of. Moments will arise where data is insufficient or even nonexistent – we can refer to other alternatives, such as generating synthetic data. Some examples of generating data in our current system environment are as follows:

- Generating authentication credentials to test security mechanisms

- Generating product purchase workflows to test spikes in workloads

Figure 7.9 depicts the selected journeys, their SLI type, and a brief description of the associated workflow, which includes the targeted expectation based on customer feedback and data emitted in various applications and tooling such as application, client, and platform logs.

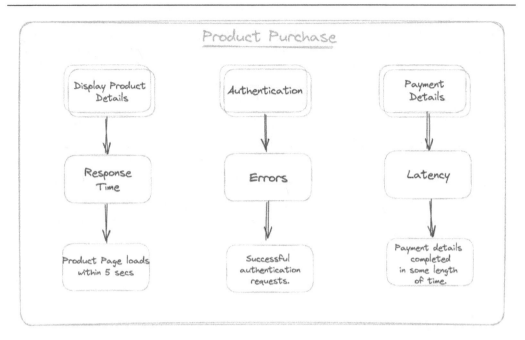

Figure 7.9 – SLI specification details

Based on the data analysis process, we might conclude the following for each specification:

- Customers, on average, submitted tickets to the support team after numerous attempts at reloading a slow-loading product page. However, after the debugging process with the support and customer success teams, customers noticed issues with loading, when the page took seven seconds to load.

  - **Response time**: The team would like to remain conservative and decides it is best to ensure the page loads within five seconds or less.

- The organization has also had complaints to the internal technical account managers from their top enterprise accounts regarding failed authentication attempts. In addition, the IAM security team experienced an outage related to authentication.

  - **Errors**: The successful authentication rate becomes a critical priority, with the expectation of maintaining a 99.9% success rate, with an error budget that allows for a 0.1% failure rate.

- The internal engineering team responsible for the payment service and data reports an increase in service-related incidents. They also include complaints being escalated from the support team regarding the processing of payment systems. As a result, there have been numerous customers abandoning product purchases after several attempts with payment processing failing or experiencing a delay. Customers report it is hard to purchase because, in some instances, there have been duplicated charges reported via their payment method.

  - **Latency**: As a result, it becomes increasingly critical to define a clear SLO based on specific thresholds for successful performance. In this instance, we would not want to focus solely on the length of time for payment processing but be able to provide a concrete SLO that ties directly to an SLI. For example, the payment service should successfully process 99% of payment requests within 2 seconds.

Now that we have successfully identified the problems we want to address, the measurement types, and the internal data and metrics that we can use to support our reasoning, it's important to seamlessly move from specification to implementation and focus more on the architecture and technical details of the system.

Implementing SLIs with accurate touchpoints based on the system specifications

The SLI implementation stages shift the functional details of the specification process to the architecture and technical details. The goal of this step is to redirect from the "what" toward the "how" and "where." This also helps to ensure what is measured, via metrics, reports on the customer experience or a specific workflow versus reporting on a single specific detail that reports technical information for the backend team. That's what monitoring is for.

Figure 7.10 depicts the shift from specification, related to SLI types, toward implementation related to the technical details. Based on the data referenced in the previous section, we know we want the following:

- The product pages load within 5 seconds
- Successful authentication requests
- Payment attempts are successfully processed within 2 seconds

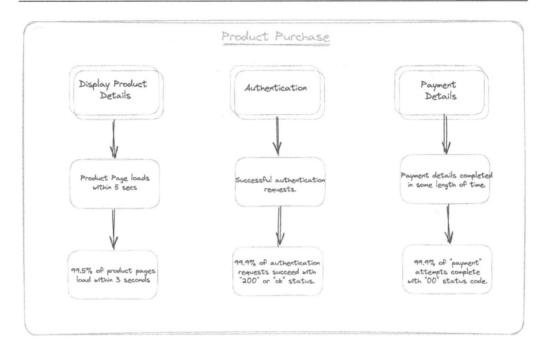

Figure 7.10 – SLI types that are good starting points when building your SLIs

If we refer to the architecture and service deployment in *Figure 7.1*, then we understand the following services are deployed related to each SLI specification that we want to implement:

- **The product pages load within 5 seconds**:

  - Website UI

  - Inventory service

  - Inventory database

  - Client-side request

- **Authentication success rate**: The percentage of authentication requests that successfully authenticate users within an acceptable time window (e.g., 99.9% success rate):

  - Client-side request

  - Authentication service

  - Authentication database

- **Payment processing latency**: The time it takes to process payment details from the client-side request to the completion of payment confirmation. A reasonable SLO for this might be 95% of payments processed within 3 seconds:

  - Client-side request

  - Order database

  - Order service

  - Payment service

  - Payment database

We now want to think about each of these services as providing an outcome for the respective persona and their journey. We can also refer to this as a system capability.

Understanding required considerations when prioritizing SLIs and SLOs

SLIs and their respective SLOs should be prioritized based on business impact and feasibility. Business impact refers to how directly an SLI contributes to customer experience, revenue, and customer satisfaction. Feasibility includes technical complexity, cost, and resource availability, as well as how easily the team can monitor and respond to the metric. For instance, prioritizing authentication success rate over payment processing latency may have a greater business impact if authentication issues are causing users to abandon the workflow. When considering the business impact, we want to ask ourselves the following questions:

- What is the level of impact this change brings to the following?

  - Our customer bases

  - Our team

  - Our organization

- Does the impact affect the business from a monetary standpoint?

  - If so, how?

    - Is this a SaaS offering?

    - Is this a licensed offering?

- Have we assessed industry competition?

    - If so, does our solution offer something that everyone else's does not?

- Regarding feasibility, consider the following:

    - On a scale of 1 to 5, how easy is the technical implementation?

    - What does feasibility mean to the technical team members?

    - Are there other solutions available to achieve the desired outcome?

        - This also includes weighing the number of engineers and other staff the implementation might require

The ranking system is based on internal dialogue between the individuals leading the initiative and the technical staff responsible for the respective technical components or designs. In our instance, we might consider the following:

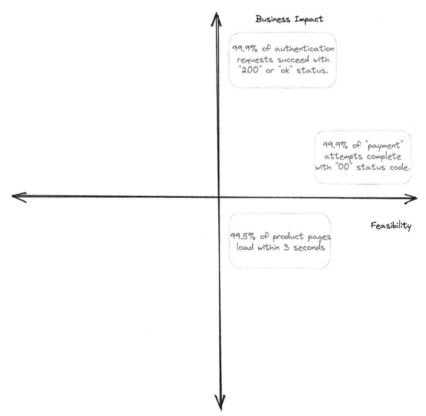

Figure 7.11 – SLI prioritization based on business impact and feasibility

There is no prioritization focused on which trait is of importance. That should be determined by the team based on the business and technical requirements of each SLI and SLO. In this example, we focused on building out three SLI and SLO metrics. However, it is also possible to work through this same flow, add items to the prioritization chart, and then loop through the process again, increasing the number of items the team will manage before implementation.

Summary

In this chapter, we reviewed our example application and infrastructure architecture, worked through identifying personas, created journeys, and gained an understanding of the application boundaries to build SLIs and SLOs in a workshop setting. In the chapters that follow, you can expect to do the same while shifting the focus to different layers such as cluster and data components.

As you continue through the book, I hope you can think of several implementation ideas and other use cases internal to your organization.

Further reading

Here, you can review and read the referenced articles and books for additional reading about concepts mentioned in this book:

- Dambrine, F. (2022, December 14). *Kubernetes Icon Set*. Retrieved from Excalidraw Libraries.

- DoxyGen. (2024, August 22). *Status codes and their use in gRPC*. Retrieved from: `https://grpc.github.io/grpc/core/md_doc_statuscodes.html`.

- Google, Inc. (2017). *Monitoring Distributed Systems*. In B. Beyer, & R. Ewaschuk, SRE-Book. O'Reilly Media.

- Luzar, D., & Gian, P. (2023, April 18). *Stick Figures Collaboration*. Retrieved from Excalidraw Libraries.

- The Linux Foundation. (2024). *Kubernetes Components*. Retrieved from: `https://kubernetes.io/docs/concepts/overview/components`.

8

Scenario 2: SLIs and SLOs for Distributed Systems

In previous chapters, we covered the history of reliability engineering, SLIs and SLOs, and the importance of establishing a reliability engineering team for your SLO process. In this chapter, we plan to shift the focus toward building SLIs and SLOs for distributed environments. When SLIs and SLOs are mentioned, the conversation typically shifts toward applications. This may steer the conversation in the direction of topics surrounding client requests via HTTP request and response, latency for page loads, or overall application availability and uptime. In distributed environments, it is equally important to consider the following when reporting on application availability:

- How the underlying infrastructure can impact application availability and uptime, with an emphasis on how control over infrastructure differs between on-premises and cloud environments. In cloud environments, the provider typically manages the infrastructure, which influences the performance of SLIs and SLOs. For on-premises infrastructure, organizations have full control, allowing them to implement tailored solutions that affect the performance and reliability SLIs.

- The difference between reporting on SLI and SLO metrics for infrastructure hosted on-premises versus with a cloud provider.

- The impact of networking on data processing; thus, impacting storage metrics and CRUD database operations and performance.

- Consideration of how multi-region deployments and load balancing impact latency, availability, and reliability SLOs. Load balancing between regions can optimize traffic routing, reducing latency and ensuring high availability, but also needs to be measured by appropriate SLIs (such as response time and error rates) to align with the SLOs for system reliability.

There are numerous other considerations that we should consider that may not immediately come to mind. However, it's important to continuously structure the conversation in a way that encourages the team to build performance measurements and thresholds for various tasks and activities used within the system and daily operations.

This chapter uses the same steps outlined in *Chapters 6* and *7*, which include the following:

- Understanding the application architecture
- Identifying personas and the persona journey
- Establishing application (system) boundaries
- Specifying SLI types based on the identified system boundaries
- Implementing SLIs with accurate touchpoints based on the system specifications
- Understanding required considerations when prioritizing SLIs and SLOs

So, let's get started!

Understanding the application architecture

For this chapter, we'll extract the specific components and shift our focus toward SLIs and SLOs for the distributed parts of the system architecture. The architecture is depicted in *Figure 8.1*.

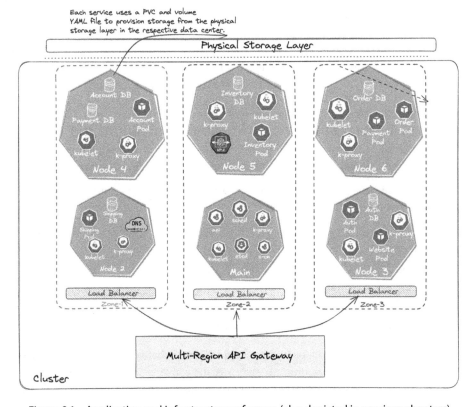

Figure 8.1 – Application and infrastructure reference (also depicted in previous chapters)

If further details for the application and infrastructure architecture depicted in *Figure 8.1* are needed, please reference the *Understanding the application architecture* section of *Chapter 7*.

Chapter 7 focuses on the application layer components while this chapter focuses on the distributed components of the cluster, which include some of the cluster components responsible for orchestration. The goal is to highlight how the deployed services can play a role in your application meeting external agreements or SLAs. Therefore, the application services are not mentioned here but expect the chapter to follow a similar flow.

The cluster depicted in *Figure 8.1* also includes a load balancer within each region to route traffic or requests to the appropriate service. The external storage provider is configured using the storage class CRD and is the storage provider for persistent volumes and volume claims. More information on the latter can be found in the Kubernetes website documentation linked in the *Further reading* section.

Now that we have reviewed the architecture at a high level, let's understand which personas play a key role in our distributed environments. At any point, please review *Chapter 7*'s application architecture to understand the role of a specific component in the text.

Identifying personas and the persona journey

In a normal workshop, the conversation would start after an assessment of internal data and team members to understand the various personas. This includes a ranking system to follow to establish which personas are most critical to start. For this chapter, we will begin the conversation of identifying and defining the persona journey by focusing on specific personas. In this distributed environment scenario, each persona plays an integral role in developing, configuring, or managing the components that make up the infrastructure platform that hosts the application services. These personas are as follows:

- **Cluster administrator**: Responsible for ensuring the cluster is available within defined SLOs and configuring security to meet security and performance SLIs. Availability targets should be defined in terms of uptime, such as 99.9% or 99.99%, with measurable metrics for system reliability (e.g., node uptime, cluster health status).

- **Developer**: Responsible for deploying applications into the cluster, ensuring deployments meet established SLOs for availability, response time, and reliability. Developers should monitor and optimize SLIs such as deployment success rate, time to deployment, and service response time, to ensure that the application performs within defined reliability targets.

- **DevOps tooling**: Operational tooling that integrates with the cluster to improve developer productivity and cluster maintenance.

Each persona might appear on our whiteboard, as follows in *Figure 8.2*:

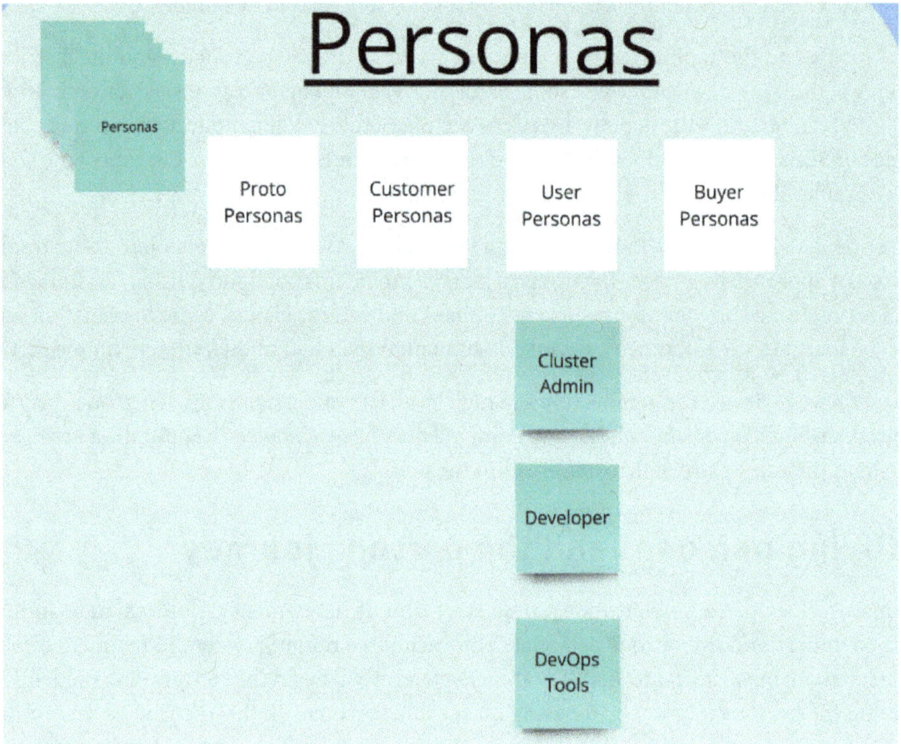

Figure 8.2 – Personas identified by the team

It's important to highlight that the DevOps tooling persona is a bit too broad. In a workshop setting, we'd want to investigate the importance of this persona and narrow it down to a specific tooling. We'd then highlight the significance of needing to measure the tools, possibly based on some interactions with our application. Based on previous experience, there has been mention of tooling such as CI/CD pipelines and credential management tooling. It's mentioned here to serve as a reminder of the various integrations from internal tooling to third-party integrations and other APIs that can and should also be included in the team brainstorming or analysis sessions. This helps to identify gaps that impact performance measurement but may immediately appear as the offender of performance degradation as it relates to the application service.

Moving forward, let's imagine the cluster administrator and developer personas are the two personas we need to focus on to improve infrastructure immediately. In addition, we know first-hand that there have been numerous reported issues regarding the underlying infrastructure impacting application availability and performance. Therefore, the team decides it is best to focus on both and generate as many journeys as possible to gain better insights and immediately make technical decisions. The engineers have enough experience with the platform and customer-facing outages to immediately begin gauging performance and identify short-term wins.

We then decide to move the selected personas over to the persona journey section of the virtual whiteboard. In a live workshop, the team or individual(s) running the workshop would have likely established a ranking system to eliminate bias and shift the correct personas to the next stage. See *Figure 8.3*.

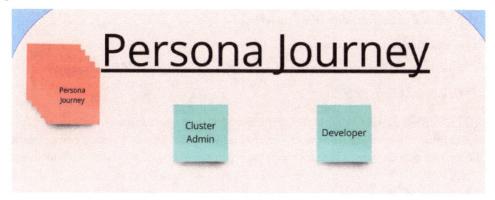

Figure 8.3 – Distributed systems persona and journey template

We then want to collaboratively work together to determine the various journeys each persona utilizes when trying to achieve some outcome in the system. If the team has developed a backlog of internal data from various sources, this can be used to make assumptions. This includes monitoring systems and other dashboards or charts that are currently configured. However, let's start by assuming we need to take the following flows into consideration:

- Applications that the respective persona deploys or manages within the cluster.
- Tasks completed to manage the cluster and respective configuration settings.
- Resource consumption measurements that the respective persona measures and monitors.
- Native objects created, deleted, or updated by the respective persona. This includes cluster and infrastructure components.

Based on discussion among the team, we determine each role is responsible for the following journeys to complete the tasks previously mentioned:

- **Cluster administrator**:
  - CRUD operations
  - Node addition/deletion
  - Cluster IAM access
  - Storage utilization
  - Cluster resource utilization

- **Cluster developer**:

  - Incident management

  - Application deployment

  - Namespace resource utilization management

  - Application resource scaling

  - Ingress management

  - Dashboard management

We might then update the whiteboard to include the following journeys in alignment with the respective persona. The information depicted in *Figure 8.4* represents the persona journey and should be established from the internal data and metrics in place with the organization and developed by team members.

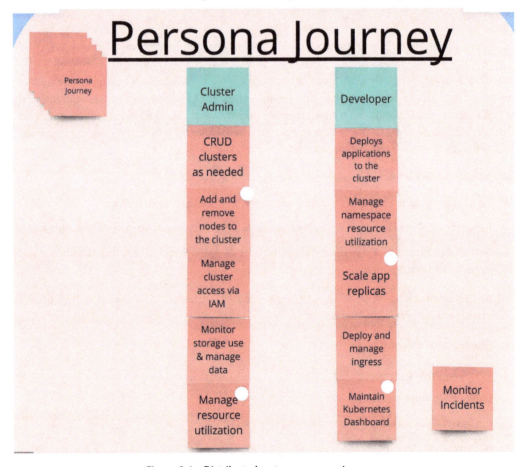

Figure 8.4 – Distributed systems persona journeys

After further discussion, we might then have the team select a few journeys that are critical or great candidates to start with. In *Figure 8.4*, critical journeys are marked with a dot on their sticky note. In this scenario, we will select four journeys that we believe are critical to start based on an assessment of internal data. For each journey, we might pose additional questions to better understand what we are trying to capture and measure for each journey. It's important to probe for additional information through dialogue to better understand the requirements. For the marked journeys, we might pose the following questions and information for additional clarity:

- **Node addition/deletion**:

  - The workflows for adding and deleting a node should exist independently as they are on opposing ends of the spectrum.

  - For each operation, there should be a clear SLO for latency and success rate. For example, a node addition should have an SLO for how quickly the node reaches a "ready" state (e.g., within 5 minutes).

  - Similarly, for node deletion, the SLO should define how quickly workloads are rescheduled without downtime, and ensure that all workloads are relocated successfully, meeting a defined success rate (e.g., 99.9% success rate).

- **Cluster resource utilization**:

  - What does *manage* mean in the sense of this journey?

  - Is this a cluster- or namespace-scoped resource? Are resource quotas an option?

  - Are there specific resources we are gauging? Databases deployed via statefulsets? Or standard deployments?

  - Of those resources, has either been involved in an excessive number of incidents?

  - Network throttling and node outages due to resource consumption.

  - Has either caused friction in the customer experience to an unacceptable degree?

- **Application resource scaling**:

  - What encourages the team to focus on "scale"? Has there been an excessive number of outages in a specific time zone? At certain hours?

  - Is there a decrease in performance or website accessibility when there are a certain number of replicas for the respective application workload?

- **Cluster dashboard management**:

  - What does *maintain* in this instance mean?

    - Does it relate to the charts and dashboards?

    - Is the deployment via automation and YAML?

  - Is there a specific deployment or resource that the team can monitor?

  - When is this deployment most critical for the targeted persona?

Upon further discussion, the team may decide on the identified journeys and raise additional questions. They may even identify certain journeys that should function independently, such as node addition and deletion. Although similar but opposing transactions, there are different tasks required to complete both. Some journeys may function independently to better track and reflect the value they bring to the organization and customer experience. We might restructure the previous journeys and end with the following journeys, which include customer expectations, requirements, or indicators the journey was successful. The restructured journeys appear as follows:

- **Node addition**:

  - Node displays a "ready" state.

  - Node accepts new workloads.

- **Node deletion**:

  - Node no longer displays in cluster output.

  - Node workloads have been rescheduled.

- **Application resource scaling**:

  - Deployments scale when performance accessibility decreases:

    - Network throttling.

    - HPA is already deployed.

- **Cluster dashboard management**:

  - Deployed dashboard is readily available:

    - *Readily available* is determined by the respective pod being in a healthy and running state.

- **Cluster memory utilization**:

  - A percentage of the memory needs to remain available for application scaling and rescheduling.

  - Resource utilization metrics are available in the cluster node output.

- **Cluster CPU utilization**:

  - A percentage of the CPU needs to remain available for application scaling and rescheduling.

  - Resource utilization metrics are available in the cluster node output.

If we regress back to the journey phase map, we might also walk through each of the journeys and develop the following artifact for each identified journey to better outline the process. For the sake of the text, we will utilize a single example, as depicted in *Figure 8.5*.

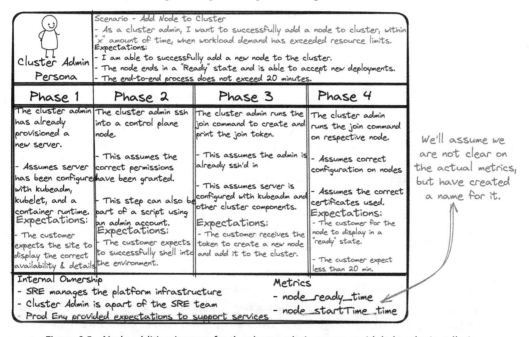

Figure 8.5 – Node addition journey for the cluster admin persona with kubeadm installation

In addition, it's important to mention again that the team can start with the most critical personas and journeys. If a persona or persona journey is not completed in the first run, it is best to iterate through the process again to identify the next group. In the iteration to follow, there will not exist a need to identify personas and journeys again. You'll hear this restated in each of the chapters in this part of the book as a gentle reminder. As it relates to the text, we are going to keep moving forward! Our team has settled on the journeys and expectations previously mentioned! It is time to understand the technical implications of the workflow.

Establishing application (system) boundaries

Now that we have identified the critical personas and their respective journeys, it is time to understand a bit more about how this translates to the technical aspects of the distributed environment. How do the components interact with one another to achieve an outcome within the system to help developers achieve their respective goals? At what touchpoints do we collect metrics? How do we aggregate these metrics in a way that reflects our SLIs and enables the team to determine whether we are meeting our SLOs? This helps to quickly assess whether we are meeting the agreed-upon service levels (SLAs) and whether corrective action is required. This is ultimately the sort of thinking as dialogue continues during the workshop.

We can utilize the customer journey map from *Figure 8.5* to assist with creating a visual diagram of the interactions between the technical components, to clearly understand how the components interact with one another and where. This step within the process can be accomplished through collaborative talking points, but occasionally, it will help to visualize the process and ensure that all individuals are on the same page and agree. We should also take this into consideration when trying to consider individuals who maintain different learning styles. The interpretation of what is discussed can be left to the imagination only if you allow it to be. We might utilize a sequence diagram to visualize the technical flow of interactions while ensuring that key touchpoints are aligned with relevant SLIs, such as request latency, error rates, or availability, which directly contribute to SLOs, as depicted in *Figure 8.6*.

This does not indicate that this is the best diagram or the recommended approach. Experience has shown that talking through workflows has worked. Sketching system architecture through talking points has also worked. Many organizations may already maintain in-depth design documentation to pair with the workshop. The best approach is the one that makes sense and should be considered in the early stages of developing or scheduling your workshop. Let's look at the interactions displayed in *Figure 8.6*.

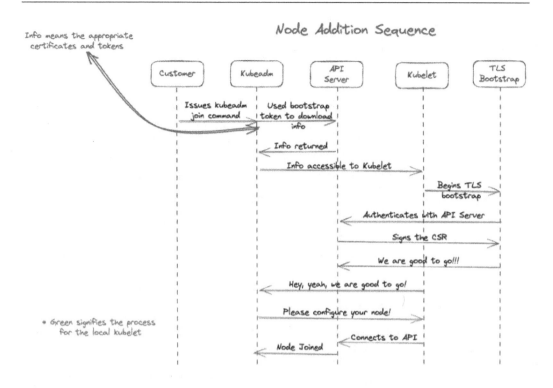

Figure 8.6 – Node addition sequence diagram

Figure 8.6 displays the various components from the container orchestrator deployed within the cluster. The orchestrator is responsible for scheduling and running the various services deployed to the cluster, ensuring that workloads remain in a healthy state and consistent with the desired state configured in the resource's deployment YAML file.

Within the interaction, we have touchpoints that begin with the customer utilizing the kubeadm bootstrapping tooling for cluster deployment and node join management. In addition to the networking communications that happen with the API server, a Kubernetes component and kubelet resource are deployed on all nodes within the cluster. Behind the scenes, various tasks occur to add and remove a node to and from a cluster, respectively. The sequence diagram helps to visualize the touchpoint to better understand where we may need to measure what.

When approaching this step, the goal of the discussion is to dissect at a lower level what takes place on the backend to better understand the metrics you want to collect, metrics you need to collect but that may not be established, and what and how different or several components work together to achieve the end goal. If your organization has an internal architecture or design team or is evaluating software and technology from another organization, much of this information is likely readily available to you.

If we redirect to the *application resource scaling* persona journey, we can dive a bit deeper into the journey to better understand the technical components and architecture.

However, upon further review, we realize the team mentions it has a solution deployed within the cluster that it has not fully implemented yet. It is the HPA that is native to the Kubernetes orchestration layer. The HPA automatically scales a workload based on resource utilization metrics (such as CPU or memory usage) to meet the desired SLOs, ensuring that response times and availability are maintained under increasing traffic. These metrics are gathered through the metrics API and should be monitored to ensure they align with our established SLIs for optimal service performance. If our application experiences an increase in traffic during the holidays, we might want to add additional resources to the cluster, with which we can balance the load.

Initially, we listed this journey in reference to the developer persona. If we think of the scaling process done by a developer, it might happen through a deployment file, some script, or a third-party integration deployed into the cluster or local infrastructure code base repository. It's important to differentiate between the persona being a tool, API, or some integration versus being a human role. It will help the team direct the conversation in the right way when we differentiate between the types. For the sake of the text, we will leave it categorized the way it is.

Therefore, our customer journey map might appear as follows for HPA, and with the developer persona, since they are the ones implementing or configuring the functionality:

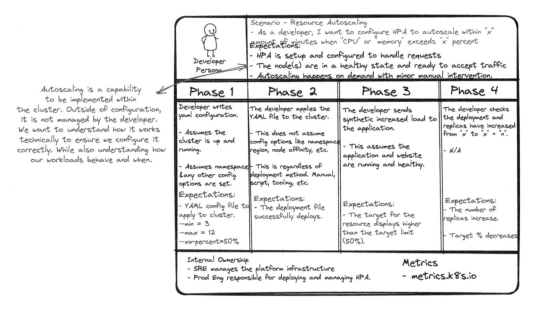

Figure 8.7 – Resource autoscaling journey

We might then determine that our journey ended up being too process-oriented and want to put together a quick sketch of the components that monitor, notify, and scale workloads to better understand what component logs we need to search, what metrics are currently available via `metrics.k8s.io`, and what metrics are reported to the server running in our cluster.

At a high level, the communication channel begins with a request sent from an external client. The request is routed to and through the API gateway for request filtering and authentication and is then routed to the load balancers, deployed on their own nodes within the cluster. The load balancers serve as a mechanism to route traffic to the appropriate backend service using ingress capabilities. Once the configured details have been reviewed, the request is routed to the backend service, which, in this instance, is our inventory service to retrieve information regarding a specific product from the inventory database. You can review additional details in *Figure 8.8*:

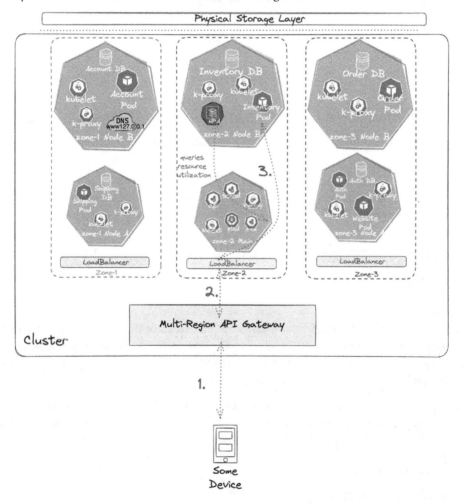

Figure 8.8 – Client-to-service and HPA communication flow

Asynchronously, the HPA service, which is deployed within the same region and on the same node, runs through a loop at an interval set by the development team to query the resource utilization metrics within the HPA definition file. It then identifies the respective objects and retrieves the appropriate metrics from the metrics API to decide whether it needs to scale resources up or down.

Because we had our original design documents available, we decided that we no longer needed to go through the process of creating a sequence diagram to loop through the communications between each object.

What we have found is the HPA functionality enables the team to set configurations such as the following:

- `--horizontal-pod-autoscaler-sync-period` to pass the time interval that the team would like for the controller to query resource utilization for the respective objects.
- HPA uses the metrics server. The metrics server retrieves its data from kubelet and exposes it in the API server through the metrics API. This means there are no additional configurations or deployments in the cluster:
  - `Metrics.k8s.i`
- It also handles aggregated APIs, which enables us to implement external and custom metrics:
  - `Custom.metrics.k8s.io`
  - `External.metrics.k8s.io`

With that being said, the team decides it best to move forward with both journeys mentioned during the mapping process as well as an additional journey that is a bit simpler to implement.

Specifying SLI types based on the identified system boundaries

Before we move on to specification, in *Chapter 7*, we outlined the SLI types. If a refresher is needed, please review *Chapter 7*'s *SLI specification* section for reference. For the context of the chapter, it is simply used to remind us of the types available before we begin the brainstorming session. As your team and organization get used to the process, they will develop a natural ability to immediately identify the appropriate types during discussion.

As a refresher, the persona journeys that we have agreed to focus on SLI development for are referenced in the following list. For the purposes of this section, we will not provide or go over definitions or descriptions. Each of the aforementioned is available for review in *Chapter 7*'s text:

- Application resource autoscaling
- Cluster resource utilization:

- CPU

- Memory

- Node addition

- Cluster dashboard management

It's important to be mindful of the journeys that you attempt to implement SLIs for. It impairs the group's ability to focus on the quality of specification and implementation. In addition, if there are any blockers or too many unknowns, it can cause the team to shift from one SLI to another, and on to another, without giving much attention to the end-to-end process and ensuring the end goal is achieved.

In this instance, there is an overlap between the resource utilization journey and the autoscaling journey. It was thought best to add the CPU and memory requests under the umbrella of the autoscaling journey. In addition, CPU and memory utilization metrics should be considered as part of the system's reliability measurements (SLIs) that affect the end user's experience. These should not only be monitored but also mapped to the SLOs to measure the ability of the system to meet a customer's needs, such as response time or availability under load. While resource utilization can indicate system health, it should be linked to the desired SLOs rather than treated as isolated operational metrics. Considering our persona in this instance is our developer managing the infrastructure and deploying the application workloads, we are going to keep it in the conversation and see whether anything comes of it. Here are some questions that we may want to keep top of mind:

- Can we incorporate each of these into the HPA journey and, by default, the SLI?

- Can we structure this in a way that internal engineers and developers are the customer persona, focusing on their experience?

This may not be the ideal method for solving this problem. Please do remember that when you and your team are running your workshops, it is ultimately up to you to do what is best for all parties, including stakeholders, that are involved. With that being said, let's do some initial brainstorming to set a better stage for what we need to measure:

- **Application resource autoscaling**: The team would like to measure the performance of autoscaling capabilities in a way that lets the dev team know the customer is benefiting from this. Based on the metrics design process review, we find much of the information and metrics are logged via the kubelet and timestamps are available in component logging:

  - **Throughput**: The team would like to capture the requests at some rate and during some given period.

  - **CPU resource utilization**: It is important that CPU utilization limits across nodes do not exceed a certain percentage. This may require additional configurations at the namespace or pod resource levels.

- **Memory resource utilization**: It is important for memory utilization to not exceed certain limits. This may require resource limit configuration at the namespace, pod, or node levels.

- **Node addition**: This is important to the team, due to scaling nodes up and down frequently, including during peak hours. The team cannot afford a cluster that is too unhealthy to adapt to the frequently changing demands with prolonged delays in scaling operations:

  - **Timed-event**: The length of time it takes to complete the additional operations, from initiation to readiness.

  - **Availability**: The cluster should remain in a ready state, to accept new workloads and manage current workloads during node operations.

- **Cluster dashboard management**: The web-based user interface is used as one of the several first lines of defense when attempting to debug live incidents. The deployment consists of a multi-container deployment via Helm installation and deploys the workloads into the system namespace. Therefore, we can look toward the deployments remaining available:

  - **Error rate**: Maintain a specific error rate during normal operational conditions.

  - **Pod startup**: The time it takes for a new pod to start and become ready to serve.

An SLI specification flow is depicted in *Figure 8.9*.

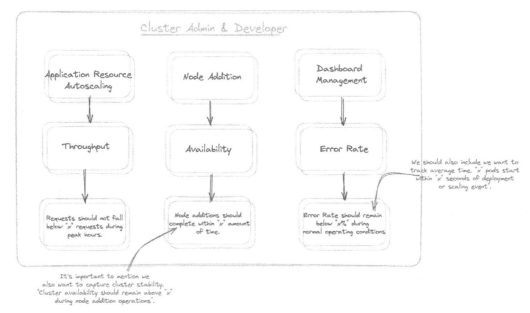

Figure 8.9 – Cluster admin and developer specifications

Now that we have an understanding of what we want to measure, it is imperative that we determine the following:

- Where current configurations allow us to measure the "what"

- What configurations are in the current environment that help to capture the limits of the "what":

  - Event logging

  - System and workload logging at the cluster level

  - Probing for additional data

  - Implementing a new observability layer

In addition to answering the preceding questions, we also want to look at internal data to begin to understand what the limits or thresholds are. For instance, if we are calculating the error rate remaining below a specific threshold during normal operating conditions, we may want to first define what normal operating conditions are and then look to the data to answer related questions.

If normal operating hours are Monday to Friday 8 a.m. to 4 p.m. EST, we should define the expected SLOs during these hours, such as availability or response time. Once SLOs are defined, we can analyze these hours. For example, we might look for peak hours that could indicate a higher-than-normal load and whether the system can handle this load without breaching the availability or latency SLOs. These are the questions we want to investigate using current and historical data. Much of this information may not be available at this stage but it is important to consider. The data investigated at this stage will inform the team of the metrics and components that need to be considered during the implementation stage. With that being said, let's shift our direction to how we measure the "what."

Implementing SLIs with accurate touchpoints based on the system specifications

Once we specify our SLIs, we want to shift the conversation toward the technical implementations, which we discussed in the previous two sections of this chapter.

The more dialogue that happens between team members and stakeholders in the beginning stages, the easier the conversation and implementation is in the later stages due to the data having already been gathered. This is under the assumption that the respective architectural or design documentation has already been reviewed and analyzed by the enablement team.

Now, how do we transition the narrative from specification to implementation? As we did in the prior chapter, the goal of this section is to redirect the conversation toward "how" and "how much." *Figure 8.10* displays the high-level shift from specification to implementation.

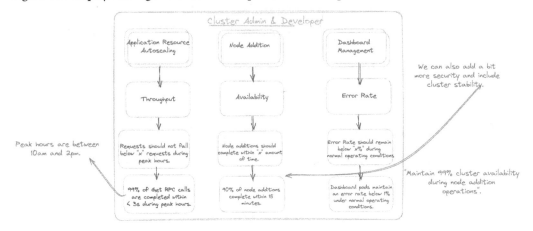

Figure 8.10 – Cluster admin and developer specifications

The structure of each persona journey, starting from defining the SLI type, shifting toward SLI expectations to specifications, and finishing with SLI implementation, should also naturally guide us toward defining the corresponding SLO. The SLO defines the target or goal for the SLI, ensuring that the SLI is not only measured but also aligned with the desired level of service that reflects the customer experience or business needs. In some instances, the data available will consist of enough information during earlier phases. In other instances, it may take a lot of dialogue between the team in phases to determine the appropriate SLO.

If your data does not immediately indicate a clear pattern, it's often useful to start with an agreed-upon initial SLO based on team consensus, or historical performance data. From there, monitor the system's performance over a defined period (cadence), adjusting the SLO as more data becomes available. This iterative process ensures that the SLO is both realistic and aligned with customer expectations and service reliability. The length of cadence greatly depends on the criticality of the SLO development and the need to report on it.

For our SLIs, we understand we are capturing service performance for workflows and resources within the cluster or infrastructure. SLI and SLO implementation focuses on which components and existing metrics within a system are best to use and measure a specific user journey. In this instance, we are focused on the measurement of throughput, availability, and error rate. For this section, we'll focus on the node addition SLI and SLO, which is as follows:

- 90% of node addition operations are completed within 15 minutes.

  This is indicated by the node status reporting `Ready` and the node `StartTime` reporting a time within the last x minutes.

In an earlier section, adding a node to a cluster is triggered by an action completed by the developer. This results in an event between the client and API server, of which a timestamped event populates in the logs. The timestamped event ends with confirmation information being sent from the local kubelet resource to the API server and then to kubeadm. For an end-to-end measurement of the node, the closing timestamp should post a time less than or equal to 15 minutes after the initial timestamp triggering the workflow. Through our observability tooling of choice, we will be able to query and populate the length of time to configure an SLI and SLO.

It is important to understand the architecture of the system you are measuring to formulate these decisions. For our SLI, we want to track the ability to spin up a node, and the node reports a `Ready` state within a certain amount of time, to indicate we can immediately deploy workloads to it. We can use a more reliable metric, such as `kubelet_node_startup_duration_seconds`, which reports the node startup time in total, or the `kubelet_node_startup_post_registration_duration_seconds` metric, reporting the node startup time post-registration activities. Registration, as it relates to Kubernetes, provides the API server with metadata about the node, so workloads are scheduled to it accordingly. In this scenario, post-registration communication is ideal, as we want to track the readiness to accept workloads versus merely being available.

In this instance, we can utilize a readily available metric to calculate a node's readiness to accept workloads and we would want to kickstart the SLI and SLO through it. In other scenarios where a metric is not readily available within the system, we would capture the logs available from the mentioned components to build a single metric. Thus far, we know that `kubelet_node_startup_post_registration_duration_seconds` should remain less than or equal to 15 minutes.

Understanding required considerations when prioritizing SLIs and SLOs

The ranking system is based on internal dialogue between the individuals leading the initiative and the technical staff responsible for the development and management of the technical components or designs. Like the previous chapters, and likely to be mentioned in the following chapters, the prioritization phase should occur between the decision-making teams and through natural conversation and communication with relevant stakeholders. In our instance, we might consider the following assumptions:

- Resource scaling during peak hours, especially the holidays, has a larger impact on the number of sales completed, number of carts abandoned, and number of customers that redirect to a competitor due to poor performance.

- Node additions, completed within a certain timeframe, impact business metrics in the long term. Although feasible, it is not as critical to business as ensuring scalability during peak business hours.

- For our third SLI, it is feasible and critical to the teams handling on-call responsibilities, thus having a business impact. However, its impact is not directly tied to business, as with the initial two SLIs, so we will rank it as a lower priority and consider it to be associated with ongoing maintenance.

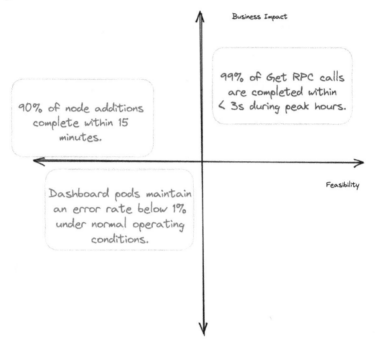

Figure 8.11 – SLI prioritization based on business impact and feasibility

Prioritization is and always should be a collaborative effort, while the processes and technical analysis aspects help to structure and shift the prioritization phase in the most accurate direction. When prioritizing your SLIs and SLOs, it's important to focus on feasibility, as it relates to your engineering teams and business impact, broader organizational goals, and contributing to meeting strategic goals and enabling other initiatives. As a reminder, be sure to include relevant stakeholders in the discussion, as they are likely to understand the internal business impact from a broader perspective.

Summary

When implementing SLIs and SLOs, it is common to immediately shift toward thinking about applications and the typical metric measurements that you'd expect to see from a frontend application. This statement is opinionated based on discussions and publicly available content. However, I hope that this chapter not only reinforced the steps or starting points for building and running your workshops but also highlighted the importance of measuring the components' performance in your distributed environment, including the infrastructure your applications run on. If a measurement or metric does not exist, it's imperative to consider the abilities of observability solutions to create and implement the necessary metrics and queries to quantify the customer experience and service performance.

Another thing that is not immediately mentioned throughout but should be considered is how the underlying infrastructure plays a critical role in the performance of your services. This especially includes when an organization is deploying their workloads with a cloud provider who can only commit to a specific level of service already defined within their SLAs, as well as application integrations from third-party providers that may have some dependency. It is critical to not over-commit to a level of performance beyond what the provider can commit to. These are also discussions that should take place as a part of your workshops.

How do we inject these dependencies into our own indicator measurements? Is it appropriate to simply commit to a level of performance that replicates their SLAs? Let's have a look at that in the upcoming chapter.

Further reading

You can review and read the referenced articles and books for additional reading about concepts mentioned in this book:

- *Kubernetes documentation*: `https://kubernetes.io/docs/concepts/overview/components/`.

- *gRPC status codes*: `https://grpc.github.io/grpc/core/md_doc_statuscodes.html`.

- *Custom Backend Metrics*: `https://grpc.io/docs/guides/custom-backend-metrics/`.

9

Scenario 3: Optimizing SLIs and SLOs for Database Performance

As we continue to build upon the process of developing SLIs and SLOs, you can expect this chapter to focus on SLIs and SLOs for database performance. *Chapter 7* focused on centering service level measurements around web applications specifically, while *Chapter 8* shifted the focus toward distributed systems, incorporating infrastructure a bit more.

This chapter is all about the backend database and focuses on other SLI types that may not immediately come to mind or you are less likely to see examples of. Like the previous chapters, the goal is not to prescribe a one-size-fits-all process or default SLI types. Instead, it is to help you and your team define specific **Service Level Indicators (SLIs)** that align with your **Service Level Objectives (SLOs)**, focusing on measurable aspects that directly impact the user experience. This ensures that all parties involved agree on the right metrics so that performance and reliability goals are clearly defined and measurable, which ultimately improves customer satisfaction.

This chapter outlines the process as follows:

- Application architecture
- Creating personas
- Identifying and mapping the persona to their journey in your system
- Establishing application (system) boundaries
- Specifying SLIs
- Implementing SLIs

Let's get started!

Application architecture

In previous chapters, we referenced the web application deployed in cloud infrastructure architecture throughout the respective scenarios. *Chapter 6* elaborated on the process with a bit more detail. Expect this chapter to focus more on the backend of your application and the platform's performance. If additional detail is needed, please review *Chapter 6* of this book for reference.

Our application is hosted across three availability zones of data center infrastructure, which we will refer to as zone-1, zone-2, and zone-3. Each zone is fronted by a load balancer and hosts some microservice in our application layer, as well as the components to run the orchestration layer. In a real-world scenario, we'd consider multi-regions with multiple availability zones, as needed, and have our services run with replicas running in multiple zones. In this scenario, we are not focused on replicas or zones, only that we have single instance microservices that reside in the assigned zone to reference.

Within the multizone cluster, we have a seven-node cluster running Kubernetes orchestration. One node acts as our main node running the workloads, or services, required to ensure the cluster is in a good state. For this chapter, we will focus on the performance of the database services and some of the storage layers. Each node within the cluster is hosting the associated applications and databases:

- Zone-1 node:

  - Account app

  - Account DB

- Zone-2 node:

  - Inventory app

  - Inventory DB

- Zone-3 node:

  - Order app

  - Order DB

The cluster also includes a load balancer within each region that is hosted in its own nodes, which routes traffic to the appropriate backend service. External storage is our storage provider for persistent volumes and volume claims. This architecture is depicted in *Figure 9.1*.

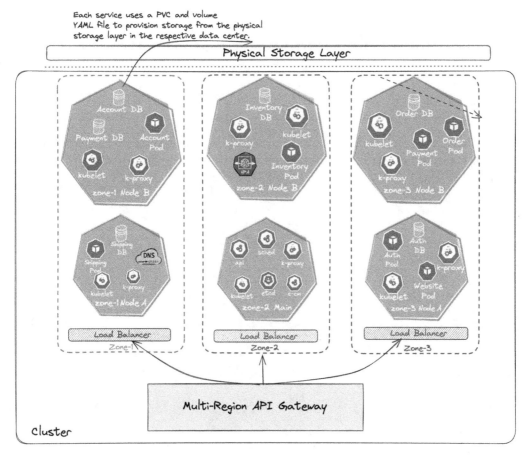

Figure 9.1 – Multi-region cluster and application services

Each service deployed within the cluster maintains its own database service that is responsible for **create, read, update, and delete** (**CRUD**) data transactions of information for its respective application services. As previously mentioned, for this chapter, we will focus on SLIs and SLOs for the database aspects of the application architecture. This chapter encourages you to think beyond just availability and uptime when measuring database performance, though these remain foundational SLOs. In addition to availability, consider incorporating SLIs such as latency, throughput, and error rates to ensure a comprehensive view of database performance and service reliability.

Personas and the persona journey

We will begin the development of SLIs and SLOs as we did in previous chapters, by establishing the critical personas and their respective journeys within our system. In the initial scenario, we began the discussion by heavily focusing on understanding the data and how to incorporate it into the discussion while asking the right questions to elicit the right information. In this chapter, we will not focus on that aspect so much, as our architecture is a continuation of the previous chapters, just on the data layer.

If we remember in our initial scenarios, we mentioned four persona types. In this scenario, we are focusing on the "user" persona type and have the following personas, of which we will focus on their journey as it relates to the database application and its performance:

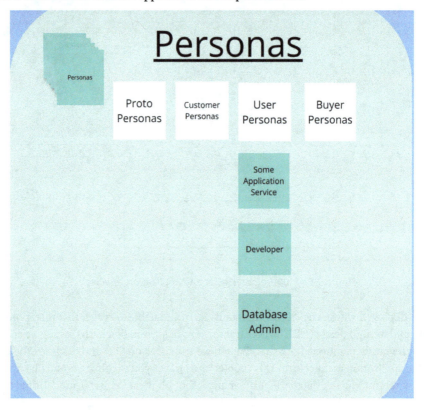

Figure 9.2 – Personas listed under their respective persona type

In this scenario, the database is a crucial service involved in numerous workflows. As previously mentioned, it is responsible for retrieving and updating inventory. Therefore, for many users, it's important that information is accurate, retrieved within an expected amount of time, and updated when needed with the appropriate security implications in place. Each application within our service architecture emits information to its own backend database application, which integrates with a physical storage layer.

The physical storage layer points of presence are within a location associated with the respective region listed in the architecture. Each zone consists of hardware within a data center in the region that is responsible for database services associated with the region. We can also go a step further and include each service and node deployment labeled with the region, so it understands to only schedule and run services with the appropriate labels.

The identified personas that are concerned with the process and are critical to the workflows within our system, referenceable in *Figure 9.2*, are as follows:

- **Application service** – Each service within the deployment is coupled with its own database. For simplicity, we will focus on the shipping app service and database.

- **Backend developer** – For this scenario, the team decided they wanted to get more specific and focus on the backend database, as full stack and frontend developers within the organization are typically focused on the frontend services. They are also responsible for the design and implementation phases.

- **Database admin** – Once the database has been developed, the database admin or engineer is responsible for maintenance and has various concerns surrounding database performance.

Since we have identified the personas critical to our application(s), we want to take a minute to understand the various workflows that help each persona achieve some outcome in our system. The team has also expressed some concerns regarding performance during peak hours and with increased traffic during holidays. Therefore, this is something that we want to take note of when working with the team through the various workflows. It's also a good idea to incorporate it on a sticky note. Also remember that much of the information will stem from the engineers included in the workshop and any internal data that may be relevant to the discussion, such as incidents, application/service logs, support cases files by the external customer, and so on.

Now, let's take a step back and shift our focus toward identifying the respective workflows and converting them into the persona or customer journey. For each persona, we will define measurable SLIs that represent key aspects of their workflow. We will then align these SLIs with SLOs, ensuring that expectations are clearly defined for each phase of the journey and that we can measure success in terms of user experience and system performance.

Defining the persona journey

In *Figure 9.3*, you'll find each persona listed with the possible journeys. Critical journeys are dotted on their respective sticky note. This indicates that the journey is critical, and we will move it toward the next phase of our SLI and SLO process.

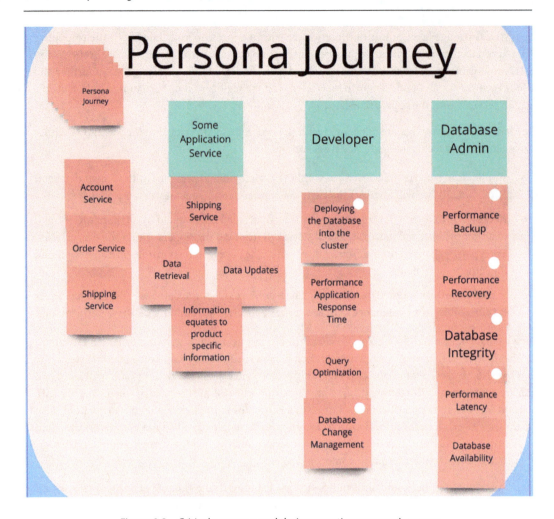

Figure 9.3 – Critical personas and their respective persona journeys

Of the journeys listed, we find the following persona journeys to be important and would like to flesh out more details to further break down each journey into more detail during the expectations phase. For each journey, we identify the respective persona's expectations and define the associated SLIs that represent those expectations. These SLIs will then be used to set SLOs that ensure each persona's expectations are measurable and aligned with the overall service reliability goals:

- **Shipping service persona**:

  - **Data retrieval** – The shipping service retrieves customer and product information from the order service to calculate shipping details such as pricing. The database then connects to an additional and external facing service to provide the necessary information to calculate shipping ETAs. The external service then provides the calculated shipping ETA via the API:

- We could even extend this to an additional consideration of API requests returned based on status codes.

- Data retrieval can also be included when a customer requests and views the ETA for product shipment. In this case, a freshness SLI should be defined to measure the latency between the most recent read transaction and the corresponding write transaction.

- **Developer persona**:

  - **Database deployment** – Deploying the initial database into the cluster.

  - **Query optimization** – Queries to the inventory database are completed successfully without errors.

  - **Database change management** – Integrated automation processes read compute resources and apply the necessary changes to the database, rolling out a new YAML file. The dev team would like to ensure that the method implemented is completed successfully.

- **Database admin persona**:

  - **Database performance backup** – The database successfully completes and is replicated at a specific cadence in preparation for recovery.

  - **Database performance recovery** – The team would like to ensure the external SLAs to the customer are met regarding data restoration.

  - **Database integrity** – Data is consistent through replication of primary and secondary storage systems.

  - **Performance latency** – Ingestion rates perform without degradation:

    - This can also extend to saturation, or the amount of storage utilized in comparison to storage that is available.

Each persona journey in the previous list is an ideal candidate regarding business criticality to the team, according to the internal research and analysis process used to determine customer pain points and temperature. Therefore, we'd want to further analyze and assess each item to identify what the customer expects within each phase of the journey. This step includes the team shifting the selected journeys over to the next section of their whiteboard or the tooling of choice being used to organize the conversation.

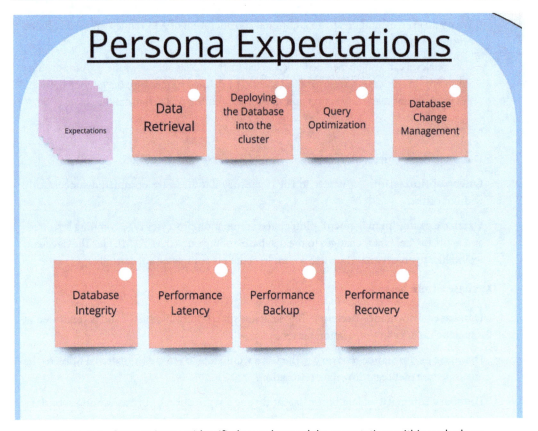

Figure 9.4 – Persona journey identified to understand the expectations within each phase

Now that we have a better understanding of the persona journey and additional context, we can shift the discussion toward expectations. For each persona journey, what does the data inform us of regarding expectations of the system? Are there specific cadences or time lengths? Let's dive into the next phase of persona expectations.

Setting journey expectations

In *Figure 9.3*, you will find the persona journey list in preparation for persona expectations. The team is starting to feel a bit more comfortable and decides to add additional items to the board to do the following:

- Add additional discussion points
- Gain a little bit more traction
- Establish a larger pool of journeys to pull from when they iterate through the initial batch of SLIs and SLOs

Our board might include the following information after group discussion, elaborating a bit more on each of the journeys and persona expectations:

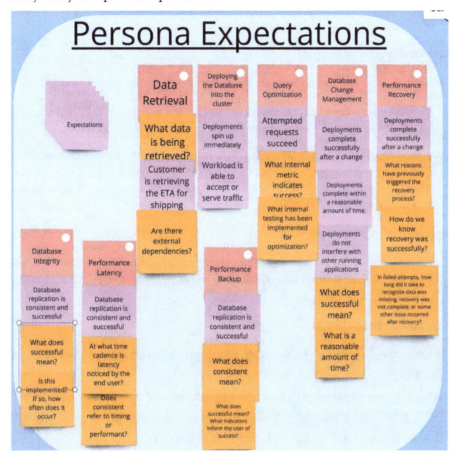

Figure 9.5 – Persona expectations for each persona journey

The team is confident in defining SLOs for the following journeys and expectations, with each SLO to be tracked via SLIs, ensuring measurable performance goals that align with user expectations. For the purposes of the text, we'll walk through the persona journey phase mapping to prepare for the next step in our process. We'll start with the expectations for the following persona journeys without the technical and process implications to be established in later steps:

- **Data retrieval**:

  - What is the format and type of data being retrieved from the system?

    - Customers have complaints regarding the reporting of the estimated time of arrival for their product shipments reported in their profile.

- Are there external dependencies that contributed to the success of the journey?

  - Yes, the dependency is with the third-party system owned by the shipping provider communicating the ETA back to our system.

- **Database change management**:

  - What does *successful* mean regarding the deployed workload?

    - The statefulset is deployed into the cluster and reports back to a healthy and running state. All associated resources are ready and able to accept and consume traffic.

  - What is a reasonable amount of time?

    - The support and SRE teams noticed a pattern of customers filing tickets, on average, between 12 and 15 minutes.

  - Are there any other expectations?

    - Internal engineering teams want to encourage engineers to review and submit clean code. Therefore, they want to roll out configuration and other changes without having to resubmit code for the same change.

- **Performance recovery**:

  - What incidents have previously triggered the recovery workflow and for which parts of the system?

  - What SLAs are in place to trigger recovery processes and how do they define acceptable downtime or data loss for each component?

  - How do we know and validate that recovery was successful?

  - If there were failed attempts, how long did it take to notice data integrity issues?

- **Query optimization**:

  - What internal metric indicates that a query is successful?

  - Which query are we most concerned with to start?

  - Are there already internal optimization or reporting mechanisms implemented for specific queries?

To better answer the previous questions and better align the expectations with the respective workflows, let's start with a persona journey visual for data retrieval. As previously mentioned, this is not a required step. It is a single method that can be utilized quickly during a workshop to ensure that an accurate description of workflows and tasks within each flow is captured.

Customer Persona	Scenario - Data Retrieval - Shipping ETA - As a customer, I want to place an order and an accurate ETA shipment for my product is provided within 24 hours. Expectations: - An accurate ETA for product shipment is provided within 24 hours - The ETA is specific to shipment, not necessarily the actual arrival date. - A new notification is sent to the customer via email within 24 hours		
Phase 1	**Phase 2**	**Phase 3**	**Phase 4**
The customer places an order. - Assumes the purchase is successful. - Assumes they have an account in good status. Expectations: - Receive confirmation response. - Requests shipment Details.	The customer provides shipment details. - Assumes the correct details have been provided. - This is regardless of deployment method. E.g. Manual, script and tools. Expectations: - Shipment details are validated and accepted. - The customer requests payment details.	The customer provides payment information for processing. - Assumes payment details are correct. - Assumes payment method is accepted. Expectations: - The payment is processed. - Confirmation is sent.	The customer receives an email with confirmation of purchase. - Assumes payment method was accepted and successful. Expectations: - An accurate ETA of shipment is provided. - Product ships on the provided date.
Internal Ownership - Product Engineering manages the local shipping service and database. - The external provider manages the pickup, shipping, and delivery of the product.		Metrics - shipment_ETA - delivery_DOA	

Figure 9.6 – Customer journey visual for shipment ETA

In *Figure 9.6*, we can immediately see at a high level the phases or steps that are taken for a customer to retrieve data regarding the estimated shipment date. It's also important to note that the current workflow includes an immediate email notification to the customer regarding successful order completion and potential shipment dates.

However, it does not update the customer regarding what the actual shipment date is once a tracking number has been assigned to the product and a shipment date calculated. The customer is requesting an accurate ETA within 24 hours of product purchase. This has a dependency on the process and integrated APIs with the shipping partner. Let's shift toward understanding the system boundaries, and how each component works together to achieve the necessary functions for the critical persona.

Establishing application (system) boundaries

Now that we have identified the critical personas and their respective journeys, it's time to dissect the database architecture a bit more to understand how each component works together to achieve some outcome. This will help us to ensure that we are measuring the right things in the right way. As previously mentioned, this scenario is going to focus on the database functionality as opposed to the infrastructure layers.

Let's revisit our persona journey map and sequence diagram to understand the functional and technical steps required to reach the journey's end. Let's look at the *Data Retrieval – Shipment ETA* workflow to further establish the components and system boundaries.

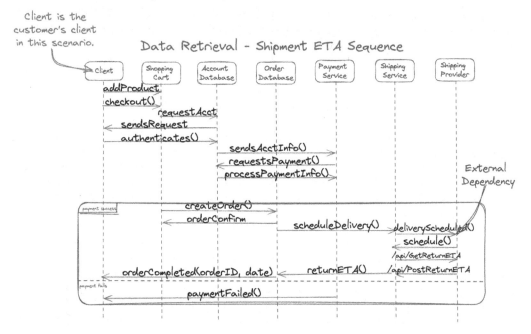

Figure 9.7 – Shipment ETA sequence

The sequence diagram for this specific persona journey helps to visualize the flow and understand the order of operations between the individual services deployed within the cluster. It's important to remember that each individual service consists of a service pod and a database pod that encapsulates the container(s). In some instances, both a service and database exist for the same workflow, but we are more concerned with the database and flow of the data to measure performance.

This is mentioned as the pod will host the container, which includes the underlying code from the local or external code repository and any other application dependencies. For a quick reference of the view between the services and cluster components, see *Figure 9.8*.

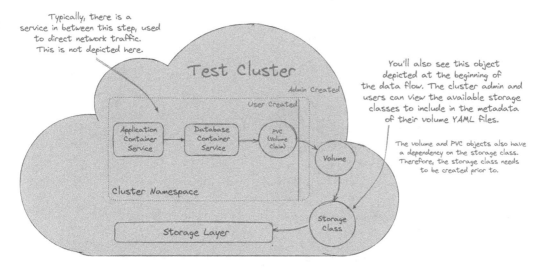

Figure 9.8 – The network traffic flow from application to storage

The flow between components includes the application container, which includes the application code and relevant application dependencies. This container or pod is configured with a service object that is configured with networking options to route traffic to specific objects within the cluster based on configuration rules. The service object directs toward the database service, which consists of the database code and configurations for the required database. The database will then direct to a **persistent volume claim (PVC)**, which consists of the metadata to request storage via the volume object. The volume is an abstract of the physical hardware utilized for storage. The architecture is not the focus of this section but is mentioned to serve as a reminder of the flow of data and ensure that you and the team understand the communication flow.

Another consideration worth noting is the numerous types of storage configurations and architects that can be configured for a cluster. When the kubelet on the node attempts to start the container, the provisioning phase will occur, and the underlying storage will mount to the pod's container via the volume. This is also important to take into consideration the changes that happen when we complete a task as simple as changing the configuration in the YAML file of an object associated with the database flow.

In this scenario, the object workflow might appear as depicted in *Figure 9.9*.

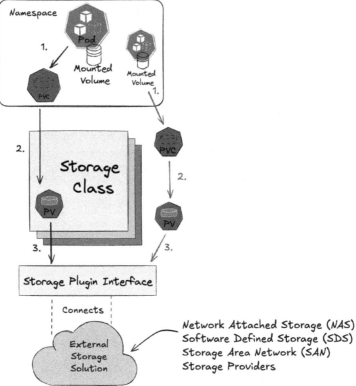

Figure 9.9 – Network flow for storage provisioning and attachment

Figure 9.9 depicts the flow of the storage provisioning through both dynamic and static volume provisioning at a high level. Each flow follows the same pattern, except for in *Step 2*. Dynamic provisioning will flow through the storage class object, which is configured by the administrators. The storage class provides a set of configuration options that are available and mounted when the application and PVC are deployed, and sends the request.

On the right-hand side, you'll still see the flow shift starting with the reference of the application (pod) to request storage through a PVC. The referenced claim requests a **persistent volume (PV)**, which it successfully binds to if all objects are available and in a healthy state. The PV in *Step 3* is provisioned through the storage class on the left-hand side, while on the right-hand side, the YAML files are written and deployed requesting the appropriate volume.

The storage plugin interface will connect to the external storage solution, located within the respective data center. Although this is not the focus of this chapter, it is important to mention it to ensure that the overall architecture and workflow are understood. Let's shift toward the specification step with this in mind.

SLI specification

As done in the previous chapters, upon understanding the underlying architecture, we want to ensure that the expectations associated with each journey are associated with an SLI type to help guide the conversation and take into consideration the various measurements possible outside of uptime and availability, although both are equally important.

To serve as a reminder, you can view *Figure 7.8* in *Chapter 7* to revisit a brief list of the common SLI types used within this chapter as well.

Based on the previously mentioned architecture and description, we'll conclude that the team has decided on the following SLI types to work through the specification process:

- **Data retrieval**: Data retrieval in this instance is the estimated shipment date that customers feel should be reported within 24 hours of placing a purchase. The shipping process has an external dependency on the shipping provider, of which their SLAs commit to 48 hours based on the architecture. In this instance, it is important for the organization not to commit to a measurement that does not align with the business completing the task. Based on this information, the team agrees to 72 hours to leave room for error between both organizations, and after analyzing the data and agreeing that 24 hours is simply unreasonable. Therefore, they decided on the following SLI types:

  - **Response time**: The customer is requesting a specific piece of data to return within an allotted amount of time. Regardless of the time we commit to, it's ideal to have a metric that ensures we honor the time set if it is outside of the parameters requested.

  - **Freshness**: This metric should ensure that the data being retrieved is up to date within a defined timeframe. Freshness is a critical SLI when the system relies on external data sources, such as APIs, to ensure that the most recent data is captured and used in processing.

> **Note**
>
> Freshness is an SLI type that is not typically mentioned, nor was it covered in the SLI types mentioned in *Chapter 7*. Therefore, it is important to note here that it focuses on the recency of stored data. This is especially important when retrieving information regarding shipping dates, to ensure the most recent data is captured and being used. In some environments, it can be simply comparing referenceable timestamps of some objects within the system, or in more elaborate environments, it can include other scraping techniques and tooling or a focus on time-based series and measurements.

- **Database change management**: This is with regard to direct changes made to the database via the local code repository and then applied through the respective YAML files. The team also notices the rolling update feature for stateful sets and decides this is a good feature to leverage, which also supports rollbacks:

  - **Errors**: To ensure reliability, we need to track the failure rate of deployments, specifically for database-related changes. This SLI will include tracking the error rates during deployments and code changes, such as failed rollouts, failed database migrations, or failed readiness probes.

  - **Deployment success rate**: The percentage of successful database deployments without rollback.

  - **Error rate**: The percentage of deployment failures (e.g., due to failed pods, and unready replicas). This information is made available through the following:

    - **Ready field**: The number of replicas configured deployed and in a ready state

    - **Up-to-date field**: The number of replicas updated to achieve the configured desired state

    - **Available field**: The number of replicas ready and available to users of the deployed objects

  This is in addition to utilizing the probing capabilities to periodically run checks on containers.

- **Database performance recovery**: The team aims to ensure data consistency and availability during recovery operations due to storage-related bottlenecks. This results in a limitation on the performance of the system network. To meet this goal, the following SLOs should be established:

  - **Replication latency SLO**: Define an acceptable time for data to be replicated across multiple availability zones (e.g., data should be replicated within "x" minutes).

  - **Recovery point objective (RPO)**: The maximum acceptable data loss in the event of failure (e.g., data loss should not exceed 15 minutes).

  - **Throughput**: Measure the throughput for data transfer rates to and from the storage to ensure that it meets expected performance levels under varying loads, particularly during recovery scenarios.

It may also serve best to configure the metric based on the complaints via support tickets and data logged by your incident management team to create an SLI and optimize it along the way. The goal is to test and monitor various loads to determine methods for the database to continue to recover after peak usage.

> **Note**
>
> It's important to include (and may have already been mentioned in earlier chapters) that some SLIs will make sense based on the persona's expectations of the journey and the architecture without having sufficient data internally or monitoring and observability configurations to gauge an accurate starting point.
>
> In instances such as this, the team, with agreement from stakeholders and the respective engineering team, can configure a metric and SLO starting point based on incidents and monitor it over a given period for additional optimization at a later point.

- **Query optimization**: Optimization in this instance focuses on the quality, speed, and correctness of the product information requested by the customer or end user on the website. There have been complaints of slowness and missing product-related details, of which the team has already identified metadata discrepancies within the database:

  - **Errors**: At this stage, the team does not have sufficient data to focus on ideal speeds. To start, the team agrees to track the error rate or that of the backend database queries that succeed or fail as a starting point.

> **Note**
>
> Based on the original requests related to this persona journey, it is also ideal to focus on correctness. However, correctness and query speed/optimization are SLIs that the team can iterate upon once they have spent some time tracking the error rates. This is ideal in this instance where there is not sufficient monitoring or data available to build a solid starting point.

Tracking the success and failure rates of the queries run will help the team identify specific behaviors through errors and which application workflows are associated with specific issues to improve issue resolution. This will also passively help your incident management and support teams in the long run, as it relates to debugging and troubleshooting live incidents.

Based on discussions with the team and the items identified in the previous lists, we might depict our specifications diagram, which includes the SLI types and SLI specifications shown in *Figure 9.10*:

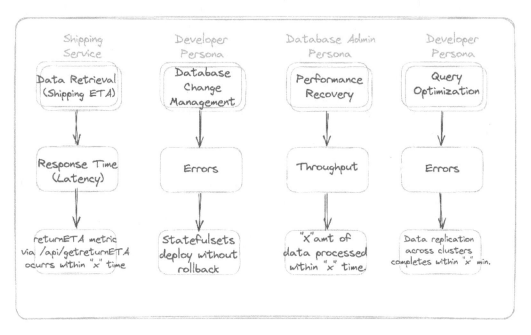

Figure 9.10 – SLI specification flow from persona journey to SLI specification

In previous chapters, we focused on a single persona journey and created SLIs and SLOs for each. In this chapter, we have identified individual personas and selected a persona journey for each to focus on creating an SLI type. We'd formulate our SLI specifications with the following conditions:

- **Data retrieval (shipping ETA)**: *Figure 9.7* depicts the sequence diagram, showing the flow of traffic and data while placing an order. An external dependency exists, requesting and sending the shipping ETA via the `/api/getReturnETA`, `/api/PostReturnETA` API constructing the `returnETA()` method and metric. This might lead us to request the following:

  - Responses from `/api/getReturnETA` are sent within a certain amount of time

  - The `returnETA` metric is updated with information from the API within a certain amount of time or at some cadence via the shipping service's `/api/PostReturnETA` API

- **Database change management**: Due to the reporting of application/container status via the container orchestration and the ability to complete readiness checks as a feature, this might lead the team to request the following:

  - Database deployments occur without rollbacks

  - Database deployments are available

In this instance, we might err on the side of a readiness probe due to the handling of data, but not in the sense of needing to load large amounts of data during the startup phase. If that were the case, we might err on the side of implementing a startup probe.

- **Database performance recovery**: High availability and data recovery are important aspects of this organization. Therefore, replication and data protection are a high priority. The team agrees, and based on customer incident reports, reporting on data integrity and consistency is a key SLO for brand and reputation improvements. They are requesting the following:

  - Replication across availability zones at some cadence for recovery processes

  - Consideration of primary and secondary storage system performance

- **Database optimization**: To start, the team may want to capture success versus failure rates for certain queries, as replication efforts for load balancing will contribute to improving this SLI and SLO.

> **Note**
>
> We'll rename this SLO *Database Optimization vs. Query Optimization* to reflect the database activity versus narrowing the activity to optimizing a specific query.

It is imperative to focus on understanding each customer's persona and journey, so that when you are figuring out why you are measuring a specific component and where, your team does not experience scope creep and stray away from customer centricity. The specification stage of the process aids in ensuring that alignment stays intact. Let us shift toward the next stage and focus more on the implementation phase.

SLI implementation

Now that we have specified "what" after identifying the "why," we want to navigate the "how" and "where" a bit more in depth. How do we go about implementing SLI types and determine where it's best to measure, while also incorporating SLO thresholds? This phase simply allows us to ensure and transition the specification in a way that helps to structure and ensure we are measuring the right things in the right place, in the right way.

It's important to understand that in a live workshop, the flow is going to shift through conversation and numerous updates. This is not depicted within the text but is mentioned as a reminder for you to incorporate things to add or remove during your own internal workshop, whether in person or virtually.

The figures from the specification toward implementation just serve as a visual aid of the actual flow. You should feel free to incorporate as much or as little information as is needed for your team to synthesize and hypothesize. Now, let's shift toward understanding how we should incorporate the implementation details.

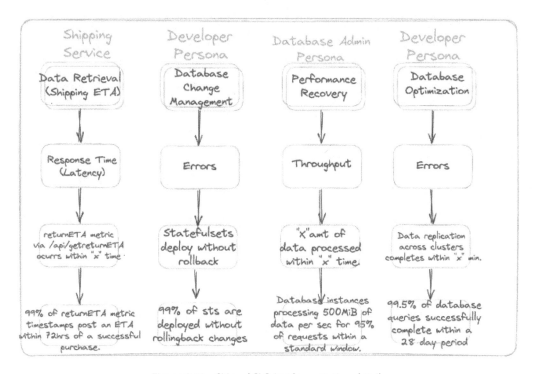

Figure 9.11 – SLI and SLO implementation details

In the previous section of this chapter, we were able to identify the criteria and technical details surrounding what we want to measure and how. In a live workshop, much of this section is covered through collaboration and conversation among the engineering team and the SRE leadership team. In some instances, final sign-off may be required by stakeholders and other internal leaders to ensure the components measure up to and validate internal KPIs, organizational strategy, business unit OKRs, or any other criteria agreed upon in earlier phases of the process.

Now, let's imagine our SRE leaders signed off and agreed to the SLOs as well as implementing any architectural changes to support their implementation. In *Figure 9.11*, we identified the following SLOs based on previous data synthesis activities done in earlier sections of this chapter:

- **Data retrieval (shipping ETA)**: 99% of `returnETA` metric timestamps post an ETA within 72 hours of a successful purchase.

- **Database change management**: 99% of **StatefulSets (STSs)** are deployed without a rollback.

- **Database performance recovery**: Database instances should process 500 MiB of data per second for 95% of requests within a rolling 28-day window. This ensures performance is consistently measured over a dynamic, continuous time period, rather than a fixed past window:

- Database replication across clusters is successfully completed within 45 minutes

- **Database optimization**: 99.5% of primary database queries successfully complete within a 28-day period.

For the `returnETA` SLO, we accidentally covered much of the technical detail in the specification step. There is nothing wrong with that. However, I want to revisit and cover implementation for the remaining three:

- Database change management
- Database performance recovery
- Database optimization

If we revert to the technical architecture covered in *Chapter 7*, in *Figure 7.1*, it's helpful to remember the cluster is deployed across regions and *database performance recovery* requires the implementation of additional secondary storage and database instances in separate regions for failover operations. The team understands this will take the engineers some brainstorming and time and agrees to later prioritize it as high business impact, due to several outages, with less feasibility.

For *database optimization*, the team will track query success rates by measuring the ratio of successful database queries to the total number of queries within a defined time window, such as 28 days. This metric will calculate the SLO for optimization as *(successful queries / total queries) * 100%*. Let's depict these changes in the prioritization chart of our visual board!

SLI prioritization

Prioritization in this scenario will follow a similar workflow used in the previous chapters. However, in this chapter, we will need to focus on how the database impacts the respective journey and prioritize based on how the SLI and SLO will impact the broader business and strategic goals. In this instance of prioritization, we have a single SLO for data processing. We must evaluate its impact on system reliability by analyzing past incidents, outages, and the frequency of breaches in the SLO. This will help in understanding how much it affects the customer experience and business outcomes.

To begin, we will want to open discussions with the team to determine how feasible it is for the team to implement. What components within the system are directly involved in the success of the workflow? How do upstream, downstream, and third-party dependencies (e.g., cloud provider services) affect the ability to meet the SLOs? It's important to assess whether third-party services can meet the agreed SLOs and define their impact on your own system's SLOs. In the scenarios used within this chapter, we were able to identify and discuss the dependency shipping ETAs have due to being established by the shipping partner.

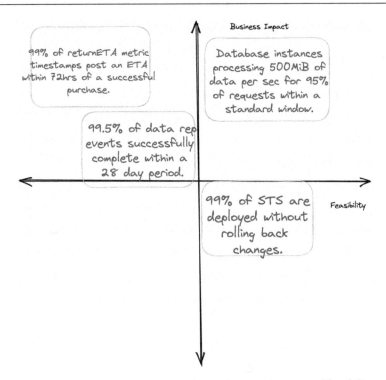

Figure 9.12 – SLI prioritization according to business impact and feasibility

In this instance of prioritization, we have a single SLO for data processing, which requires revisiting the process use and iterating on incidents and outages. On the other hand, two SLOs exist, which will include collaboration and a dependency on a third-party organization and new components added to the system architecture. When prioritizing, the team will want to work closely with engineering to determine the length of time it will take to implement. If looking for short wins, the team may want to identify additional SLIs and SLOs they are able to implement while other tasks are being completed.

Summary

When building SLIs and SLOs for your application and infrastructure architecture, it's important to think of the various components at the data and storage layers, and how each can be measured to ensure reliability for your customers. Often, the mind will immediately shift toward measurements surrounding availability and uptime, which are critical to system performance.

However, I hope this chapter has at least highlighted some of the areas and components that need to be taken into consideration to foster thinking outside of the previously mentioned measures of performance.

I also hope that the structure of this chapter helps you to foster an environment where these conversations can be had to efficiently identify areas of importance, and which are central to the success of your customer's experiences. In the chapter to follow, we will shift the attention toward focusing on new features within your system, as well as iterating through established backlogs. We will focus on making traction using new features identified in this and previous workshop chapters.

Further reading

Here, you can review and read the referenced articles and books for additional reading about concepts mentioned in this book:

- Authors, T. K. (2024, August 26). *Kubernetes Components*. Retrieved from: `https://kubernetes.io/docs/concepts/overview/components/`.

- Dambrine, F. (2022, December 14). *Kubernetes Icon Set*. Retrieved from: `excalidraw.com`.

- Luzar, D. G. (2023, April 18). *Stick Figures Collaboration*. Retrieved from: `excalidraw.com`.

10
Scenario 4: Developing SLIs and SLOs for New Features

This chapter focuses on developing SLIs and SLOs for new features within your current system. Despite how available the system is, customers will always have new and changing needs, resulting in a requirement for new features. We can also assume the customer is going to expect enhancements to current features and other improvements within the system as time goes on. How do we then incorporate SLIs and SLOs for new features to report on their availability and performance? Additionally, how do we define and measure the reliability of new feature rollouts using the appropriate SLIs, such as the percentage of successful requests or feature adoption rates across targeted user segments? How do we then strategically decrease downtime and outages that impact long-term objectives? You can expect the answers to these questions in the sections that follow.

In previous chapters, we focused on centering service level measurements around other areas within a system's architecture. The goal of this chapter is to shift the focus and narrative to adding new features that may have developed during the workshop session, from external customer requests, or by simply iterating through your product backlog. The overall goal remains the same: to provide you and your team with a starting point for developing service-level measurements within your organization.

This chapter covers the following topics:

- Application architecture
- Creating personas and the persona journey
- Identifying application (system) boundaries
- Specifying SLIs
- Implementing SLIs
- Prioritizing SLIs by business impact

We will follow this flow throughout this chapter and focus on new functionality and feature improvements for our hypothetical system. With this in mind, let's get started!

Application architecture

In the previous chapter, we introduced a simple website that offers products to individual customers making a purchase and businesses looking to purchase products in bulk for resale. We'll continue with this example and scale it to include infrastructure and additional availability zones.

In previous chapters, we highlighted the overall architecture. In this chapter, we will not focus on the overall architecture but simply on the process as it relates to the new feature. The application and platform architecture are depicted in *Figure 10.1*.

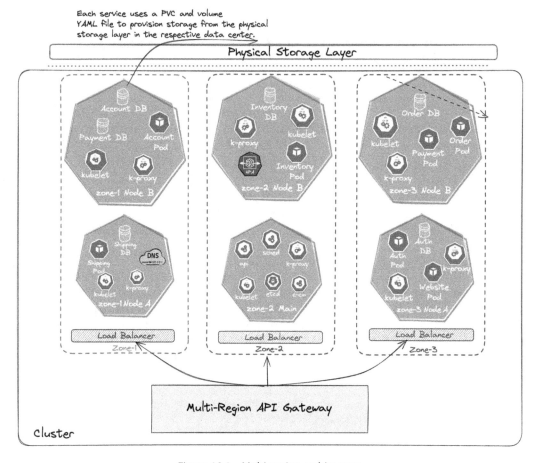

Figure 10.1 – Multi-region architecture

For additional information or application references, you can refer to *Chapter 6*. For now, the referenced architecture has been provided here as a refresher.

Creating personas and the persona journey

At this point in the book, you will be familiar with what a persona is, persona types, and the persona journey. In this section, and sections to follow, you can expect to work through the process for adding new features and determining how to do the following:

- Build and implement SLIs and SLOs for new features.
- Implement SLIs and SLOs that cater to the usability of the system as it relates to the functional purchasing process versus the technical process in the system.

If we revisit the personas and persona journeys from *Chapters 6* through *9*, we navigated through the application and platform architecture to select the critical personas and their respective journeys through the system. During the persona and journey mapping process in *Chapter 6*, we identified two expectations that could potentially exist as new features of the system. At a high level, the feature requests were as follows:

- A guest account workflow used when a customer is checking out:

  - As a customer, I want to create an account.

  - As a customer, I want to log in to my account during the checkout process so that I can add personal information.

  - As a customer, I want to check out as a guest without logging in to or creating an account.

  - Additional method of payment:

    - As a paying customer, I want to make a purchase using accounts other than a debit and/ or credit card (e.g., Google Pay, Apple Pay, Shopify, PayPal).

- Additional email notification regarding the date of arrival once the product is shipped:

  - As a paying customer, I want to receive a secondary email once my product has shipped, related to the predicted time of arrival.

- Measurement of custom application SLIs, such as request latency and error rates, using custom metrics exposed via `metrics.k8s.io`:

  - As an internal engineer, I want to measure the performance of custom metrics.

> **Note**
> The initial request is related to aggregated custom metrics.

Now that we have a better understanding of the customer requests from previous chapters, we can shift toward fleshing out the personas and their respective journeys in the systems.

Personas

To ensure that we understand the definition of each persona, let's consider the following short descriptions as refreshers for each persona:

- **Customer purchase**: The customer purchase persona identifies as a customer who is making a typical purchase from the business website.

- **Shipping service**: The shipping service persona represents the shipping service deployed to the cluster that interacts with an external third-party service to provide details regarding product shipment.

- **Metrics service**: The service deployed to the cluster.

- **Buyer method of payment**: The buyer can make a purchase via multiple third-party payment methods (Google Pay, Apple Pay, Shopify, PayPal, etc.).

Based on the high-level expectations identified from the prior chapters, we can now update our visual dashboard to display the respective personas, which will help move us into establishing the respective journeys, as depicted in *Figure 10.2*.

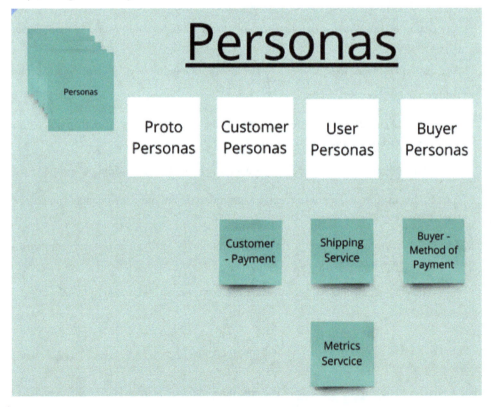

Figure 10.2 – New feature personas based on persona type

As we shift toward defining the persona journey further for customers and other types of users, we also want to consider metrics that measure engagement, completion, feedback, and other experience-related workflows. When considering service-level measurements, it is easy to focus on the technical details. However, there are various other customer-centric measurements that help to capture experience-related details. We hope to highlight them within this chapter.

Following the brief descriptions that aid in providing an improved understanding of what each persona means on our visual board, we want to investigate, through collaborative discussion, the various workflows a persona can take in attempting to achieve an outcome within the system. *Figure 10.3* depicts the user journey for the respective persona.

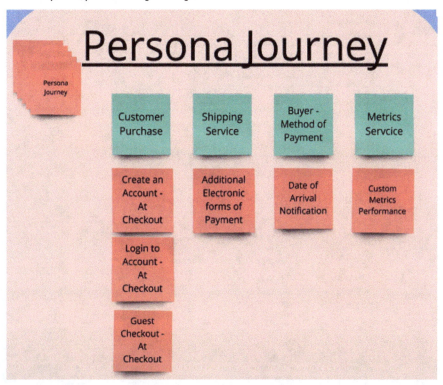

Figure 10.3 – New feature persona journey based on new features requested by customers

By the team maintaining effective communication with design engineers and product managers, regarding historical information related to feature requests, we are able to immediately capture the initial user stories and several other technical documentation artifacts surrounding the new implemented features. The details were mentioned in previous sections.

The next step in the process is to flesh out the details surrounding what the customer expects versus the technical architectural details. This shifts us into the expectations chart within the visual board. The *expectations* section of the discussion helps the team define measurable SLOs based on customer expectations, such as response time, success rate, and frequency of service interactions, to measure the system's performance. This helps to transition to a smoother path for mapping these expectations to the different system boundaries in the next phase. Based on the discussion, we define the customer expectations of the selected journeys as follows:

Figure 10.4 – Updated journey expectations

We might find ourselves discussing several aspects of the journey as it relates to how the new feature was implemented within the system. We might also discuss what the customer experience has been or what feedback was provided to gain a better understanding of customer sentiment regarding what is realistically occurring within the system. In addition, like in previous chapters, sorting through the workflow will only help to better understand how the underlying components are working together to achieve the ultimate end goal. In this instance, you might also find yourself answering some of the SLI specification questions as you get more comfortable moving through the process.

Create an Account – At checkout

To better showcase an example, let's use the *Create an Account – At Checkout* journey and walk through the process. Based on *Figure 10.4*, we have already identified the following related to the workflow.

Description: The business' "new" customer base requested a feature where they can check out; enter all personal, payment, and shipping information; and end with the option of creating an account. Previous functionality created the account prior to submitting the information; however, it caused broken links during the process and did not always log in to the account after creating the new account, which led to information not being collected and stored. Customers were finding themselves having to go through the account creation again afterward, without having a suitable link to the order and personal information. The current workflow is depicted in *Figure 10.5*.

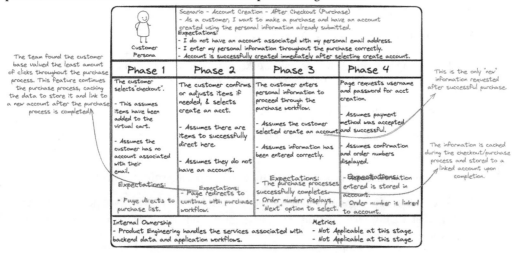

Figure 10.5 – Account Creation – After Checkout workflow/persona journey

Based on the workflow and discussion, the team identified the following steps or phases within the journey, based on the assumption that the customer has completed shopping online and added all necessary items to their virtual cart. They are now at the point of following this workflow consisting of four dependent phases:

- **Phase 1** – The customer selects the **Checkout** button after placing all items in their virtual shopping cart:

  - We assume that the customer has placed all necessary items in the cart.

  - We assume the customer does not have an account and therefore is not logged in to an account.

  - We assume, since they have no account, that their email account is not associated with any accounts in the internal database.

- **Phase 2** – The customer is redirected to a **Purchase confirmation** page where they can add and/or remove any items, and then confirm they want all items remaining within the cart. They then can select **Create an account**:

  - We are assuming there were items added to the cart and still in the cart.

  - We are still under the assumption that the customer has not logged in to the account, nor do they have one.

  - We assume they selected **Create an account**.

- **Phase 3** – The page continues the purchase workflow instead of redirecting to solicit credentials and other account information. The customer enters personal, shipping, and payment information:

  - We assume they selected **Create an account** instead of other options.

  - We assume the customer has entered the correct information as it relates to procuring their product.

  - We assume the purchase process successfully completed after the payment was accepted.

  - We assume an order number and confirmation number are provided to the customer and displayed on their screen. (An email is sent to the customer; however, this is not important to this step.)

- **Phase 4** – Customer selects **Next** to redirect and input the email (username) and password to complete account creation:

  - Assumes the customer selected **Next** on the order and confirmation page.

In the preceding diagram, we did not include a phase 5. However, it is important to mention that we could have included the following:

- **Phase 5** – Customer selects **Submit** and is redirected to the newly created account home page:

  - Assumes all information entered meets the required length and format.

  - Assumes the button is available.

  - Assumes the customer can click the **Submit** button.

Our diagram would then depict the additional phase and provide a more accurate depiction of the workflow, as shown in *Figure 10.6*. The workflow is highlighted in this manner to showcase the possibility of missing a step within a workflow when merely talking through it or not referencing architectural diagrams. This can result in a significant change to the underlying metric or measurement. See the following for the inclusion of phase 5.

Customer Persona	Scenario - Account Creation - After Checkout (Purchase) - As a customer, I want to make a purchase and have an account created using the personal information already submitted. Expectations: - I do not have an account associated with my personal email address. - I enter my personal information throughout the purchase correctly. - Account successfully creates immediately after selecting create account.			
Phase 1	**Phase 2**	**Phase 3**	**Phase 4**	**Phase 5**
The customer selects "checkout". - This assumes items have been added in virtual cart. - Assumes the customer has no account associated with their email. Expectations: - Page directs to purchase list.	The customer confirms or adjusts items if needed, & selects create an acct. - Assumes there are items to successfully direct here. - Assumes they do not have an account. Expectations: - Page redirects to continue with purchase workflow.	The customer enters personal information to proceed through purchase workflow. - Assumes the customer selected create an account. - Assumes information has been entered correctly. Expectations: - The purchase processes successfully completes. - Order number displays. - "Next" option to select.	Page requests username and password for acct creation. - Assumes payment method was accepted and successful. - Assumes confirmation and order numbers displayed. Expectations: - Account information entered is stored in account. - Order number is linked to account.	The customer selects "submit". - Assumes correct info is entered. - Assumes button is available. - Assumes customer can click submit. Expectations: - Page redirects to the new account home page.
Internal Ownership - Prod Eng handles the services associated with backend data and application workflows.		Metrics - Not Applicable at this stage - Not Applicable at this stage		

Figure 10.6 – Account Creation – After Checkout workflow/persona journey
incorporating redirection after clicking the Submit button in the UI

In addition, we can highlight an example of identifying a possible new feature during the discussion. Let's use the redirection to the newly created account home page. We can easily argue there is a lack of security in place here, if a customer places a one-time order using someone else's email address. The team would be interested in implementing the following:

- While security is critical, this feature also impacts availability and user experience. Therefore, introduce an SLO for the feature to ensure a balance between security and usability:

  - For example, the team may also consider implementing an activation link so the customer must log in to the account and confirm that the email belongs to them, as well as the account being created by the owner of the email.

  - To ensure a seamless user experience, we could define an SLO where 99.9% of account activation links should be delivered within 30 seconds.

- Redirect to a login page, if there is no activation link, and request that the customer logs in with the newly created credentials to access the account that contains personal and payment information.

Since the goal of the workshop is to outline the process and foster communication regarding features and functionality where we want to measure performance, we should define relevant SLIs, such as checkout page load time and time to complete account creation. Ideas such as this can be added to the "parking lot" for later triaging, ensuring performance tracking aligns with reliability goals. As the team further develops and acclimates to their own process, it may be beneficial to have a product manager included in the discussion who is able to manage and add items to the product management or engineering backlog. For the purposes of this chapter, we will continue to the next section and begin to familiarize ourselves with how the workflow maps to the underlying services and data layers.

Establishing application (system) boundaries

Previous chapters have highlighted that once we have identified the critical personas and persona journeys, we want to then triage the persona journeys in a way that helps us to better understand the application logic. This includes other backend and platform components to gauge how they work together to achieve an end goal. In the previous section, we focused on a single persona journey, *Account Creation – After Checkout*, for the customer persona.

Let's shift our attention to understanding the workflow as it relates to completing a product purchase when completed by two different customer personas. This will help us to understand which microservices work together to create the workflow. We need to first ask ourselves the following:

- What is it that we need to measure?

- Where do we need to measure it?

- Are there metrics currently available that capture items established on answering the prior two points?

Considering we are working within the remaining system, the team is already aware that we have the necessary information and various design and architecture documents to help understand the flow of backend components deployed within the cluster. Let's start by revisiting our handy sequence diagram to understand the flow and then break down some of the underlying application components if necessary. Depicted in *Figure 10.7* is our product purchase sequence diagram, explained in *Figure 7.7* of *Chapter 7*.

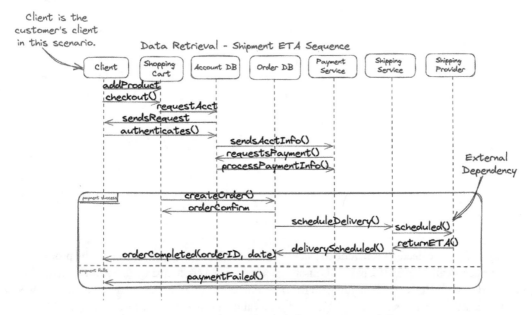

Figure 10.7 – Depicting the product purchase sequence of Chapter 7

In the diagram, there are no references to the creation of an account or guest checkout due to the focus of the discussion being on the purchase process for a customer who already has an account. If we consider the flow as it relates to a customer without an account, wanting to make a purchase, it will appear as in *Figure 10.8*.

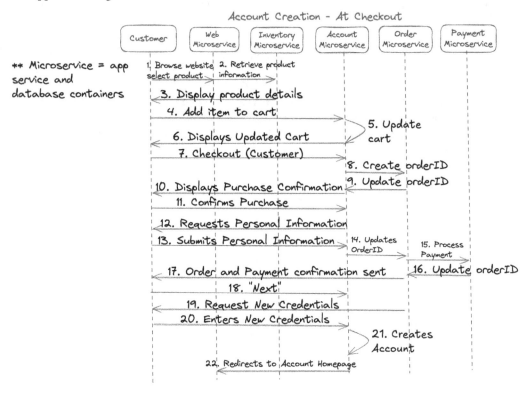

Figure 10.8 – Account Creation – At Checkout sequence diagram

In *Chapter 7*, we neglected to include the steps for the checkout option; however, in the process, it did not necessarily impact the main discussion points as we were focusing on accounts that were already logged in. However, depending on the flow, functionality, and architecture of a system, this could drastically impact the accuracy of the indicators and objectives you are measuring, resulting in inaccurate reporting against your SLOs, which in turn may affect compliance with your SLAs.

While many teams, organizations, and individuals may disagree, documentation and technical writers are extremely important where they can be supported. They can better aid in legacy and other historical information, as well as with iterative approaches where knowledge sharing among various individuals and roles is a must. This is not within the scope of this chapter but is important to keep top of mind. Let's now focus on the specification process.

SLI specification

The purpose of the specification process is to help the team work toward developing an understanding of "what" they want to measure, without the technical details. In previous chapters, we focused on critical journeys and identified SLIs for those journeys that were critical despite the persona journey. In this chapter, we will focus on a single journey and identify SLIs specific to it that provide the ability to report on performance or some other critical metric.

For the *Create an Account* persona journey, we can refer back to the expectations and journey chart to identify key pieces of functionality that happen between the microservices that are critical to the overall success of the workflow. Functionality referenced in previous sections of the book included the following:

- Successfully being able to click the **Create an account** button to create an account.

- A new account successfully being created.

- The new account populating and successfully redirecting to the home page, after credentials have been submitted.

- Customer information gathered during the purchase process being cached and written in the new account service after creation.

This provides the team with more than enough data points to leverage and improve the customer experience. We can then structure each piece of functionality in a way that assigns the function a name and SLI type, as depicted in *Figure 10.9*.

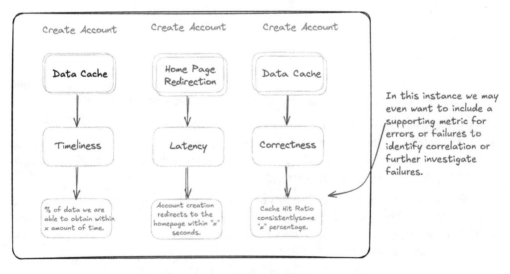

Figure 10.9 – SLI specification with SLI types

Based on the previous discussions and descriptions, the team decides that there are a few areas to further synthesize that will aid with determining the performance levels of the create an account functionality.

Let's review the following persona journeys to better understand the new features and SLI types to develop additional insights for understanding what we should measure:

- **Data Cache: Data Retrieval** – As part of the new account creation feature, improvements were made to the data cache system to better fulfill data retrieval when a customer selects **Create an account** at the point of completing the purchase and submitting new credentials. Upon submitting new credentials, the information entered during the purchase process is captured and retained to store in the account database without having to redirect back to the order database to fulfill the request:

  - **Timeliness**: To better improve the availability of data, it's best to capture the timeliness or the lag between when data is entered versus when it is being written.

  Timeliness is an SLI type that exists but was not referenced in the SLI type chart mentioned in other chapters. It's important to have conversations with others, thinking outside of the box and capturing several SLI types and performance metrics, to ensure that we do not isolate our thinking to those mentioned in the list.

- **Home Page Redirection** – The timeliness SLI type, associated with the creation of an account, is focused on capturing the timeliness of redirecting the consumer's request from the order fulfillment page, where credentials are also captured, to the home page of the newly created account after credentials have been submitted. Considering improvements were made to the cache system, and data read and writes will occur potentially across regions and between different backend services, the team would like to ensure the redirections occur within a certain amount of time and with accuracy:

  - **Latency**: Captures the time it takes for a request to be processed from end to end, from initiation to response, typically measured as request-response time or tail latency (e.g., 99% latency) to account for worst-case performance scenarios.

  If we refer to the previous section, where we mentioned an external customer being able to select **Create an account** to submit information and the account being created on the backend, the time it takes for the account to be created, given fields and values are entered according to build in policy, is the period for fulfillment.

  In this instance, we want to focus on this process as it relates to the cache system: the point where data has been entered, via the purchase process; written into the cache system; and retrieved after the purchase is completed, credentials are provided, and it is submitted so data can be written into the account backend.

- **Data Cache: Data Processing** – Within any cache system, there are metrics specific to gauging performance. To ensure that the speed of data caching enables fulfilling incoming requests, the team will focus on the cache hit ratio, which captures the ability of the cache system to fulfill user data requests without passing the request off to the origin server. In this instance, we understand the order service will capture the information from the customer, and the cache system will ensure this data is available for the account service to capture at the end of the purchase process.

- **Correctness** – Another important aspect when handling data is having a validation mechanism in place. Due to the underlying architecture, it is important to capture and validate the correctness of data:

  - In this instance, and in reference to handling the data cache, we will focus on version-based invalidation, or what is also known as validating on access.

- **Error Rate** – Capturing errors will help the team to pinpoint an area of focus when some leg in the workflow fails. We can think of this metric as simply capturing a request that failed. This is important for gaining better visibility of data reads and writes, as well as the failure of any other component.

Each of the identified areas will provide the team with a good starting point to effectively gauge the customer experience of the new changes surrounding creating an account during a purchase within the customer portal. We can now shift our focus toward implementation to better understand what processes we have in place to capture the metrics and information related to each component; we need to measure service performance in a way that captures the customer experience.

SLI implementation

The purpose of the implementation process is to help the team work toward developing an understanding of "how" they want to measure the "what," and "where" it is best to measure it. It simply incorporates the technical details into the specification process, as we have done in the previous sections. This prevents the team from jumping directly into the technical details, shifting the focus on monitoring what is more important to the engineering team versus what is important to the customer base and experience.

Now, let's work a bit backward here and start with the implementation details, which incorporate information from the specification process. In the product world, this would be considered back-casting. Back-casting, in product management, is where we define the desirable future or end goal and then work backward to identify the steps and processes the team or individual needs to take to achieve it. This process is beyond the scope of this book but explains how we are handling this step, which is different from the previous chapters. *Figure 10.9* depicts the ideal end goal.

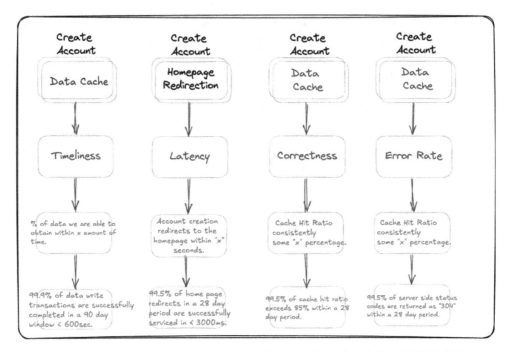

Figure 10.10 – Create an Account implementation depicting the end goal of our SLI/SLO definitions

Hypothetically speaking, we've implemented a new caching system and configuration method to handle data transactions during the account creation process in a way that best serves our internal process. We will term this data gathering (caching) during the purchase process to then pass the information along to the account service to ensure the customer is not requested to enter the same data twice and data is captured at the end of the process.

In our current architecture, we know from previous chapters that logging is enabled at the application and infrastructure layers. We also know that we have event logging enabled at the container orchestration layer through our Kubernetes Deployment. Much of the event information as it relates to the applications will exist in the `kubelet` component deployed within each node in the cluster. We should keep this in mind as we flow through the implementation of each item of the specification process.

In previous chapters, we focused on application services and their backend databases, as well as container orchestration components deployed in clusters within a multi-regional cluster setup. Here, we are going to zone in on the web application component and focus on the cache process and home page redirection.

Figure 10.11 displays the data process as it relates to caching for the account service. A service, the account service in this instance, sends a request to the backend database to request some data. The database service will then send a response to the application to provide that information to the appropriate application or UI for the end user.

Figure 10.11 – Account application request and response to the account database

The cache system integrates in the middle of the request/response process to ensure data is available for faster read/write transactions due to not having to send the request to the origin server, as shown in *Figure 10.12*.

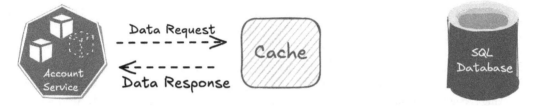

Figure 10.12 – Account application request and response via the cache system

Our main goal is to capture performance, and to ensure data reads and writes at various stages are successful and occur within the specific cadence, including during peak hours. The cache system ensures this happens at a faster pace. Therefore, it's important to capture aspects of speed, success, and correctness as it relates to data.

Data cache timeliness

The main goal of the cache system within the workflow is to focus on making data accessible at a rapid speed so that the following is achieved:

- It is captured correctly
- It is saved efficiently
- It is retrieved quickly
- It is safely copied

This ensures the data entered by the end user is captured, saved, retrieved, and copied from the order database within the account database. This should occur within a time frame that is reasonable to the customer when making a request. Initially, the team did not have a metric to gauge performance. However, if we view the timestamps within both services' application and database logs, the team can gauge the approximate time it takes to complete the respective task.

In our web application, we know that on average, it takes the customer approximately five minutes, from end to end, to submit all fields with accurate information. We also know we have the **Time to Live (TTL)** configured at 10 minutes due to previous complaints from external customers regarding web page refreshes when breaking from the page. The team might decide to stick with the current TTL configuration, as a constraint, but the actual SLI should measure the percentage of successful data writes completed within a predefined latency threshold, for example, 99% of writes within a 600-second (about 10 minutes) period.

Home page redirect latency

The main goal of the home page redirect latency SLO is to ensure that 99.9% of user redirections occur within 3,000 ms. Once a customer places an order, a confirmation page is displayed. The page provides the opportunity for the customer to create a new account, retrieving details from the order process and storing them in the new account. At this step, the customer is only required to enter the credentials to perform the account creation process.

It is important to not confuse redirection at this stage with the customer receiving a 301 or 308 response code. The focus in this phase is on creating an account with the supplied credentials and retrieving cached data from the respective database to provide to the account process to create a new account for the customer. It is not an error that needs addressing.

We can think of this step here as utilizing conditional HTTP headers to route the request. If the customer supplies credentials and opts to create a new account (conditions are met), then the data from the order is retrieved and used to populate the new account. This removes additional requirements for the customer to reenter data later.

Data cache correctness

When working toward determining data correctness, it can prove to be a bit more difficult. However, let's pretend the team agrees that although fast data processing is ideal, it should not occur at the sacrifice of data correctness. It's equally important to their reputation and brand for the implemented processes to output the correct data. The handling of data retrieval within the system, outside of just the built-in data policy on data field values when customers are inputting relevant data, is even more important. The data that is stored within the system account and returned to the customer must be valid, secure, and consistent.

When determining correctness, we don't want to necessarily focus on the input but the output. The customer, with guidance from a built-in policy, is responsible for the input, so the team wants to validate whether the output, which is data written to the cache and then updated to the account database, is correct as well. In this instance, we will use the cache hit ratio since data is validated upon being entered and written to the cache.

$$\text{Cache Hits} / \{\text{Cache Hits} + \text{Cache Missed}\} \times 100\%$$

Figure 10.13 – Cache hit ratio equation

The cache hit ratio measures the effectiveness of being able to fulfill the user data request without passing the request to the origin server (Cloudflare, 2023). *Figure 10.12*, displayed earlier in this section, describes a cache hit. A cache miss is depicted in *Figure 10.14*.

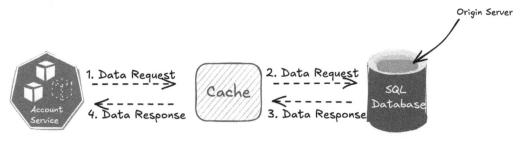

Figure 10.14 – Cache misses sending the request to the origin server

For static content, cache effectiveness is on average between 85% and 89%, while dynamic content will have a lower average. To start, the team agreed to aim for 85% and gauge the metric as it relates to developing a normal consistency. However, since this is a critical piece within the workflow, it's important for the SLO to aim for a higher number of nines, of which is achievable.

Data cache error rate

As another mechanism to aid in effectively measuring data performance, the team also wants to implement SLIs and SLOs surrounding error rates, to validate whether cache data is still valid. If a user sends a request to the application and thus the backend data source, the browser will validate whether there is a valid copy before sending a response back to the requestor. If the data is not valid, the browser will send a request to the original server, which is considered a cache miss, and shift through a flow to update the cache after the request to the origin server.

The prior SLI focuses on improving the cache hit ratio; therefore, we want to capture the errors thrown to better gauge when failures occur, how frequently, and where. The cache system consists of **Entity Tags (ETs)**, which serve as unique identifiers for specific resources by the respective server. We know we can use the headers to compare the tags of the current version of a resource with the cache version of a resource. In the event that the two match, the server will respond with a 304 Not Modified status, where the data can still be used.

In this instance, the SLI should measure the cache freshness by tracking the percentage of cache reads that return stale data. Additionally, an error rate SLI should be defined as the percentage of requests that failed due to stale or invalid cache responses over a rolling 28-day period.

Prioritizing SLIs by business impact

The final stage of our process is prioritization. This helps the team gauge how to implement the build process for the respective SLIs and SLOs. We won't go into as many details as we have done in previous chapters. At a high level, the prioritization process helps us to capture the business impact of an SLI against feasibility. *Figure 10.10* provides a representation of our SLIs as they relate to team and broader business unit prioritization.

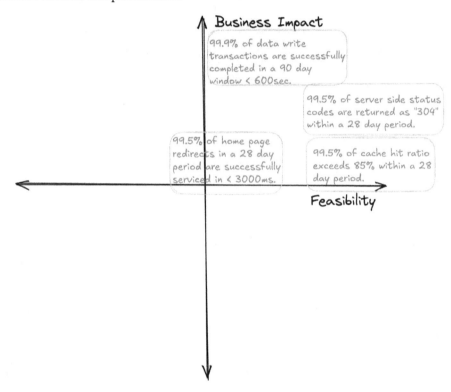

Figure 10.15 – New feature SLI prioritization based on business impact and feasibility

As it relates to prioritization, each component being measured is part of a single workflow or feature implemented within the system. The team agrees that each SLO is feasible to implement based on the SLIs, and prioritization should be driven by business impact. For the purposes of the text and flow of the workshop chapters, determining what to implement based on business impact versus feasibility does not require as much work as in previous chapters. However, it's imperative to remember that the prioritization process should consist of a ranking system identified by the team running the workshop and signed off by the team doing the work. This ensures that the system is unbiased and helps provide organization regarding the order in which items are implemented.

In addition, some teams will have internal processes that are currently used to manage existing backlogs and items in progress to report up the management pipeline. It is helpful, especially in a virtual environment, if the team utilizes as many practices as possible that resonate with the team's working style.

Summary

In this chapter, we have focused on building SLIs and SLOs for new features. This includes new features identified by the customer base, internal backlogs, or iterating through items identified ad hoc during a workshop. In addition, we've also reiterated the importance of using visual aids such as sequence diagrams and internal architecture diagrams to help understand your system boundaries. It's important that your team establishes various ways to work through the process in a collaborative environment.

This chapter concludes the workshop portion of this book. The goal of the workshop is to help teams, business groups or units, and organizations structure conversations with the right stakeholders, ensuring that the right SLIs are measured and corresponding SLOs are defined to improve service reliability and meet customer expectations.

In the next section of the book, you can expect to shift the conversation toward daily operations and additional topics that will help you to maintain SLOs. You can also expect to cover topics that will help you to decide how to package much of it as a solution, whether that is internal or external to your organization.

Further reading

You can review and read the articles and books referenced in this section for additional details about concepts mentioned in this chapter:

- Baker, K. (2023, November 10). *Page Load Time Conversion Rates*. Retrieved from: `https://blog.hubspot.com/marketing/page-load-time-conversion-rates`.

- Connolly, T. & Begg, C. (2013). *Database Systems: A Practical Approach to Design, Implementation, and Management*. Boston: Pearson.

- Dambrine, F. (2022, December 14). *Kubernetes Icon Set*. Excalidraw Libraries.

- Luzar, D. & Gian, P. (2023, April 18). *Stick Figures Collaboration*. Excalidraw Libraries.

- Ricardo, C. (2011). *Databases Illuminated*. Sudbury: Jones & Bartlett Learning.

- Cloudflare Inc. (2023). *What is a cache hit ratio?*. Retrieved from: `https://www.cloudflare.com/learning/cdn/what-is-a-cache-hit-ratio`.

Part 3:
Help! We've Identified Our SLIs and SLOs... Now What?

In this part, you will gain insights into maintaining and refining SLIs and SLOs, with guidance on iterative processes and informed decision-making for monitored services. Additionally, you will gain insights into establishing internal processes to foster the adoption of an SLO culture and available tooling that offers capabilities to simplify the deployment process for you.

This part contains the following chapters:

- *Chapter 11, SLO Monitoring and Alerting*
- *Chapter 12, Service Level Performance Metrics: Daily Operations*
- *Chapter 13, SLO Preservation and Incident Management*
- *Chapter 14, SLIs and SLOs as a Service*

11
SLO Monitoring and Alerting

In previous chapters, we discussed the history of reliability engineering and the positive impact it has on a team and organization. We also took the opportunity to work through hypothetical system environments to build SLIs and SLOs for an internal distributed system focusing on different touchpoints within. However, once our metrics are in place, how do we proceed when the customer experience has decreased due to some incident? How do we notify the team of an issue that has occurred or is about to occur with respect to the customer experience thresholds identified? What is the appropriate cadence, timing, and levels of sensitivity to avoid overwhelming on-call engineers or interfering with other consumption-based alerting configured for product engineering teams and their respective on-call rotations?

These questions are answered and resolved through the principles of monitoring and alerting specific to SLOs. You might ask, what are the fundamental principles for configuring SLO alerting? Are they like traditional monitoring practices? In earlier chapters, we mentioned the differences between black box and white box monitoring, as well as building SLOs that represent the customer experience versus alerting on a technical metric that our internal engineers care about.

In this chapter, you can expect to work through best practices for setting up monitoring and alerting for your SLOs. You can also expect to visit examples from previous workshop chapters to work through implementing alerting for SLO thresholds. Best practices surrounding monitoring and alerting configuration already exist. Several concepts within the practice are used as guidelines for standard monitoring. If observability is considered in your organization, then the tooling of choice and language to structure your queries will impact this process as well. Therefore, it is important to understand the goal of this chapter is not to reinvent the wheel but to provide you with sufficient information to leverage the information and configure alerting and monitoring specific to SLOs.

In this chapter, we will cover the following topics:

- Monitoring and alerting for SLOs
- Monitoring and alerting for web application SLOs
- Monitoring and alerting for distributed systems SLOs
- Monitoring and alerting for new features SLOs

Now, let's review a few topics to ensure that we begin the discussion on the same page. No pun intended.

Monitoring and alerting for SLOs

In earlier chapters, we defined monitoring as the process you put in place to gather data about relevant systems and check for events that indicate the component being measured is healthy and operating as expected. If monitoring is gathering relevant system data and event checking, alerting is the practice of notifying the relevant on-call engineers of performance degradation, unexpected events, and changes in behavior within the system that have occurred. No quote here, simply a summation.

In *Chapter 4*, we defined observability as the methods used to aggregate relevant data in a consumable manner to investigate some issue or outage. Observability, which includes logs, metrics, and traces, provides the ability to debug and understand unknown failure modes. Monitoring, on the other hand, focuses on predefined SLIs that track system health in alignment with SLOs. While both are critical, monitoring enables proactive alerting, whereas observability aids post-incident debugging.

In *Site Reliability Engineering: How Google Runs Production Systems*, it was mentioned, "*Without monitoring, you have no way to tell whether the service is even working; absent a thoughtfully designed monitoring infrastructure, you're flying blind*" (Google, 2016). However, without the appropriate level of visibility into your systems, how do you know you are monitoring the right things, in the right place, in the right way? This questioning led to the belief that the hierarchy of reliability engineering (in *Chapter 1* of this book) is best when incorporating observability as an individual pillar and setting the tone for monitoring capabilities. This is depicted in *Figure 11.1*.

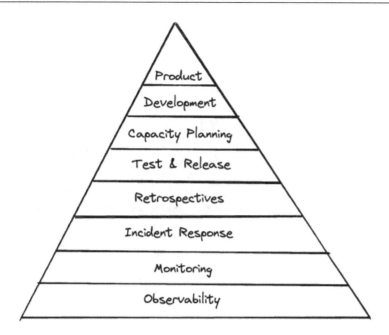

Figure 11.1 – Hierarchy of reliability engineering with observability as the initial building block

Without the appropriate levels of observability and tooling, which includes querying functionality, coupled with a set of practices as guidelines for gathering and aggregating data, how can we ensure the right level of observability in internal systems to proactively assess system events? How do we ensure internal teams are able to immediately make sense of the data as opposed to collecting random logs and spending hours sifting through debugging and troubleshooting system issues?

As much as I enjoy researching and sifting through logs to debug, it's never been fun during a live customer-impacting incident, when an immediate response and resolution are expected. This is not the goal of this chapter; however, it is important to mention to correlate certain points from earlier chapters with those within this chapter. It is also to help embed the importance of effective observability, monitoring, and alerting practices to ensure a healthy reliability engineering organization. Now, let's redirect back to monitoring and alerting.

Within monitoring, we first need to differentiate between two types of monitoring behaviors:

- **White box monitoring**: Monitoring based on metrics exposed by the internals of the system.
- **Black box monitoring**: Testing externally visible behavior of the system from the customer persona.

In *Chapters 7* through *10*, we referenced application and cluster architecture within a distributed environment where the system is multilayered. This means that a single symptom of one behavior is likely the cause of another behavior. For instance, if a node in the cluster is undergoing penetration testing, and a single workload is consuming excessive memory, the on-call engineer would receive an alert of high consumption usage. Asynchronously, there is a pod running on the node experiencing **out-of-memory (OOM)** or **OOMKilled** error messages due to insufficient memory resources.

If monitoring and alerting are not in place, the on-call engineer might experience a longer period of debugging the OOM errors and reviewing logs to understand what events are occurring for specific components. They'd then need to determine which resource is overconsuming and stemming from which application workload, if applicable. In an environment where observability practices and white box monitoring are in place, the on-call engineer can immediately review a configured dashboard and see the increase in memory usage occurring before the incident. In another instance, they'd receive an alert that consumption has increased, and the chart would ideally point them directly to the respective workload. In both scenarios, alerting simply on the amount of consumption being used is ideal for notifying staff of an active issue.

When monitoring on SLIs and SLOs, we need to focus on customer-impacting symptoms rather than purely technical resource metrics. In the previous example, alerting on OOM errors reflects a system health issue but does not capture customer impact. Instead, monitoring SLIs such as request latency, error rates, or availability helps correlate high memory usage to actual service degradation, which aligns with SLOs.

Think of it this way: if you or a loved one is sick, we can monitor your high temperature, (a symptom) or we can monitor the behaviors that occur daily that caused the cold and thus high fever (the cause). Are you wearing a jacket outside? Do you wear socks on your feet? Are you eating healthily and taking supplemental vitamins? If we think of the predictability of SLO dashboards with respect to our example, we could monitor behaviors (customer centricity) by monitoring the degradation of eating the typical number of meals and the increase in the number of hours a person is sleeping to predict the onset of sickness. It's similar thinking.

We can monitor the application workloads and the errors they produce, which remains important to do, versus monitoring the underlying metrics that play a role in providing critical functionality to customers. With regard to SLIs and SLOs, we want to monitor and alert on the features and attributes that help us to understand the *why* behind an application with high resource consumption to help determine whether resource quotas are sufficient, or application architecture and dependencies are at play. We can utilize observability practices to monitor and aggregate data in a way that helps to determine what actions were completed to prompt a negative behavior within the system.

In some cases, we might monitor one, multiple, or all attributes critical to health restoration in a singular manner, which may be sufficient for the staff monitoring your system(s). However, creating SLOs and monitoring on each will help you to naturally aggregate data in a way that focuses on the critical components and impacting behaviors that are important to your customer base and experience. This is done through implementing alerting frameworks that help to detect issues of service degradation prior to an incident occurring or within time periods prior to the customer experience being impacted. This is the overarching goal of monitoring and alerting for SLOs.

While several observability platforms support telemetry collection, not all provide native SLO management. Tools such as Google Cloud's operations suite, Nobl9, and Datadog offer direct SLO tracking, whereas OpenTelemetry primarily acts as a framework for collecting and exporting telemetry data. Selecting the right tool depends on whether you focus on data aggregation or direct SLO enforcement. The following are some observability tools:

- **Elastic Observability**: A full stack observability solution, which unifies monitoring across cloud applications and platforms, providing visualization capabilities.

- **Datadog**: A real-time observability platform providing infrastructure and application monitoring and log management.

- **Dynatrace**: An end-to-end observability platform that provides unified observability, security, and business analytics capabilities, which include intelligent automation.

- **OpenTelemetry**: An observability framework and toolkit used to structure how you generate, collect, and observe telemetry data.

- **ServiceNow Cloud Observability**: A cloud-based observability platform providing similar capabilities to the prior tooling mentioned. However, ServiceNow consists of a broad product portfolio, making it more appealing to current enterprise customers.

Most of the tooling previously mentioned provides similar capabilities: the technical implementation on the backend and third-party integrations with other platforms and application solutions. As with anything, understanding your own architecture and initiative needs will help you to procure the right products.

There is also an increasing presence of platforms focusing on providing capabilities of pillars within reliability engineering, which includes SLI and SLO creation and management. The goal of this chapter is not to sell to you or raise awareness of any specific product, platform, or tool available. It is to inform you of the importance of its existence and encourage you to navigate the market with fundamentals in mind to procure the right solution for your organization. In *Chapter 14*, we will cover additional information related to this.

When you find the right solution, the goal is to ensure the appropriate features provided are the features needed to direct your team or organization in the direction of reliability. In the event that there is no solution, I hope this book helps you to begin your SLO journey and build the proper process and system that best suits your organization. Now, let's circle back to monitoring and cover some concepts specific to SLO management.

SLO monitoring concepts

When creating SLOs for their respective services and indicators, you want each SLO to maintain a performance level that exceeds the level committed to or expected by the customer. As mentioned in an earlier section of this chapter, the expectation is the threshold where a customer notices the degradation of a service or feature. The objective is an internal mechanism that provides a way to maintain accountability internally and affords the team an opportunity to make some decisions prior to an incident or outage occurring.

SLOs are one effective solution for monitoring your systems or services to maintain your agreed-upon commitments. If we regress to the SLIs and SLOs from *Chapters 7* to *10*, our SLOs consisted of the following components:

- **The SLI itself**: A measurement of the level of performance of the service.
- **The SLO threshold**: The ideal level or goal for service performance we want to achieve.
- **Time cadence**: The SLI length of time for the ideal level of performance to remain at or above its threshold. This is also referred to as the compliance period (Google, 2018).

If we reflect on our SLOs, each fits into one of the following categories: it is categorized as being request-based or windows-based. Request-based takes a *good request versus bad request* approach, while windows-based focuses on measurement intervals that meet a specific level of performance. The components of our final SLO and the category type are information that we need to take into consideration when deciding the best type of alert to configure.

In addition to understanding the structure and categorization type of the SLO created for the creation of our alerts, we also want to focus on another aspect as it pertains to configuration, the relationship types:

- **Event cadence**: The relationship between the alert and the number of SLO events:
  - **Precision**: When the alert triggers, is it an event the on-call staff needs to receive notification for?
  - **Recall or sensitivity**: When the alert triggers, what fraction of events are resulting in an alert? Is this necessary?
- **Event cause**: The relationship between the alert and a specific event that caused it:
  - **Detection time**: What time length exists between the start of the event that triggered the alert and the time the alert was sent to on-call staff?
  - **Reset time**: What is the time length between the period of the event ending and the time of the alert resetting?

We'll focus on using the mentioned criteria in future examples within this chapter to determine the best SLO alert configurations. It is important to understand that sending alerts too often or for less significant events can result in less sensitivity among the on-call team or other internal staff handling incidents. Like paging within any on-call environment, we want each alert to mean something and require an actionable event. The mention of it here might seem tedious. When considering internal response rates and the handling of active incidents in combination with the health of your on-call staff, dismissal of its importance can have negative long-term results for your reliability engineering organization, and thus internal systems and customer base.

This directs us toward the type of alert we want to use to alert on our SLO. We'll need to consider the following types of alerts, which are ideal for SLOs (Google, 2018). This does not mean that there are not more types out there, or that your team will not identify additional alerting types and configuration options that work best for your systems.

Alert Type	Definition	Pros	Cons
Target Error Rate	Alerting on a small time window (a few minutes) exceeds the SLO	Good detection time	Decreased precision
Increased Alert Window	Alerting on an increased time window, whether time or budget spent	Improved precision and detection times	Low reset times
Increment Alert Duration	Alerting on the time length the SLO is in violation.	High precision	Low recall and detection times
Burn Rate Alert	Alerting on the speed of the SLO violation occurring	Good precision and detection times	Low recall times; longer reset times than ideal
Multiple Burn Rate	Multiple burn rate alerts configured	Good precision and recall times	Long reset times
Muti Window & Burn Rate Alert	Multiple burn rate alerts with a decreased window	Good precision and recall times	Increased level of complexity and manageability

Table 11.1 – Alert type chart referencing pros and cons from the Google SRE book

Although there are various pros and cons for each alert type, it is important to understand the initial criteria mentioned, related to your SLOs, to ensure that you get off to a good start with alerting configuration. In addition, this book focuses on SLIs and SLOs, but we've also mentioned error budgets in earlier chapters. Your error budget is the opposite of your SLO. A 99.5% SLO will imply a 0.5 error budget. The burn rate indicates the rate at which your service is consuming its error budget in relation to its SLO. A burn rate of 1 means that the service is on track to consume its entire error budget within the compliance period, necessitating corrective actions if the trend continues. It's essential to monitor this closely to ensure that the service maintains reliability and does not exceed the acceptable error budget.

Now, let's revisit SLOs from previous chapters and flow through the alerting and monitoring configuration.

Scenario 1 – Monitoring and alerting for web application SLOs

In *Chapter 7*, we flowed through a series of steps for building SLIs and SLOs for web applications, as depicted in *Figure 11.2*. For future reference, the persona journey is labeled at the top of the figure, with information about the SLI and SLO to follow.

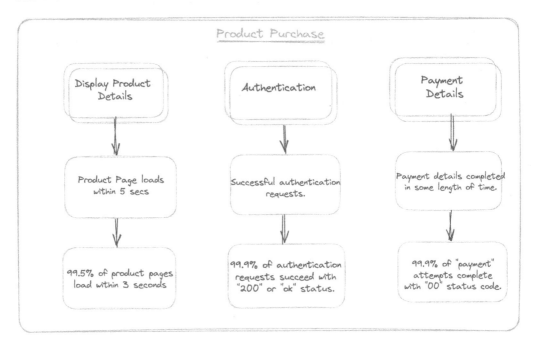

Figure 11.2 – Persona journey with SLI and SLO information from Chapter 7

Before structuring each SLO, we were able to define the persona journey and workflow through system components to better map the system flow to the phases within the persona journey. This enabled an improved understanding of which components and metrics played a critical role in measuring system behavior. This process resulted in the following SLOs:

- **Display Product Details**: 99.5% of product pages loaded within 3 seconds.

- **Authentication**: 99.9% of authentication requests succeed with a 200 or OK status.

- **Payment Details**: 99.9% of payment attempts complete with a 00 status code.

Within each of the identified SLOs, we immediately notice a common theme. The compliance period is missing. In the previous section, we mentioned the compliance period referencing the length of time the service should meet or exceed its performance threshold. The compliance period is typically measured from one point in time to another. Previously, the term *standard window* was mentioned, and I believe that was more of an opinion. The compliance period should be defined based on the service level expectations and the frequency of performance measurement. For example, it can range from daily, weekly, or monthly, depending on the criticality of the service and customer impact. Rather than using an arbitrary 28-day period, the compliance period should reflect actual data-driven insights, ensuring it aligns with customer expectations and service behavior.

If our data does not provide us with this information, we might simply commit to a 28-day period to utilize it as a base or good starting point. If our internal data signals that customers are experiencing high levels of service degradation, then we may want to adjust the monitoring and alerting thresholds, potentially using shorter compliance periods (e.g., weekly) or more frequent monitoring intervals to capture the degradation more quickly. In other events, the data may inform us that we need to configure a shorter compliance period.

In this instance, we'll agree to start our alerting for each of the SLOs based on a 28-day period. We want to assess the following criteria for each alert to determine the type of alert we want to start with:

- Does the SLO consist of all three components expected in an SLO? If it does not, do we have sufficient data to assume the missing component?

    - For example, during the missing compliance period, we can utilize the standard 28-day period. We'd answer yes to this question.

- Is the SLI/SLO variation request-based or windows-based?

- Is the relationship between the alert and SLO events or the alert and the event that triggered it more important?

    - This response to this question should guide you toward determining which type of alert you want to focus on, using the *Pros* and *Cons* columns of the alert type chart (*Table 11.1*).

    - If you already have an established monitoring system implemented, much of the data available through it will provide you with the necessary information.

We might then redefine the structure of each SLO to include the compliance period and any other information we feel might be missing. If a workshop process is followed, this will likely arise while finalizing and documenting the SLOs prior to setting up monitoring and alerting. This is not a tedious step, but to serve as a reminder to ensure you capture relevant details of the SLI and SLO prior to deployment, our *Payment Detail* SLI and SLO would then consist of the following information:

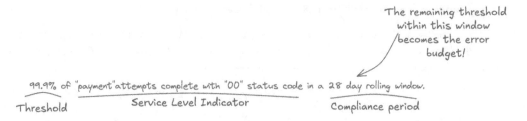

Figure 11.3 – The ideal structure of SLOs to ensure each component is captured

Let's redirect and flow through other SLOs created in the workshop chapters of this book to review SLO criteria.

Scenario 2 – Monitoring and alerting for distributed systems SLOs

In *Chapter 8*, we went through a demo for building SLIs and SLOs for distributed systems, as depicted in *Figure 11.4*. We were also able to identify potential SLIs and SLOs.

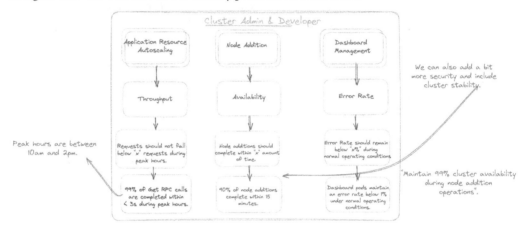

Figure 11.4 – Persona journey with SLI and SLO information from Chapter 8

Before structuring each SLO, we were able to define the persona journey and workflow through system components to better map the system flow to the phases within the persona journey. This process resulted in the following SLOs:

- **Application Resource Autoscaling**: 99% of Get RPC calls are completed within 3s during peak hours:

  - **SLI**: RPC calls completed within 3s during peak hours.

  - **Threshold**: Greater than or equal to 99% error rate.

  - **Compliance period**: Within a 28-day rolling period.

  This generates a client-side request to the website, which interacts with the web microservice API to fetch data from the inventory microservice, and the performance of this interaction is measured by the SLI such as response time or error rate.

- **Node Addition**: 90% of node additions are completed within 15 minutes:

  - **SLI**: Adding a node to a cluster completes installation within 15 minutes.

  - **Threshold**: Greater than or equal to 90% error rate.

  - **Compliance period**: Within a 28-day rolling period.

  Authentication implemented with an auth SDK and sidecar container using gRPC for event-driven communication between services.

- **Dashboard Management**: Dashboard pods maintain an error rate below 1% under normal operating conditions:

  - **SLI**: Dashboard pod maintains a low error rate.

  - **Threshold**: Less than or equal to 1% error rate.

  - **Compliance period**: 28-day window.

  Implemented by using a token system for the payment process via the payment API. We'd also need to identify possible status codes that are returned when a pod is unavailable and not able to accept workloads.

In the previous section, we noticed the compliance period missing from our SLOs, of which the same can be said here. However, our initial SLO for resource autoscaling also includes an additional time parameter. If we refer to *Figure 11.4*, we'll notice that peak hours are between 10 am and 2 pm. For the purposes of the text, we will not focus on time zones or anything of the sort. However, in a live session and depending on the makeup of your organization and the structure of the team, you'd want to ask the following questions:

- Is this metric specific to a time zone, or is there an expectation to implement an SLO per time zone?

> **Note**
>
> If we refer to the earlier multi-region architecture depicted in *Chapter 7*, *Figure 7.1*, the infrastructure spanned three regions. This is in addition to the notation of increased traffic being specific to the time zone, to factor this into our query. This will heavily rely on the observability or monitoring tooling capabilities currently in place.

Scenario 3 – Monitoring and alerting for new features SLOs

In *Chapter 10*, we went through a demo for building SLIs and SLOs for new features, as depicted in *Figure 11.5*.

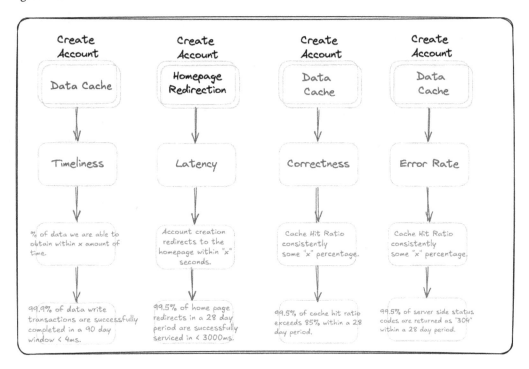

Figure 11.5 – Persona journey with SLI and SLO information from Chapter 10

Before structuring each SLO, we were able to define the persona journey and workflow through system components that were defined to better map the system flow to the phases within the persona journey. This process resulted in the following SLOs:

- **Data Cache Time**: 99.9% of data write transactions are successfully completed in a 90-day window < 4 ms:

  - **SLI**: Data write transactions successfully complete and are verified against metadata

  - **Threshold**: Greater than or equal to 99.9% success rate

  - **Compliance period**: Within a 90-day rolling window

- **Home Page Redirection**: 99.5% of home page redirects in a 28-day period are successfully served in < 3,000 ms:

  - **SLI**: Home page redirects successfully complete in less than 3,000 ms

  - **Threshold**: Greater than or equal to 99.5% success rate

  - **Compliance period**: Within a 28-day window

- **Data Cache Correct**: 99.5% of cache hit ratio exceeds 85% within a 28-day period:

  - **SLI**: Cache hit ratio metric exceeds a performance rate greater than 85%

  - **Threshold**: Greater than or equal to 99.5% success rate

  - **Compliance period**: Within a 28-day rolling window

- **Data Cache Create**: 99.5% of server-side status codes are returned as 304 within a 28-day period:

  - **SLI**: Server-side transactions return a 304 status code

  - **Threshold**: Greater than or equal to 99.5% success rate

  - **Compliance period**: Within a 28-day rolling window

In this instance, each of our SLOs includes a standard 28-day period for the rolling window. However, it's important to distinguish between SLOs and SLAs. While SLOs are internal targets for performance, SLAs represent external agreements with customers, often including penalties for non-compliance. It is important to include that it is not the only period. There are instances where a 30-day period is sufficient. However, each month within the calendar year consists of 28 days (about 4 weeks), which makes it more realistic when needing to determine between a calendar month and a rolling window. Whichever option your team decides to use, ensure that you have evaluated possible options to better determine what will work best and reduce having to restructure over the long term.

Establishing SLO alerting criteria

For the purposes of the text, we will focus on creating alerts using information from two SLOs mentioned in earlier chapters and sections of this chapter. There are continuously new products within the software industry being created to improve the adoption of reliability engineering practices and efficiently manage the data consumed and emitted to evaluate the performance of internal systems and processes. Prior to selecting a product that is suitable for you, you'll need to understand the criteria used to implement SLIs and SLOs, including monitoring and alerting, to compare to internal tooling available to you and products you're considering for procurement.

In this instance, we'll use Grafana's integration with Prometheus as a monitoring and alerting toolkit. While Grafana provides visualization, the actual alerting mechanism relies on Prometheus' alerting rules and queries. **PromQL** is the language used to query consumable data from Prometheus into Grafana. This chapter does not focus on these aspects nor is the goal to persuade you each is better than a competitor. It's an important mention to flow through the process.

In this scenario, we'll shift our focus toward deploying the SLO and configuring an alert for the *Data Cache Time* SLO. In *Chapter 10*, we mentioned the importance of reading and writing transactions during workflows such as guest checkout. If you need to familiarize yourself with the process and data flow, please revisit the chapter. Our SLO of focus from this chapter is as follows:

- **Data Cache Time**: 99.9% of data write transactions are successfully completed in a 90-day window < 4 ms

For the *Data Cache Time* SLO, there is an expectation for data to be consumed during the purchase process and emitted to the caching system. This improves data efficiency and reduces having to duplicate data entry. Data is updated within the caching system with final changes being sent to the database when needed. The final details are heavily dependent on the configuration and flags used to determine success, but we'll use the `HTTP 200` status code to confirm a write-back and successful write transaction to the cache system.

The ideal timing for this to happen is within 5 ms, but our SLO is set for 4 ms to ensure we meet a high-performance target. Since the SLO is defined based on a performance threshold (99.9% of requests), setting it at 4 ms ensures that we are consistently exceeding expectations, even under load or anomalies. This also ensures that if a user is using the guest checkout feature, any information captured through user input during a purchase is cached and available for retrieval as soon as possible.

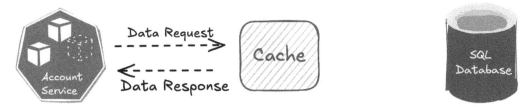

Figure 11.6 – Account application request and response via cache system

In the previous section, we outlined the SLO criteria. However, we want to answer questions surrounding the event cadence and cause to help determine the type of alert we want to configure:

- **Event cadence**: The cadence will ensure we are firing the alert for necessary events happening at a frequency that requires on-call staff's attention:

  - **Precision**: When the alert triggers, the focus is on the speed performance of the caching system. We expect cache miss and have enough data to report an average of 3.5 ms, which is more performant than we need it to be at 5 ms.

- **Recall or sensitivity**: When the alert triggers, it's ideal for there to exist several events for some duration of time. As it relates to precision, we expect to experience cache misses that are anomalies, so we want lower sensitivity levels.

- **Event cause**: Focusing on the cause of an event will ensure that when an alert is fired, it is related to causal events. An important aspect of the right cause is also supported by where you measure your SLI within the system:

    - **Detection time**: When the alert triggers, we want it to have been caused by a similar event, with high precision. We are already aware of anomalies; therefore, we want a certain number of events to occur to ensure that when an alert is triggered, it is due to a relevant cause. Detection in this instance is of moderate priority.

    - **Reset time**: When the alert triggers, we have moderate feelings toward how long it takes to reset. We'd want to focus on the average length of time it takes for the events that cause the longest duration of anomalies.

In this instance, we'd want to focus on high precision with lower sensitivity and recall times. If anomalies exist at a frequent cadence, resulting in the team having moderate feelings regarding detection times, we want to focus on an increment alert duration, where the focus is on the length of time the SLO is in violation. Since anomaly errors were already mentioned, which occur for different types of system events, it's ideal to focus on the length of time the SLI is not performant in comparison to the set thresholds.

SLO configuration and deployment

When details have been fleshed out formally, the team should use their tooling of choice to deploy the set SLO. In this instance, we are using Grafana's SLO app integration with Prometheus to track and visualize SLOs. Grafana itself does not manage SLOs directly; it relies on Prometheus or other monitoring systems to gather data for SLO calculations:

- **SLI definition**: Our first step is to configure the SLI information, which provides the ability to input the necessary information from your configured data source. Configured in the following figure is the time window, data source, and SLI query using a time series and reporting the rate of change or deviation from 4 ms. A few things to point out: our SLI was set for a 90-day window, which fell short of the 2,116 hours or 88 days configurable in the system. Although we can easily include the calculations in the query, it is an example of understanding how you want to measure your SLIs and configure your SLOs when procuring a platform.

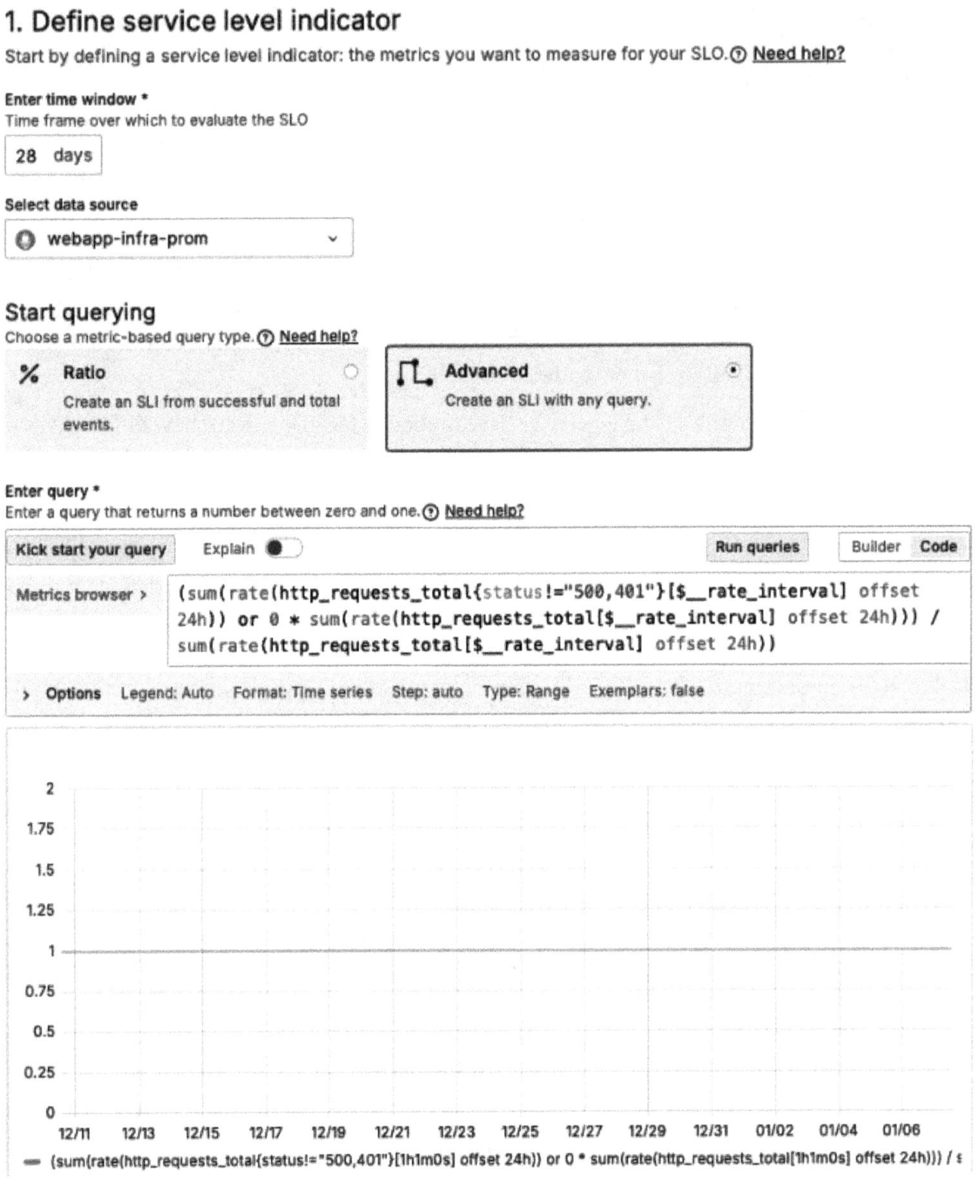
1. Define service level indicator
Start by defining a service level indicator: the metrics you want to measure for your SLO. Need help?
Enter time window *
Time frame over which to evaluate the SLO
28 days
Select data source
webapp-infra-prom
Start querying
Choose a metric-based query type. Need help?
Ratio
Create an SLI from successful and total events.
Advanced
Create an SLI with any query.
Enter query *
Enter a query that returns a number between zero and one. Need help?
Kick start your query
Explain
Run queries
Builder
Code
Metrics browser >
(sum(rate(http_requests_total{status!="500,401"}[$__rate_interval] offset 24h)) or 0 * sum(rate(http_requests_total[$__rate_interval] offset 24h))) / sum(rate(http_requests_total[$__rate_interval] offset 24h))
> Options Legend: Auto Format: Time series Step: auto Type: Range Exemplars: false
2
1.75
1.5
1.25
1
0.75
0.5
0.25
0
12/11 12/13 12/15 12/17 12/19 12/21 12/23 12/25 12/27 12/29 12/31 01/02 01/04 01/06
(sum(rate(http_requests_total{status!="500,401"}[1h1m0s] offset 24h)) or 0 * sum(rate(http_requests_total[1h1m0s] offset 24h))) / s

Figure 11.7 – The first step of SLO deployment; entering SLI metrics and query

Other fields provided on this page are related to your internal system and architecture. References to the cluster and appropriate container are highlighted. Usually, you will notice options such as the region and namespace provided. In this instance, and since there is a single database handling CDN responsibilities for us, a direct reference to the "frontend" service label is used as a filtering option. Let's move on to the SLO configuration.

- **Threshold and error budget**: Like the SLO configuration, we want to enter the requirements for our threshold.

2. Set target and error budget

Set the target for your SLO. Enter a target as a percentage to indicate an acceptable level of service. The error budget allows for a certain percentage of failure within the target and is updated automatically. ⑦ **Need help?**

Enter target *   **Error budget**
Enter a target between 0 and 100%.   An automatic calculation of 100% - target.

| 99.5   % | 0.5 %

Remaining error budget
View your remaining error budget over the last 28 days.

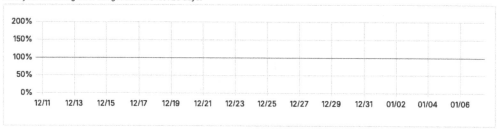

Figure 11.8 – Entering the target and error budget (the error budget is the inverse of the SLO and automatically calculated in Grafana)

This page will collect the target threshold for your service and automatically calculate the error budget for you. This number is the number of 9s the service needs to achieve to remain compliant. Error budgets are mentioned but not highlighted throughout the text. As a reminder, our error budget is simply the inverse of our SLO (1 – SLO). It is also important to note that the number of 9s you would like to achieve will guide you and your SRE team toward determining the number of on-call staff you will need to support this goal. The increase in the number of 9s will result in more overhead, for budget and staffing. Do not confuse yourself by thinking it is not worth the investment. It is to highlight that with an increase in reliability, there is a correlation to an increase in expenses. This further highlights the importance of understanding internal system architecture, reliability engineering capabilities, and ensuring appropriate resource allocation.

- **Metadata**: Once SLI and SLO information is inputted into your platform of choice, the likelihood is naming conventions or additional metadata is requested. As simple as this might seem, naming conventions are extremely important to the success of SLO management as you iterate over time. In addition, if you plan to offboard your process to internal product engineering teams or other SRE teams, the transition will alleviate some confusion that can arise. In addition, when SREs are on-call, this provides easier abilities to reference the appropriate charts and dashboards during a live incident.

3. Add name and description

Add an SLO name and description to organize and identify your SLOs.

SLO name *
Displays on the SLO dashboard and in SLO alert rules.

> Data Cache Time

SLO description
Make sure the description clearly explains what the SLO measures.

> Successful completion of write transactions to cache database, completed within a certain period of time (4ms)

Folder
Choose a folder where you want to store the SLO.

> SLO Alerts   ⌄   or   + Create folder

SLO labels
Add labels to identify your SLO with a team or service name, or use custom labels. ⑦ <u>Need help?</u>

| team_name ⌄ | Select a value ⌄ |
| service_name ⌄ | Select a value ⌄ |

+ Add custom label

| ← Set target and error budget | → Add SLO alert rules | | Cancel |

Figure 11.9 – Name and description fields to attach metadata to your SLI and SLO

In addition, if your team plans to manage SLOs as code, it is likely to utilize infrastructure tooling such as Terraform, Ansible, Puppet, Saltstack and so many other solutions available today to deploy your configurations in your platform of choice. If your solution consists of multiple SRE and other development teams within it, it will help to serve as a reminder related to which objects were created internally to the platform or created by an external tool. This will also help to ease the debugging and troubleshooting process in the event issues arise unrelated to your SLIs, SLOs, and other internal metrics.

Maybe soon, we'll begin to see more SLO platforms with dedicated plugins or external modules created specifically for them. Grafana maintains a plugin to control its alerting system.

SLO alerting rules

After submitting metadata for your SLOs, your platform should request information to configure SLO alerting rules. At the time of writing this, most SLO and observability platforms allow you to create fast-burn and slow-burn alerting rules. These rules are used to alert on different rates of error budget consumption over defined time periods, such as rapid (fast-burn) or gradual (slow-burn) consumption. Multi-window and multi-burn rate alerting are also available in the Grafana SLO app. However, there may be a case where alerting is not integrated into your solution, or these are not the standard alerting rules provided. As mentioned throughout various chapters in the book, it is best to understand your SLIs and SLOs, the goals you want to achieve, or problems you want to solve, to better understand which platform or app will provide you with the capabilities your organization or team needs:

- **Fast-burn alert rate**: Fast-burn alerts will configure an alert using the criteria set by the provider. In this instance, the burn rate is at least 14.4 or 6 times the error budgets over x minutes and over the last 6 hours:

SLO alert rules

If you select the option to create SLO alert rules, two SLO alert rules are generated: one for a fast-burning error budget, and one for a slower burn.

Fast-burn alert rule
Over short time scales, Grafana sends alerts when the burn rate is very high. This alerts you for very serious conditions.

ⓘ View alert conditions

Name	Data Cache Time SLO High Burn Rate
Description	Error budget is consuming 14 times the error budget over the last 3 hours
Labels ⓘ	grafana_slo_window=28d
	grafana_slo_severity = critical
	+ Add label
Annotations	+ Add annotation

Slow-burn alert rule
Over longer time windows, Grafana alerts when the burn rate is elevated but not critical. This alerts you to ongoing issues that require attention.

ⓘ View alert conditions

Name	Data Cache Time SLO Burn Rate
Description	Error budget is consuming 6 times the error budget over the last 6 hours
Labels ⓘ	grafana_slo_window=28d
	grafana_slo_severity = warning
	+ Add label
Annotations	+ Add annotation

Figure 11.10 – Grafana and most other SLO apps will allow you to generate fast- and slow-burn alerts

In this chapter, we mentioned *Data Cache Time* as experiencing anomalies, more frequently than we'd expect, in addition to experiencing cache misses, for non-trivial reasons. In addition, we know it takes frequent and various misses to occur when the issue stems from the backend or source database. The engineering team has alerting specific for them, but we want to know when/if this impacts the frontend. A multi-burn-rate alert configured under the fast-burn alert within the app is likely ideal for this.

- **Slow-burn alert rate**: On the other hand, there is also the capability to configure a slow-burn alert, which follows similar rules to fast-burn alerts with a lower expectation of the burn rate and a larger window for the application to experience the burn. If the *Data Cache Time* alert proves to be less important than initially thought, it may be appropriate to adjust the alert's threshold to a slow-burn rate, allowing for more gradual consumption of the error budget before considering depreciation.

Alert routing is a capability that is not included in the text but is a capability provided by most apps and platforms providing alerting capabilities. This is important to take into consideration if your organization integrates with various apps and tooling during the incident management process. It will help to ensure seamless and unified processes with other teams you need to collaborate with for SLO Management.

SLO review

A formal SLO review screen will display to provide you with the ability to review and then save your SLOs to a folder of your choice.

5. Review SLO

Review each section of your SLO and once you are happy, save it.

Information — Edit section

SLO name	Data Cache Time
SLO description	Successful completion of write transactions to cache database, completed within a certain period of time (4ms)
Folder	SLO Alerts

Service level indicator — Edit section

Data source	🔵 webapp-infra-prom
Query	`(sum(rate(http_requests_total{status!="500,401"}[$__rate_interval] offset 24h)) or 0 * sum(rate(http_requests_total[$__rate_interval] offset 24h))) / sum(rate(http_requests_total[$__rate_interval] offset 24h))`

Target and error budget — Edit section

Target in **28 days**   Error budget remaining

99.5%   **0.5%**

SLO alert rules — Edit section

✓ Alert rules are turned on.
SLO alert rules are created when you save the SLO.

Figure 11.11 – Verifying entered data on the SLO review page

There is no specific functionality to highlight here, other than the ability to view the SLI, SLO, and alert on a single page. It is also important if your team utilizes an external documentation system to maintain track of information regarding what is configured for later iterations.

It also serves as a last-minute review to ensure everything is in alignment. If nothing more, it is an indication that your SLO journey is heading in the right direction!

Summary

Monitoring and alerting on your SLOs is as important as effectively implementing observability practices to improve visibility into your systems. To do so, we need to ensure the appropriate mechanisms are put into place to better align with the practices instilled within the specifications and implementation phases. In simpler terms, we need to ensure we have the underlying criteria for our SLIs and SLOs to make more informed decisions regarding the applications and platforms we integrate with for SLO management.

The goal of reliability engineering is to improve the customer experience, but it's equally important to highlight the impact on your on-call staff and development teams. The monitoring and alerting practices we put in place greatly contribute to reducing on-call and engineer fatigue and improve the efficiency of resolving issues as they arise. When we build better processes to investigate, remediate, and communicate with increased observability, we are better equipped to improve the overall customer experience when we fall short.

Now that we have covered creating SLIs and SLOs and SLO management with alerting and monitoring, we'll discuss best practices for SLO daily operations in the next chapter.

Further reading

Here, you can review and read the referenced articles and books for additional reading about concepts mentioned in this chapter:

- Google. (2016). *Site Reliability Engineering: How Google Runs Product Systems*. Sebastopol: O'Reilly Media, Inc.

- Google. (2018). *The Site Reliability Workbook*. Sebastopol: O'Reilly Media.

- PagerDuty. (2024). *Best Practices for Monitoring*. Retrieved from: `https://www.pagerduty.com/resources/learn/best-practices-for-monitoring/`.

12
Service Level Performance Metrics: Daily Operations

In previous chapters, we discussed the history and importance of reliability engineering. We also navigated through examples of an SLI and SLO workshop for various aspects of your system environment, highlighting additional system features that your organization may want to raise awareness about. However, once SLIs and SLOs are implemented, what does the team do daily to iterate and improve upon them? How does the team maintain the necessary mindset to keep building upon their SLIs and SLOs in a way that is intuitive and cross-functional? In my previous experience, one of the major shifts was maintenance in a cross-functional manner while attempting to advocate for indicators and objectives.

In this chapter, you can expect the discussion to center around the iterative nature of SLIs and SLOs. The goal is to improve your understanding of how your organization can leverage various practices and processes to continuously refine and improve your reliability and performance metrics. It will also highlight the iterative approaches available for refining SLIs and SLOs, highlighting the importance of rapid iteration in response to changing business needs, user feedback, and technical constraints while adjusting over time.

To experience the short- and long-term benefits of customer-centric performance monitoring, we'll need to focus on the following:

- The appropriate approaches to leverage for iterations and adjustments

- How to create iterative processes and gain cross-functional operational perspectives

- How to improve responsiveness and enhance the organization's effectiveness

Managing your SLOs with high efficiency and effectiveness will require consistent effort and attention. However, you want to ensure that you don't fall into the cyclic pattern of managing your SLOs in the way that you would handle support requests or incidents, although the practice of each should integrate or flow into your SLO workflow. Some areas that we will cover within this chapter are the following:

- Understanding the iterative nature of SLIs and SLOs

- Monitoring for your SLIs and SLOs

- SLI and SLO iteration and continuous improvement

- Adapting to SLI and SLO changes

- Cross-functional collaboration for SLIs and SLOs

- SLI and SLO performance reviews

Before we dive into the previously mentioned concepts, it's important to understand that the current state of your organization and team is going to differ from other organizations, resulting in a different set of needs and wants. Therefore, it's important to take your current organizational structure and internal processes into consideration while reading. This will help you to gauge and compare what needs to be changed, removed, or added to bring your organization or team to the desired state.

Understanding the iterative nature of SLIs and SLOs

When considering the rapid development of software and technology in today's world, practices such as reliability engineering have become increasingly important. Businesses will need approaches to increase the speed of the delivery of software, reduce the amount of customer-impacting incidents, and improve the efficiency of the processes and tooling their development and engineering teams use to deliver software.

Even as a business grows and adapts to these advancements, there will always exist new integrations and feature requests from customers requiring additional adjustments. This increases the need for customer-facing staff to understand the iterative nature of concepts such as SLIs and SLOs to aid with quantifying how customer-centric services and systems are. Through iteration, teams can incorporate lessons learned from past experiences, address emerging issues, and adjust SLIs and SLOs to better align with organizational goals and user expectations. By embracing an iterative approach, organizations can build agility, resiliency, and responsiveness into the dynamic nature of modern software systems.

Monitoring your SLIs and SLOs

In the previous chapter, we discussed monitoring and alerting configuration options available for monitoring the customer-centric features of your system. The end goal was to transition the focus from consumption-based resource monitoring to customer-centric resource monitoring. However, your team still maintains the responsibility of managing the processes used to improve your SLI and SLO life cycle. This is especially important if you expect to offboard your process to another team. If your team opts to build internal tooling versus investing in a platform dedicated to managing your SLOs and metrics, this can end up requiring increased effort and dedication from your team(s) and organizations.

SLIs and SLOs enable us to regularly monitor and track system performance and reliability, but how do we then increase the reliability of the processes we use to deploy and maintain? You can expect to see this discussed in more depth in the sections to follow. Teams should ideally utilize monitoring tools and dashboards to collect real-time data on each of the SLIs and their respective SLOs, ensuring that the monitoring is tailored to the agreed service reliability objectives, such as availability, performance, and latency. The same level of sensitivity used to secure processes that focus on monitoring security features and data traffic through automation pipelines and internal databases should be used to ensure compliance with relevant security standards.

SLI and SLO iteration and continuous improvement

When considering ongoing monitoring for continuous iteration and improving upon your SLIs and SLOs, you want to "treat your SLOs as code." This suggests handling the SLI and SLO process with similar processes and tooling that you would use to manage the source code for applications and services. By treating SLIs and SLOs like code, teams can leverage familiar concepts and tools, making the process smoother for internal engineering teams and enhancing the overall efficiency of service-level management. If you plan to potentially offboard your process to another team, this will greatly simplify doing so. On a team where you are deploying and managing software code for your system and services, your team is likely doing the following:

- Developing SLIs and SLOs with distributed teams (in some cases).
- Using a version-controlled system for version control and code management.
- Building and testing code in a development, staging, or testing environment.
- Handling various dependencies in preparation for packaging your code for deployment.
- Utilizing various security mechanisms for deployment to a production server.
- Monitoring the software code and validating the success of its deployment.
- Have implemented a process for rolling back code changes.
- Have CI/CD pipelines that streamline all the preceding steps for you.

For SLI and SLO development, it is important to follow a structured process to define SLIs, establish SLOs, and implement monitoring before beginning iterations. Consistency in these steps ensures that the service levels are well defined and can be tracked effectively. Consider the following list as areas of focus when developing your internal process or SLO management infrastructure:

- **SLI and SLO objectives and definitions**: Determined during the workshops, documented in a technical format, and prepared for consumption via automation.

- **Automation**: The process we use for SLO change management to consume SLO objectives to make available for our platform of choice.

- **Platform**: The platform we use to host and manage our SLOs and dashboards, which consumes SLO definitions through our automation to present to our audience.

In *Chapter 11*, we referenced observability platforms and SLO management platforms. Consider the automation focus as the process and tooling used to efficiently deploy your SLOs to your platform of choice. In some instances, an SLO management platform may not provide certain capabilities or calculate your SLOs in a way that is meaningful to your organization. You may then want to utilize internal platforms, such as an observability platform already integrated into systems you are using with internal metrics available to your dashboards. The automation step then becomes even more important to your process.

If we flow through the mentioned components of our SLO management infrastructure, the technical flow will consist of the following steps:

1. Document your SLI and SLO objective configuration files using the format appropriate for your tooling of choice.
2. Upload configuration files to a repository of choice.
3. Monitor the repository for changes to and deployment of supplied configuration files.
4. Apply configuration files via the API of your platform of choice.
5. Carry out CRUD operations for the management of SLO objects hosted in your platform of choice.

Each listed step is a high-level action that needs to be taken into consideration to better determine whether a specific internal platform and tool your team is already using integrates best with existing processes. In some cases, it may prove best to procure a platform that integrates each of the following. When building your SLO management infrastructure, it will serve you best to audit and take inventory of solutions your development teams are already utilizing internally.

In many instances, taking inventory of current code management practices will solve the problem if the right process is being used. However, in the event it does not, and you find your team navigating the current market for an SLO management platform, it remains best to understand the workflow to ensure the selected solutions serve your organization best. In addition, understanding the required flow and how it relates to your current workflows and processes will help your team to better adjust to naturally updating and adjusting SLIs and SLOs as needed and when appropriate in the life cycle.

Adapting to SLI and SLO changes

A benefit of treating your SLO as code and creating an SLO management system is enabling your team and organization to naturally adapt and respond to SLI and SLO changes. We want to make sure we have processes in place, such as considering the level of observability into the systems being measured, that enable SRE to not only notice a system issue but also quickly determine whether there is an actual issue or a code or environment change that was not taken into consideration. SLIs and SLOs are implemented through metrics based on components within a system, which work together to provide your customers with specific functionality.

For instance, let's return to earlier architectures mentioned in *Chapter 7* of this book. In a multi-region cluster, we have several nodes hosting several services providing a UI for purchases to external customers. Several of the workloads consist of replicas to ensure high availability and efficient load balancing across regions. Our SRE team may have internal dashboards that monitor SLOs for specific features, such as checkout and payment processing functionality.

At the backend, the development team could push a change to the source code base, to incorporate a new method of payment. Our SLO for successful payment is being reported with a 98% success rate, and a large percentage of the user base is not using this method just yet. However, with the way the system metrics are calculated, the new payment method is not included in our data query and numerous failures are going unnoticed via SLO reporting but are being reported through the help desk and customer success channels. How do we as an SRE team implement processes that help to adapt to changes such as this? Adapting to SLI and SLO changes is a responsibility that will require adjusting over time.

Legacy systems may indeed experience fewer code base updates, but it's important to note that customer feedback should not only inform new features but also be used to reassess and refine SLIs and SLOs. As an SRE team, it's essential to continuously monitor and adjust these metrics in response to evolving customer needs and system behavior. When new features and functionality are integrated, or if your system experiences additional changes in a more agile environment, it will require the team to become more aware of how these changes impact established SLIs and SLOs. Occasionally, you may experience updates to the system, changes in user behaviors, or shifts in your business's priorities, which will also require adjusting SLOs and response strategies as needed to align with changes in requirements and other circumstances.

Being adaptable and responsive to changes in the environment means adjusting SLOs and associated response strategies as needed to align with changing requirements and circumstances. Creating SLIs and SLOs will naturally help your team to measure your services in a way that is easy to align back to business operations and strategy through practices such as the following:

- AI-driven anomaly detection

- Automated incident response orchestration

- SLO-driven chaos engineering

- SLO-driven service dependency mapping
- Dynamic SLO adjustments

An important aspect of implementing SLIs and SLOs is to improve the customer experience by quantifying service performance in a way that benefits the customer. Even more, it provides internal teams with the ability to build internal metrics that provide insight into system performance to make informed decisions when issues and downtime occur. Apart from making informed decisions when issues and downtime occur, being able to swiftly and efficiently manage incidents is also important.

Although AI is not the topic of this chapter, or book, it's an important reference to serve as a reminder when attempting to identify internal gaps for improvement. With the advances in the adoption of AI and its incorporation into various software and technology, it's important to look for opportunities to bring it into your SLO management process and platform to improve automation, detection, and other areas that may have been overlooked.

Let's read further and revisit ways each of the preceding practices can help to improve the daily operations of the SLO management process.

AI-driven anomaly detection

In *Chapter 11*, when reviewing SLOs and walking through creating the SLO threshold and alert in your platform of choice, we made mention of anomalies within the CDN system due to data cache misses. This process focuses on leveraging the capabilities of machine learning algorithms and AI-powered systems to detect anomalies that could signal potential breaches of SLOs.

Current systems focus on rule-based algorithms on the backend to detect anomalies in behaviors of your systems, lacking manual adoption. With AI-driven detection, your team will focus on the following capabilities:

- **Data mining**: Data-gathering initiatives surrounding the collection of data emitted from internal hardware systems.
- **Data storage**: Establishing a storage solution that hosts data from data gathering. This solution will align with the type of workloads you are emitting data from.
- **Building AI models**: Models built by your team or fine-tuned from existing models, which incorporate linear regression, logistic regression, decision trees, and so on to recognize patterns and formulate a decision using relevant data presented.

Although this book does not focus on the power of AI or ML, it's important to understand the evolving landscape of software and technology, while identifying areas of opportunity to incorporate such advancements. A common AI model reference is **Large Language Models (LLMs)**.

Automated incident response orchestration

Incident management is a pillar of its own within the reliability engineering hierarchy. It is also crucial to the success of a product when the product falls short of meeting the customer's expectations. Within your incident management process, your team likely uses a severity and priority system for incidents in addition to maintaining internal SLAs for incident response times and RCA.

As a part of daily operations, and to reduce response times and engineer burnout, as well as achieving set SLAs, leverage opportunities to do the following:

- Respond swiftly to incidents via automated templated initial responses to incidents.

- Promptly identify and categorize incidents that impact any SLIs and SLOs.

- Quickly update and redirect incidents to their respective queues, if applicable.

Although alerting capabilities are typically built into the platform of choice, it's important to remain proactive with the handling of incidents violating their SLO. In hindsight, merely reviewing dashboards every morning, looking for a topic to discuss, can easily become a tedious and redundant task. Within reliability engineering, SREs should naturally look to eliminate toil, when possible, to increase the amount of time available to innovate.

SLO-driven chaos engineering

Chaos engineering consists of experimentation on a system to build confidence in the system and assess its ability to withstand chaos in a production environment (Chaos Community, 2019). Essentially, we want to break things to better understand specific behaviors and test a system's capacity. A similar approach can and should be utilized to validate aspects of your system as it relates to SLO thresholds. If your team experiences unusual anomalies or spikes or SLO violations, use them to leverage and build "test cases" that challenge your system.

There are some new SRE platforms currently in development, such as the following:

- **Blameless**: Dedicated to providing solutions to SRE needs for reliably managing incidents through an incident management-based platform. It also includes an SLO manager to manage reliability objectives.

- **Steadybit**: Provides a tool for chaos engineering to test the reliability of your applications and infrastructure in cloud and on-premises environments.

These replicate some of the most common issues systems experience, while allowing the opportunity to customize test cases as needed.

SLO-driven service dependency mapping

In a later section, we'll discuss how service dependency mapping contributes toward working cross-functionally. However, it's important to mention it here as a contributor toward successful SLO management. Dependency mapping focuses on the underlying relationships between your systems to better triage issues and understand the collective goal they are trying to accomplish. Outside of engaging with the product engineering teams developing the respective services, SLO-driven service dependency mapping helps SREs display service dependencies based on real-time or historical communication data, enabling a dynamic view of the interrelationships and performance bottlenecks within the system. This improves the ability of SREs to do the following:

- Display application traffic flow and relevant dependencies within a system at a given point in time.
- Quickly differentiate between applications reporting an issue and applications causing an issue.
- Get insights into the performance of distributed systems and applications through efficient event logging.

When including service dependency mapping within your SLO infrastructure, the team will have increased visibility into the relationships between each of the services when issues arise. For instance, during peak hours over the holiday season, the services associated with ordering a product are likely to experience an increase in sales and traffic. In the event of the system experiencing throttling, and either auto-scaling occurs or load balancing routes traffic to another region, when an issue arises, the service dependency chart will route the on-call engineer to the services directly involved in throttling. Most dependency charts will provide you with metadata related to the service, while highlighting errors or provide request and response network information to further debug.

Dynamic SLO adjustments

In earlier workshop chapters, we made mention of an SLO to monitor system performance during the peak hours of sales. Dynamic SLO adjustment enables your platform of choice to tailor SLO targets dynamically based on changing circumstances. During those peak periods of high user demand or increased system load, it will service your on-call teams best to adjust SLO thresholds and prioritize service availability over response times. If your team is concerned about missing an incident, AI-driven anomaly detection can act as a filter to alleviate some of those concerns.

During critical incidents or service disruptions, it may be necessary to tighten SLO targets, ensuring swift resolution and minimal impact on the user experience. If an organization sells technical solutions with a business objective to provide a platform for developer enablement, it's not ideal for a key enterprise account to experience a critical issue during an event, such as releasing a new application to consumers. Tightening any SLO targets surrounding the respective persona journey can lead to delivering good service to loyal customers.

Cross-functional collaboration for SLIs and SLOs

When developing knowledge and experience of the SRE hierarchy and pillars within each layer, my primary experience was centered around container orchestration with vanilla and enterprise Kubernetes environments. In a microservice architecture for larger systems, we can automatically assume that there are several teams responsible for their respective service, associated integrations, and automation pipelines or processes used to deploy and manage changes.

As much as an all-hands-on-deck approach can appear to solve all our communication and collaboration issues, it can end up doing the opposite. The more teams and individuals responsible for various system components and reporting to different management chains, the more confusing it can be. This can also increase the chances of communication gaps, unclear ownership, and incorrect delegation of tasks. As mentioned in earlier chapters, how we communicate and work across teams to reduce silos and increase efficient communication greatly impacts the success of implementation and speed of adoption.

In larger organizations, you will experience an increase in the number of teams and various tooling and processes used within each team if there is a lack of unification and process streamlining. As it relates to the SLI and SLO process, you want to consider the following to foster a cross-functional communicative culture:

- Service dependency mapping
- The incident management structure
- Cross-functional touchpoints
- The offboarding process

Each of these are things you want to take into consideration during the beginning stages to improve the collaborative aspects of your SLO management process and increase the buy-in of SLOs within the broader organization. The introduction and expectations of each at the start of the conversation will contribute a great deal to the success of your SLO journey.

Service dependency mapping

Service dependency mapping will help your team navigate the system and triage incidents by identifying the root cause and understanding the impact on dependent services. In addition, during an active incident, on-call engineers are more likely to quickly engage with the appropriate team, in the event alerting and triaging are out of alignment.

When procuring an SRE platform, especially for Incident Management or Observability focused platforms, ensure service dependency mapping is a highlighted feature. On-call alerting platforms, such as PagerDuty, also provide the capability to structure alert routing in a similar manner.

The incident management structure

Incident management is discussed further in *Chapter 13*. It's the system of processes used to manage an incident's life cycle. The process you use for responding to SLO violations should replicate or at least be like that of the teams handling incident management for the respective services. SRE platforms for incident management, such as Blameless, mentioned earlier in this chapter, will combine incident management and SLO management capabilities, incorporating them into the platform, unifying the process and tooling for on-call engineers responding to incidents for different services or in different on-call rotations, but requiring a similar process and system access. Unifying incident management will improve a few areas for you and your team(s):

- Avoid reinventing the wheel and adding another process to an engineering (or on-call) team that likely already has many processes.

- It enables your team to bring value to the incident management system through process improvement. If you are in an organization where incident management is simply a bunch of alerts firing, it's an opportunity to offer other SRE services and revamp the incident management structure.

- It can improve response times. On-call teams are likely already busy. Understanding how the team runs the incident management life cycle, structure, and unifying incident response will associate your process with a process they are already familiar with – which, if operating on muscle memory, will make it easier for on-call teams to respond immediately to you.

Cross-functional touchpoints

Cross-functional touchpoints include creating a cadence to interact with the teams responsible for developing the services you are implementing SLOs for. As things change within the system, it's important to create an avenue for communication in a healthy way. The more development teams understand what you are doing and why, the easier it will be for them to adapt. There are also other benefits, such as relationship building, which helps greatly when something is needed.

Otherwise, it's likely that your team will have specific meeting cadences with stakeholders. Just don't forget about the folks who know and engineer your systems. This can include the following:

- Establishing a healthy cadence for internal meetings with development or engineering teams and management will help to keep your team on the right track. Take into consideration the schedule for meetings relating to internal teams completing the SLO work.

- Quarterly meetings incorporating management, stakeholders, and other necessary executives will ensure SRE is in sync with the strategy of the broader organization.

Offboarding process

If your SRE team or the team initially managing the SLO process is an enablement or initialization team, you'll want to ensure you have an effective offboarding process. This may even include providing enablement documentation or flowing through and documenting the SLO process in a way that is consumable later.

It's important not to consider the process as simply handing over an SLO dashboard to another team. Instead, it should include ensuring proper knowledge transfer of the technical tooling used to manage SLOs as code, along with the configuration of alerting mechanisms and monitoring practices. This has been highlighted as the more transparency and understanding of the process, the easier it will be for another team to adopt the process and SLO process. Otherwise, it can end up being a dashboard that no one pays attention to after a while.

SLI and SLO performance reviews

An additional objective of your SLIs and SLOs is to establish a system of internal accountability, encouraging collaboration between teams responsible for engineering the system components and those managing customer-facing interactions that affect service reliability. This will require each team to naturally work in a cross-functional manner. However, we are also aware that there are only so many hours in a workday where we can consistently obtain the necessary individuals for the same meeting. Working in a virtual environment only makes this a more difficult feat, requiring a strategy to ensure the individuals have the appropriate face-to-face conversations to ensure that SLIs and SLOs remain as follows:

- Performant at the level necessary for business operations.

- Relevant to the target persona and the original problem identified.

- Necessary. Even if the SLIs and SLOs are relevant to a problem, is the problem still relevant to the original stakeholder?

- Impactful to business operations through decision-making between key stakeholders and team members.

Improving the sustainability of your SLOs and their management process relies heavily on consistent cross-functional touchpoints. These touchpoints often prove more impactful than hierarchal updates for driving collaboration and maintaining alignment between teams. You have a great chance of improving adoption rates when working cross-functionally with individuals handling daily operations. We can achieve the mentioned goals through lateral touchpoints and overarching SLO performance reviews. Some things you may want to consider are the following:

- Access to tooling related to documentation

- Access related to automated tooling

- Access related to cloud provider platforms
- Access related to SSO-related product lines

Although this is not a topic with its own chapter in this book, it's important to be aware of the security-related aspects of SLO management. This includes access that relates to internal and external tooling supporting your SLOs. Your SLOs are essentially reporting the performance of the services critical to your business and should be treated as important. It's best to incorporate topics such as this during your SLO workshops as well.

Summary

A proactive and strategic approach is required for adopting SLIs and SLOs to measure the performance of your systems and services and reliably address changing business objectives, market conditions, and technological advancements. Regardless of the methodology and tooling you choose, each should be a part of a larger process that enables assessment of the alignment between SLIs, SLOs, and business goals. It's equally important to ensure there exists the ability to adjust metrics and targets accordingly. When both exist as a part of your process, your organization can confidently meet external-facing commitments, such as SLAs for high-performing services.

Implementing dynamic practices will help ensure you are consistently reliable in a way that is scalable to your organization. It will also improve your ability to remain responsive to issues over time, with SLOs at the core. Meeting user expectations and driving business success over the long term depends heavily on our ability to maintain relevant practices for effective SLO maintenance.

Monitoring SLIs in real time and responding to SLIs and SLOs through automation will improve your ability to ensure alignment between business objectives and reduce human error. You will also notice an improved ability to remain agile, adaptive, and resilient in the face of responding to new feature requests and responding to customer issues and inquiries. Through continuous iteration, improvement, and alignment with user needs and the continuous changes in market dynamics, you will uphold service reliability and deliver exceptional experiences to internal and external users and customers.

In the next chapter, we'll discuss the importance of integrating internal incident management processes to efficiently manage incident metrics, resulting in improved SLO preservation capabilities.

Further reading

Refer to the following for additional reading about concepts mentioned in this chapter:

- Chaos Community. (2019, March). *Principles of Chaos Engineering*: `https://principlesofchaos.org`.

13

SLO Preservation and Incident Management

In previous chapters, the attention was surrounding reliability engineering, SLI and SLO management, and various other topics. At the time of writing this book, the adoption of digital transformation is still a priority among many organizations. This is in addition to much attention being directed to the advancements of artificial intelligence and machine learning concepts to further advance the capabilities of software and technology.

Although none of the previous topics mentioned are centered around this book, I have a special interest in learning about and understanding new software and technology to better understand how it can improve processes in my personal and professional lifestyle. Initially, I wanted this chapter to center around how my previous team leveraged the incident management process across our product engineering domains within our organization to validate live incidents against what our SLO dashboards were telling us.

The goal of this chapter is to elevate the role of incident management within reliability engineering and better understand how to improve and leverage it to maintain improved internal housekeeping for your SLOs. We will discuss the relationship between on-call engineers and agents in incident response and resolution within SLO frameworks.

We will cover the following topics as they relate to leveraging incident management as a part of your SLO preservation process:

- Incident management and core concepts within it
- The importance of incident response within the process
- Various techniques for SLO preservation
- The importance of extending accountability to on-call agents and product engineering teams

Let's take a moment and highlight incident management as a practice as well as the role it plays within an organization as a standalone practice. In the sections that follow, we will highlight approaches for SLO preservation through your incident management practice.

Incident management in a nutshell

Your incident management system and its impact on the broader organization and your target customer base is only as good as your incident management plan and process. Understanding the significance of SLOs within incident management and incorporating on-call engineers and agents into the SLO framework helps to ensure that service reliability is maintained and measured against defined SLIs.

It passively improves the customer experience and presents to your target customer base a more uniform and aligned organization when issues arise. If we then extend additional accountability to product engineering teams, organizations can enhance their ability to respond to and resolve incidents effectively. This is done in a way that fosters the improvement of reliability and availability through development insights.

Prior to an organization considering SLOs for incident management activities, it is ideal to take a step approach to identify and ensure the following information exists:

- The definition of an incident and its life cycle according to your organization
- Incident management roles and responsibilities
- An incident management communication plan
- Incident response guidelines and a value system

Despite the size of your incident management team, it's important to ensure that all individuals are on the same page. This chapter does not take on the workshop approach seen in earlier chapters. However, you can utilize a similar structure and flow of the workshop chapters to cycle through creating an incident management plan and SLOs for specific incident management metrics.

Incident management as a practice

The practice of incident management can be implemented within an organization as a process that is used to resolve issues that arise. It can function as a practice with more elaborate processes or span across an organization where various teams and business groups are leveraging a similar process and tooling to resolve incidents seamlessly. There is no one-size-fits-all approach, only implementing what is needed for your short and long-term goals in a scalable manner.

Incident management focuses on the management of incidents in a way that helps to address and prevent future incidents through process improvement. Incident response focuses on handling and mitigation as it relates to the incident when it arises and its customer impact. This will be discussed a bit more in the section to follow. However, as a practice, incident management consists of six phases, as follows:

1. **Incident identification**: This step includes the detection and report of an incident, consisting of the metadata and identifiers to associate with the incident.

2. **Incident categorization**: This step involves classifying incidents based on predefined categories such as severity levels, which directly impact the SLOs and SLIs. Categorization should align with how the incident might affect SLA performance.

3. **Incident prioritization**: This step includes a metric system that categorizes incidents according to other items and their immediate or long-term impact on the customer and thus business.

4. **Incident response**: This is the process that is used to address mitigation and resolution of an incident. This can vary drastically within different organizations and industries.

5. **Incident closure**: This is the process or steps that follow the incident resolution. This usually sets the tone for the steps to follow to prevent the incident from occurring again.

6. **Learning and improvements**: This includes the process for improving the system from a technical or process perspective, as well as the actions taken to learn from an incident. This is typically done through post-mortems or retrospectives.

The fundamental outcome of your incident management system should be to quickly and efficiently mitigate and resolve issues in a way that fosters continuous learning and improvements. Within each step or phase, the tasks and processes followed will vary and consist of things that make the most sense to your team or organization. Fundamentally, many of the steps within incident management have industry standards or best practices available to follow or utilize as guidelines to get you and your team started. An important step within the management process is how you respond to and mitigate an active customer-impacting incident, which we will discuss a bit more in the next section.

Incident response within incident management

Incident response is a step within the incident management process. It's one of the most critical steps, as it relates to how you mitigate an issue from detection through resolution. It consists of issues that are actively impacting the customer and require immediate attention. Like incident response within other industries such as law enforcement, healthcare, and so on, the incident itself is important due to the impact it has on the target audience. How it is handled by the on-call staff is critical to maintaining the customer's or some individual's safety. Each area will thus have its own set of guidelines and rules that need to be followed to reach the end goal.

The overarching goal of incident response is to ensure the service stays within its SLOs by quickly mitigating incidents that could cause a breach in the SLA. Incident resolution should focus on restoring the system to an acceptable level of performance defined by the SLOs. With that said, the incident response phase consists of five steps, which are referenced here:

1. **Incident detection and reporting**: The stage at which your detection process or system user detects and reports the deprecation of an activity.

2. **Incident assessment**: The initial assessment of the reported incident. Additional data gathering and the establishment of communication typically happen here.

3. **Incident mitigation**: The tasks completed to mitigate and reduce the impact of the incidents. In more critical events, this can include workarounds.

4. **Incident recovery**: This step includes the restoration of specific components within the system to be monitored to ensure it is operating as expected.

5. **Post-incident analysis**: This typically includes the incorporation of a retrospective or post-mortem event. This includes gathering those involved in the incident to brainstorm through associated events.

Institutes such as the **National Standards and Technology Institute** (**NIST**) and the SANS Institute are specific to security and offer a set of guidelines for incident management. However, within your own team or organization, or even through the development of your SLO process, you might find that there are areas that require additional depth, or the removal of specific concepts is required to fit into your current narrative.

It's important to understand that best practices and guidelines are just that. If your process helps you identify something different or identifies gaps that require attention, reinvent the wheel, and contribute to elevating the role of incident management, no pun intended. So, what does all of this have to do with SLO preservation? Let's continue to find out!

Elevating the role of incident management in reliability engineering

The goal of this chapter is not to persuade you about the best practices for incident management or how to structure your organization for incident response. It is, however, to set the tone for what it is and its relationship within reliability engineering to SLOs. I prefer to start with a brief overview to ensure that we understand core concepts and terminology. With this information at hand, it should help your team to advocate for a culture where incident management is seen as a benefit and complement to ensuring a customer-centric culture with regard to service reliability.

Having experience with support and incident management within various-sized organizations, preservation through SLO is not only critical to a customer-centric environment but also to preserving your staff and reducing engineer burnout. It is equally as important as other areas due to the following reasons:

- Engineers and other staff participating in your on-call rotations are your employees too!

- On-call staff must switch between being reactive and proactive. This is difficult at times.

- They often must manage the customer temperature with minimal information during active events. This can be stressful.

- If your organization does not consist of an elaborate incident organization, chances are they've experienced engineer burnout more than a few times.

- They have a more realistic perspective of your product, service, or system, whether you like the opinion or not.

These reasons are significant enough for organizations to begin to shift their perspective on the way incidents and thus support requests are handled. For the organization to truly be considered customer-centric, we need to consider all customer-facing channels. Thus, SLO preservation practices will also be of benefit to your internal engineers and other staff.

Significance of SLOs in incident management accountability

SLOs play a pivotal role in incident management accountability. When the organization maintains clear and measurable SLOs for incident management such as response and resolution times, while linking SLO performance to incident management metrics, it will experience a correlated increase in accountability of various teams and improved reliability of internal processes outside of just your systems and services.

Clear SLOs encourage implementing teams to not only establish expectations for the services they build but also for the processes used related to incident handling, providing teams with an improved ability to prioritize tasks, allocate resources effectively, and maintain service reliability and availability. SLOs provide a tangible framework for assessing the performance of incident response teams and holding them accountable for meeting defined targets. Areas within incident management that teams can utilize SLOs for are as follows:

- Incident response times

- Incident resolution times

- Incident detection times

- Incident acknowledgment times

There are various other metrics available related to incident management and outside-of-system performance, which your team can utilize to improve incident handling internal to your organization.

The SLOs in this capacity should stem from the targets expected by key accounts, business requirements, or an established SLA provided to accounts from the organization. By setting clear objectives for on-call performance, organizations can ensure consistent service levels by creating and upholding reliability commitments through processes implemented for incident-related activities.

On-call agents are essential for ensuring timely incident response and resolution. They play a critical role in monitoring system health, detecting incidents, and coordinating efforts to resolve issues promptly. SLOs and SLO dashboarding can better aid your on-call agents in the following ways:

- Identifying issues before they are customer-impacting.
- Delegating and reprioritizing technical work as needed and based on current SLO threshold limits.
- Identifying trends over time.
- Ensuring the customer experience is in alignment with agreed-upon service performance metrics.

This increases the need for frameworks or process implementation that meets your on-call engineers' needs and contributes to avoiding agent burnout and possibly increased employee attrition resulting in increased turnover rates.

In earlier workshop chapters, we mentioned excessive customer complaints and incoming requests related to platform outages and performance degradation in specific critical customer workflows. In addition, the application maintains a global presence, which results in having to consider peak hours during holidays that span several countries and time zones. This results in a requirement for additional attention to international data centers outside of the local region, with different policies and procedures.

The current incident management teams use a *follow the sun* on-call rotation. This means instead of engineers following a 24x7 on-call rotation, on-call responsibilities are rotated between global teams during normal business hours with a separate rotation for on-site infrastructure issues. For purposes of the text, *follow the Sun on-call rotation* is when agents are distributed in various regions where the standard business hour working period is structured to maintain 24x7 coverage. Do not confuse regions with being local to the respective data center.

To increase visibility and improve clarity surrounding how teams within specific regions and agents as individuals are performing, we might consider SLIs and SLOs for incident management-related metrics. Let's have a look at how the process works with some simple metrics that we can implement as indicators and objectives to contribute to a reduction in negative impact.

SLIs for incident management metrics

In this section, we'll construct a few journeys for one incident management persona, the **on-call agent**. Like the previous workshop chapters, in a workshop setting, the team would navigate through a discussion to determine the critical personas. These personas would range between on-call engineers, engineering teams, management, and other stakeholders of the incident management life cycle. In this instance, we will focus on the main persona, the on-call agent, establishing the various journeys that exist during an incident's life cycle. The persona journey chart may consist of the journeys depicted in *Figure 13.1*.

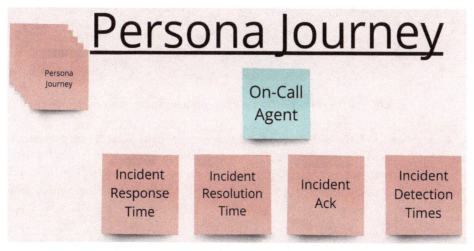

Figure 13.1 – Incident management persona journey for the On-Call Agent

In this instance, the persona is the on-call agent, and the journey is associated with the respective metric they are expected to uphold versus a workflow against a specific system. The persona journey might begin with the following expectations for each of the metrics, outlined by their respective manager or as requested through channels up the management pipeline. *Figure 13.2*'s journey displays the expectations via the virtual whiteboard.

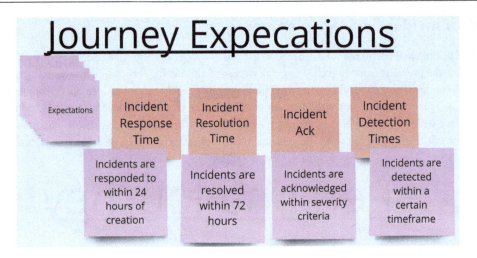

Figure 13.2 – Incident management persona journey expectations

However, we might need to define each journey and the expectations more in depth to better understand the requirements and determine whether the implemented platform for managing incidents maintains built-in features that auto-generate this information. For the sake of the text, we'll pretend it does not. If it does not, how do we then aggregate available data in the current environment to provide similar information?

We might pose the following questions:

- Incident response occurs within 24 hours of creation with the response time being tracked as an SLO, where the SLO threshold is set to respond to a defined percentage of incidents within this time frame:

  - How is the workflow for response defined?

  - Can the current system automate this process?

  - Is there a logging or event system in place to retrieve timestamps?

- Incidents are resolved within 72 hours:

  - What is the definition of resolved with regard to the organization?

  - Is there a system event or resolution metric available within the current system?

- Incidents are acknowledged according to severity and prioritization criteria:

  - What is the current prioritization system in place?

  - Is there a metric or timestamp available that provides this information?

  - Is there an incident notification tool implemented currently?

- Incidents are detected within a certain time frame:

  - What are the available methods that detect incidents?

Figure 13.3 depicts the updated whiteboard, which prompts the previous questions to the team.

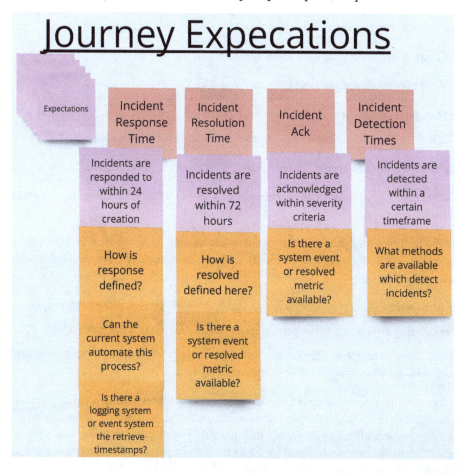

Figure 13.3 – Journey expectation requirements

Let's go over the requirements briefly.

Incident response times

Incident Response Time focuses on the time it takes to respond to an incident. Due to the prior critical issues mentioned, the team might want to implement an initial response time of 24 hours. The incident response time is going to heavily depend on a few criteria:

- The size and structure of your current team:
  - Engineer headcount, location distribution, and so on
- The size of incoming requests and the current backlog:
  - Do your incoming requests exceed the ability of the agents?
  - Is the current backlog excessive with issues breaching various deadlines?
- The workflow used to report, triage, and assign a support ticket or internal incident:
  - Are current processes handled manually or with automation? Is there an opportunity to eliminate or reduce toil?

In addition to the preceding, your team may want to set response times based on severity, priority, or criticality, which is typically logged by the reporter at issue creation. Metrics considered at this stage might be the following:

- **Incident scale** – How widespread is the outage? Is every customer impacted or some percentage?
- **Degradation coverage** – What percentage of functionality is in a degraded state?
- **Time** – At what length of time (sometimes cadence) has the event taken place? Was the issue detected a day after it happened or immediately noticed?

You can accurately measure and report on incident response times if you take an accurate and thorough assessment of its current state. In other words, if your incoming requests exceed an amount that agents can effectively resolve within a given period, then it would work against the team and organization to set an SLO on **mean time to respond** (**MTTR**) for a given percentage of responses to meet an unrealistic expectation of a 1-hour response time.

Instead, you might consider staggering the response time according to severity and priority at a time length that is realistic and where customer complaints are minimal. This can be done asynchronously while using the off-call period to identify opportunities for automation and process improvement. In addition, it's important to define what response time means. The quality of the response to the customer and the stance they take with your organization upon resolution greatly depends on the interactions made throughout the entire life cycle.

Incident resolution times

The time it takes your team to resolve an issue, often tracked through the **mean time to resolution (MTTR)**, is one of the most critical measurements during an active incident, with the resolution time being defined by an SLO that is monitored through SLIs. Many factors are at play when there is an ongoing issue, which can have a negative impact on customer satisfaction. Defining SLOs for incident resolution times is essential for ensuring timely and effective incident handling. Incident response teams can use these SLOs as benchmarks to guide their actions, streamline incident workflows, and expedite the resolution process. Often, this task is impacted by the following:

- The layers of communication that are required between the agent, customer, and other internal staff attempting to mitigate and resolve the issue

- The technical depth required to resolve the issue, including whether a code patch is needed or whether the problem stems from an upstream or third-party dependency

When considering or setting your incident resolution times, it's best to consider the internal structure, processes implemented, and roadblockers to determine the best threshold or SLO.

Time to acknowledge

Time to acknowledge focuses on how long it takes to notice and begin the work on a support request or internal incident. When considering customer success and responsiveness, acknowledgment of submission should happen as early in the process as possible, in addition to including as much information as possible. In today's industry, this typically includes an automated process that is built into the respective platform or tooling of choice. Your acknowledgments will typically include the following:

- Identifier information regarding the request

- Information regarding the agent it's been assigned to

- Expectations surrounding dialogue or communications related to the incident

- Additional information that is specific to your organization's process

Each metric is important due to its impact on the customer experience and providing the on-call agent with the necessary insights related to how an incident is impacting the customer experience. This affords the opportunity to respond swiftly.

Time to detection

Incident response, mitigation, and resolution are important phases within the life cycle. However, *when* the incident is detected plays a critical role in the success of each metric. If we regress to the concepts in *Chapter 4, Observability and Monitoring Are a Necessity and a Must*, SLO management enables SRE teams to measure customer experience with regard to the system versus a single metric such as CPU utilization, which is a metric internal engineers might pay attention to. Gauging when incidents are detected enables SREs to understand how effective the current monitoring thresholds are, with detection times being tracked as SLOs to evaluate the system's effectiveness in meeting reliability goals.

For instance, if we expect an SLI to maintain a 99.5% SLO threshold over a 28-day rolling window, the inverse of the SLO (1-SLO) is the error budget or 0.5. This equates to approximately 43 minutes of downtime over a 28-day period before the issue is noticeable to the customer and begins to impact the experience. If we fail to implement fast-burn alerting and an incident occurs without detection, we've exhausted the budget prior to the end of the period. If early detection occurs, we can preserve the budget, leaving room for errors during code release or other system changes within the compliance period.

Defining specific SLIs and SLOs for on-call responsiveness and resolution is essential for measuring and improving incident handling processes. The earlier we can detect an incident, the more error budget we are able to preserve. Incorporating on-call engineers and agents into SLO frameworks is essential for maintaining service reliability and meeting customer expectations. When clear SLIs and SLOs are defined for on-call detection, responsiveness, and resolution, we can implement effective processes for on-call agents during live incidents and leverage the appropriate tools and technologies to do so. This helps organizations to ensure timely incident handling, minimize downtime, and deliver exceptional service to customers.

Incorporating on-call rotations and escalations into SLO frameworks requires careful planning and coordination. Linking SLO performance to incident management metrics such as **mean time to detect (MTTD)** and **mean time to resolve (MTTR)** will help you to provide valuable insights into the effectiveness of incident response efforts and SLO performance. When SLO performance is aligned with incident management metrics, this provides increased visibility of performance tracking among agents and trends through increased observability and enables the broader SRE org and stakeholders to make data-driven decisions, enhancing internal accountability and performance.

Incident management and SLO preservation

Incident management plays an important role in the contributions toward ensuring the reliability and availability of systems and services. SLO preservation is achieved through incident management practices that ensure that system performance reliability is continuously monitored against SLO targets, with a focus on minimizing deviations from those targets during incident detection, response, and resolution. Preservation practices as related to your SLIs and SLOs in incident management can showcase their use as the leading indicators of potential issues and as targets for incident resolution. We'll highlight examples of this in sections to follow. The goal of this book is not to cover topics such as artificial intelligence, automation, and machine learning; however, it's important to consider the incorporation of their availability and the positive impact they can provide for SLO preservation.

Incident management is a critical component of reliability engineering and maintains the processes and procedures for detecting, responding to, and resolving incidents that impact system availability and performance. By establishing robust incident management practices, organizations can minimize downtime, mitigate risks, and maintain service reliability, ultimately enhancing customer satisfaction and trust. It also helps to create a collaborative culture where learning and continuous improvements occur in a systemic way while quantifying and measuring system performance for a customer-centric organization.

For the purposes of later discussions within this chapter, let's revisit information related to an SLI created earlier in *Chapter 8* for distributed systems. For more information related to the SLIs, please review *Chapter 8*. Highlighted here is information related to the *Cluster Dashboard Management* SLI:

- **Cluster Dashboard Management**: The web-based user interface is used as one of the several first lines of defense when attempting to debug live incidents. The deployment consists of a multi-container pod, deployed using the deployment object via Helm. Its workload is deployed into the system namespace. Therefore, there is a high expectation surrounding its availability:

  - **Error rate**: The workload needs to remain in a running state with a low error rate during normal operational conditions. Peak hours are critical.

  - **Pod startup**: During peak hours, the length of time it takes for a new pod to start and become ready to serve after failing over to another region is also critical.

Monitoring a dashboard may not immediately feel as if it is important to monitor. However, in an environment where there are numerous issues, customer complaints and peak hours vary within a region due to being globally distributed, and it's important for the understaffed on-call team to have as much relevant information available to them when a new ticket is routed from a customer. This includes when an internal incident is escalated to the engineering teams. Therefore, the team thought it best to include a metric to report on its performance and determine whether an improved solution and/or method is needed.

Our goal in this section is how we can utilize SLOs for incident management to preserve the SLOs for our system environment, thus improving the experience of our customers after various complaints related to specific outages and incidents.

Let's look at an example severity matrix for incidents. Although there is a correlation, this is not to be confused with a priority matrix, highlighting the impact on business importance. Severity focuses on the impact of an incident, such as a defect causing an entire application or platform to be down. *Table 13.1* depicts an example severity matrix (PagerDuty, 2021):

Severity	Description	Response
Sev-1	Critical issue requiring public notification and executives	Critical incident page (P1); notify internal stakeholders and the public
Sev-2	Critical issue impacting many customers' ability to use the product	Critical incident page (P2)
Anything above this line is considered a "Major" incident		
Sev-3	Minor customer-impacting issue requiring service owner attention	High-priority page to the service team
Sev-4	Minor issue, requiring action but not impacting customers' ability to use the product	Low-priority page to the service team
Sev-5	Cosmetic issue but not impacting customers' ability to use the product	Ticketing system

Table 13.1 – Standard severity matrix

During incident response and resolution, SLIs and SLOs can serve as key benchmarks for evaluating the impact of incidents on service reliability. Incident management teams prioritize efforts based on the impact of SLI deviations relative to SLO targets, ensuring that service reliability aligns with customer expectations and minimizing downtime to stay within the defined error budget. This systematic approach ensures that incident response efforts are aligned with overarching reliability objectives, ultimately minimizing service disruptions and maximizing customer satisfaction.

Delays in identifying and addressing incidents can lead to increased and ongoing events surrounding downtime, increased customer dissatisfaction, and money left on the table, resulting in reputational damage. Therefore, organizations must prioritize proactive monitoring, rapid incident response, and efficient resolution processes to minimize the impact of incidents on service reliability.

In our instance, we want to implement SLOs to ensure our on-call agents and automated processes remain in compliance with the external commitments of our customers. To ensure that teams remain responsive to the issues that arise, we want to focus on the MTTD metric, calculated by dividing the total time between failures and detection by the total number of failures. It's ideal to maintain an MTTD time as close to 0 as possible. However, it's best to use internal data to determine percentiles for buckets to calculate starter SLOs. In the next section, we'll calculate the MTTD and use this process as an example.

MTTD SLO

The following is a table providing information related to incidents with logged failed MTTD measurements for our e-commerce platform during a month period within the **Eastern Standard (EST)** time zone.

Date	Incident Start	Detection Time	Minutes to Detect
01-03	11:30 a.m.	12:00 p.m.	30
01-10	3:30 p.m.	3:47 p.m.	17
01-12	12:05 a.m.	12:22 a.m.	17
01-14	8:52 p.m.	9:35 p.m.	43
01-20	11:10 p.m.	11:16 p.m.	6

Table 13.2 – Incident detection time for on-call agents over a month period

For this month, there were a total of 20 incidents, meeting a 1-minute detection time, with 5 exceeding the expected MTTD. On-call agents, over the last 28 days, experienced a total detection time of 128 minutes. If we divide this number by the total number of failures within the same period, we reach an MTTD of 6.4.

For statistics and probability to calculate starter SLOs, the recommendation is to read *Chapter 9, Probability and Statistics for SLIs and SLOs*, in Alex Hidalgo's *Implementing Service Level Objectives* (Hidalgo, 2020). We've mentioned it's best to keep the MTTD as close to 0 as possible, but on average, the MTTD remains within 1 minute using reliable automation. This month is much higher than normal due to recent code releases.

To calculate the error budget for a 95% SLO threshold over a 28-day period, we compute the allowable downtime by multiplying the total period (28 days) by the SLO threshold (0.95), leaving us with a 5% error budget. In this case, the error budget would be 1.4 days or 33.6 hours for the period, meaning that incidents exceeding this threshold would count against the error budget. This leaves 18.25 annum days or 1.5 days per month, or 1.5 hours per day.

In this instance, it is not as simple as considering availability and latency and analyzing logs and other metrics for data on requests to determine what your SLO ought to be. You can, however, look through your incident management platform statistics and gauge from available data what it ought to be to iterate until the appropriate value has been identified.

Another option is to use statistics, and probability formulas such as **expected value, median, maximum likelihood estimation (MLE),** or **maximum a posteriori** to better determine what your SLO ought to be. There are other formulas available, and each will be applicable to the type of dataset you are creating indicators and objectives for. In this example, measuring the MTTD for a period is not as concrete as we'd like it to be as the number of incidents in each period and failed detection times varies. However, we can infer what the effects of this number "x" may or may not be and treat detection times in terms of successes and failures. Of the 20 logged incidents for the month, 5 of them are failures due to exceeding the 1-minute expected detection time.

Depending on the observability tooling implemented, we might propose "x" as a metric that retrieves the number of incidents for a 28-day window and then calculates the MTTD by dividing the total detection time (based on timestamps) for each incident in the dataset, by the total detection time for every incident with a detection time > 1 minute. The MTTD for this month for the given dataset of 20 incidents is 6.4.

Looking at this from the perspective of good requests versus total requests would result in an SLO of 0.75 or 75%, violating the SLO threshold for the compliance period.

Extending accountability to product engineering teams

When considering the impact of implementing SLIs and SLOs, it's important to realize the aspect of extending accountability to the engineering teams building the product. Depending on the structure of the incident management practice within your organization, it's likely that there is an extension that already exists to engineering teams at some touchpoint within the incident life cycle. The act of extending accountability within the product development life cycle and various workflows enhances collaboration between operations and product engineering teams by tying incident response to clearly defined SLIs and SLOs. This ensures that product engineering teams are not only responsible for building the product but also for maintaining its reliability and performance according to agreed-upon targets, improving both incident resolution and the overall product.

While operations teams traditionally handle incident response, product engineering has increased the level of visibility of system architecture, maintaining a direct impact on system performance, reliability, and availability. This level of visibility will also help SRE teams enhance the automation practices surrounding both incident management and DevOps tooling used to reliably deploy.

The incident creation flow typically starts with an end user in mind. As mentioned during the workshop chapters, this can vary from the typical user being a customer as a member of a customer account, an internal support agent, another internal SRE, or in a more elaborate organization a third-party tool creating an incident upon some notification. Regardless of who the incident is created by, it is created through some platform or your internal process and routed to the SRE on-call, as depicted in *Figure 13.4*.

Figure 13.4 – Incident creation from user to on-call SRE

This flow should ideally align with the alerting mechanisms tied to your SLOs, ensuring that incidents are triggered only when performance deviates from the agreed-upon objectives. By using SLOs as a threshold for alerting, the process avoids interfering with other workflows while ensuring that incidents that affect service reliability are promptly addressed. To increase internal adoption with other internal engineers, my team found that incorporating current processes that aligned with workflows they were accustomed to increased buy-in among engineering teams and stakeholders. Ideally, if the SRE team is handling their SLOs via their own internal process, you'd want your incidents to flow as depicted in *Figure 13.5*, shifting to the product engineering teams.

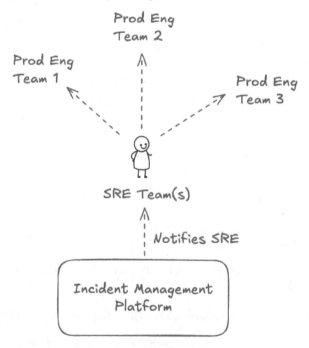

Figure 13.5 – SRE team shifts SLO violation or incident to the product
engineering team with relevant information

Incorporating incident management responsibilities into product development life cycles and workflows ensures that reliability considerations are integrated into every stage of product development. Product engineering teams should prioritize reliability requirements, conduct thorough testing and validation, and implement proactive monitoring and alerting mechanisms to detect and address potential issues early in the development process. By embedding incident management responsibilities into product development workflows, organizations can minimize the risk of reliability-related incidents and deliver more robust and resilient products to customers.

Collaboration between operations and product engineering teams is essential for improving incident response and resolution. Operations teams provide valuable insights into system performance and reliability, while product engineering teams offer expertise in identifying and addressing underlying issues. By fostering open communication, sharing knowledge and best practices, and establishing cross-functional incident response teams, organizations can streamline incident management processes, accelerate incident resolution, and drive continuous improvement in reliability and service quality.

Summary

By integrating SLIs and SLOs into the incident management process and extending accountability to your internal on-call and product engineering teams, organizations can elevate the role of incident management in reliability engineering. Along with defining clear and measurable SLOs, incorporating on-call engineers and agents into SLO frameworks, and extending accountability to product engineering teams, organizations can enhance their ability to respond to and resolve incidents effectively, ultimately improving the reliability and availability of their systems and services.

Although it is not a core aspect of this chapter or even the book, it's important to understand that the structure of the practice internal to your organization plays a key role in your ability to scale or extend accountability. The more hands on deck, the bigger the increase in the necessity of structured and aligned practice. Continuous monitoring, measurement, and refinement of SLIs and SLOs in partnership with incident management will enable your organization to drive improvements through incident management practices. In the chapter to follow, we will touch on making decisions with the information at hand.

Further reading

Here, you can review and read the referenced articles and books for additional reading about concepts mentioned in this book:

- Hidalgo, A. (2020). *Implementing Service Level Objectives*. Sebastopol: O'Reilly Media Inc.

- PagerDuty. (2021, May 18). *Severity Levels*. Retrieved from `https://response.pagerduty.com/before/severity_levels/`.

- Team Asana. (2024, Feb 16). *What is Incident Management? Steps, tips and best practices*. Retrieved from `https://asana.com/resources/incident-management`.

14

SLIs and SLOs as a Service

In chapters in the first part of this book, we discussed the history of reliability engineering, the core concepts of observability, and the importance of reliability engineering to service and application performance. In the chapters that followed, we discussed how to structure your service level indicator and objectives workshop and foster necessary discussions between the team, engineers, and invested stakeholders. This chapter can be considered a free-for-all, centering the discussion around delivering it to your target audience as a practice.

At this stage of the book, you might have already asked yourself, "What am I to do with all of this information now"? Or, even better, "How do I package this information as an internal or external service to improve customer experience"? In some cases, it may not suit you to market the information as a paid service but implement the process internally to ensure your internal engineering teams maintain an "as-a-Service" mentality. This can enable the team to effectively write code and build processes that align with the organization's broader strategy and customer needs.

In *Chapter 14* specifically, you can expect to cover the following topics:

- Developing an as-a-Service mindset

- What is X-as-a-Service?

- SLIs-as-a-Service

- SLIs-as-a-S Product lifecycle

Developing an as-a-Service mindset

The goal of this chapter is not to build another "as-a-Service" title or category but to shift the mind toward thinking about internally conducting your workshops and implementing your service level measurements with the same delicacy that you would if conducting the former with external customers. With this thinking, you can expect to internally build the following:

- Improved mechanisms that better support your external customers.

- Improved comraderies and internal processes between engineering and other teams.

- Practices that help the organization align SLOs and SLIs with external SLAs, ensuring contractual commitments are met.

- Assurance that your internal engineering teams can map their daily operations to reliability-focused objectives, using SLIs and SLOs to inform broader organizational **Objectives and Key Results (OKRs)** or **Key Performance Indicators (KPIs)** related to system reliability and customer experience.

Your team might have all or some of the goals mentioned in mind. Before we get started, I encourage you to start this chapter with your end goal top of mind. Ask yourself some of the following questions:

- What stage of the process is my team, business unit, or organization in?

- What result am I trying to achieve?

- What is the culture of the target audience I am attempting to solve this problem for?

- Is this something I want to take on and build upon?

- How much time do I have to invest to build for the goal I want to achieve?

Once you can answer the questions mentioned, I encourage you to read the text and pull from it the parts that help you to achieve the goals identified from the responses. At the end of the day, each book represents the opinions of the author and a representation of the author's experience.

In this instance, I'd like to highlight the many years I have spent working in software and platforms as a service, working in product support, and with product-focused engineering teams. So much so that I ended up enrolling in a product leadership program to challenge my own experience and knowledge outside of the technical scope. This information is mentioned to provide more context as to how we ended up here. Speaking of products, let's kickstart the conversation here.

What is X-as-a-Service?

If you made it as far as picking up this book and beginning to read it, I am working under the assumption that you are already familiar with the concept of "aaS" or as the section title suggests, "XaaS." For the purposes of the text, "X" is simply a placeholder here. "**XaaS**" is an acronym that means "**Anything-as-a-Service**". It can technically apply in this instance as well but was not the immediate goal. AaS refers to productizing or marketing something as a service, under some pricing model. You're likely more familiar with the concepts of SaaS and PaaS, meaning software and platform as a service. In this instance, we are referring to service-level measurements as a service. However, that does not mean we cannot take the necessary features and create a platform as a service. It's just not what we are referring to in this chapter.

Now that we have gotten that out of the way, why would you want to consider SLIs and SLOs as a service? To be frank, I am not sure. That is a question that only you can answer. However, when initially introduced to the concept of reliability engineering, it honestly felt like the discussion centered around infrastructure and being on call. I believe if the organization is experiencing an extreme level of incidents and constantly updating system code that is specific to customer incidents, as opposed to optimizing and refactoring iteratively, there must come a point where it revisits the fundamental practices and processes being used for service delivery.

My introduction to reliability engineering came at this peak sentiment, and after a period of my career where I witnessed an SRE team get dismantled for no reason of their own, other than being the business group that did not generate revenue. From a business perspective, this resulted in having less of an impact on the broader organization's bottom line, despite it being a critical component of running highly available systems that meet customers' reliability needs. This can sometimes happen in organizations that scale to a certain size or work in a way that does not heavily rely on research and innovation teams.

I mention this without an opinion because, at the end of the day, the business must continue to run. Having seen SLOs implemented in ways that blurred the line between monitoring and customer-centric reliability while lacking clarity surrounding how they fit into the organizations' stories and thus long-term strategies, or how to use them, it seemed like the next best step. SRE, from an engineering perspective, helps to integrate what the engineer cares about versus what the customer cares about, in a way that creates metrics important to internal stakeholders and broader business needs. And here we are! Now let's talk more about SLIs!

SLIs-as-a-Service

SLIs-as-a-Service refers to the concept of providing tools, platforms, or consulting services that help organizations define, measure, and improve their SLIs. Rather than selling SLIs directly, this approach focuses on enabling teams to establish meaningful reliability metrics within their observability and monitoring frameworks. In a typical conversation, the focus can shift toward objectives. Although objectives are important, indicators and the metrics used to build them can have a negative impact on the objectives you set if designed incorrectly. This ties into the practice of observability and developing the level of visibility into systems that is needed to accurately base other reliability dependencies upon it. If you are not able to clearly observe and report on what is happening in your systems, then you will not be able to achieve optimal levels of reporting.

If your organization aligns its internal SLOs with external SLAs, it's crucial to ensure that SLIs accurately reflect user experience. Misalignment between SLIs and SLOs can lead to incorrect reporting and impact SLA compliance. This will then lead you to believe SLIs and SLOs are not a useful practice, instead of realizing you are measuring the incorrect components and reporting metrics are out of alignment with long-term goals. You will sometimes realize that you do not have the required level of observability to begin to build customer-centric SLIs and SLOs that are meaningful to your organization. This rant is not the goal of the chapter but an important driver and thus worth mentioning.

Let's think of service level measurements as a product, instead of a service we are trying to sell. With a typical product, a customer makes a one-time purchase, whether it is online or in person, and pays the allocated price. In addition, some products exist where the customer can make reoccurring payments, at some cadence and through a subscription. In other instances, a customer can also sign a contract and purchase a product where benefits such as a warranty, customer support, or another service are included for an allotted amount of time. This is ultimately how we want to think of and treat SLIs as a Service and focus on the concepts that make up the lifecycle.

SLIs-as-a-S Product lifecycle

SLIs are generally referred to in software and technology throughout the book. In this chapter, we will shift the conversation toward software and technology product lines.

In the product world, for a product to go live and become generally available to the public, the product will go through a product development lifecycle. Once development has been completed, or asynchronously to some stage in product development, the product will also go through a **go-to-market (GTM)** strategy or cycle. At a high level, similar stages make up each cycle. The tasks that make up each stage and the strategic goal of the stage will differ between each lifecycle as one is centered around development while the other is marketing. We don't want to reinvent the wheel but pull from each lifecycle the tasks and stages that align with shaping the service-level measurement as a product in and of itself.

The software development product lifecycle

The product development lifecycle as it relates to software within the software and technology industry typically consists of seven stages, shown in *Figure 14.1*.

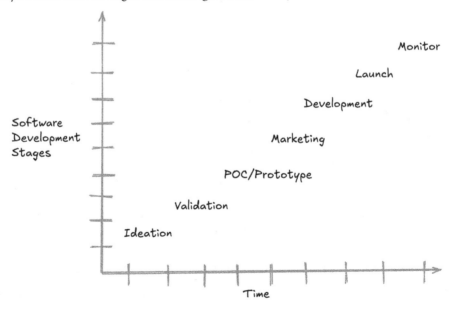

Figure 14.1 – The 7 stages within the software development cycle

Although it can vary from one organization to another, we'll stick with the standard for this chapter's purposes. As with various lifecycles and frameworks, it consists of several stages with tasks within each stage. Each stage is comprised of tasks that help the product transition from conception through to release, relating to technical development.

The standard product development lifecycle will consist of the following stages.

Ideation

Development includes the period of ideation or conception through the technical development process in preparation for release. This typically includes an organization's architects, designers, and engineering and product business groups, among various other business domains. Ideation is not limited to a specific framework but rather the best process used to help internal teams innovate in developing new solutions to address a current need or problem for the target audience.

This stage can also result in various ideas for a single solution that the team will triage to determine which is the best solution. Apart from that, a team's triaging can result in the development of a **proof of concept** (**POC**) to test whether the idea can exist as a technical solution. This stage will shift the team in the direction of validating the business and technical requirements of the solution.

Validation

Validation includes a series of processes, tests, and/or various other tasks used to validate a single or many ideations developed in the initial stage. In the product lifecycle, it can consist of surveying members of the targeted audience, interviews, and focus groups to assess which solution will perform better or confirm the solution aligns with the market need. Processes such as A/B testing are used to compare the benefits of two possible solutions. The best process for validation is the one that suits your organization and target market's needs. There are numerous case studies and frameworks within the market that can be used.

Prototyping

Once the team has internally validated the appropriate solution to the identified problem, it may make sense to prototype the solution or develop a proof of concept, as mentioned in this chapter's initial ideation section. The POC is often completed during the ideation or conception stage. However, in some instances, the two are used interchangeably. It's important to understand instances where they are used as two separate concepts. The POC is used to focus on the required processes to bring the product to life and its feasibility.

A prototype serves as a lightweight version of a product, allowing internal stakeholders and investors to evaluate its feasibility and alignment with reliability goals. When prototyping SLI-driven products and services, the focus should be on establishing the observability pipeline, defining key SLIs early, and ensuring that error budgets and alerting mechanisms can be tested before full-scale development.

The ideation process is also revisited to determine how to best bring the product to market. The prototype will include the key features integral to solving the identified problem. It also serves as an opportunity to complete another stage of validation to gather feedback and make several changes prior to development. It can serve as a point to validate the aesthetics of the UI if appropriate.

In an organization where a proof of concept and prototype are separate phases, let's consider the following: we want a platform that ingests system architecture and operational data, then programmatically defines SLIs based on measured service performance and maps them to SLOs aligned with business objectives, integrating seamlessly with industry-standard SRE tooling.

Proof of concept

The immediate request for a system where we can enter information and data regarding the system and it completes the remaining work sounds a bit foreign to all parties involved. However, a similar request came from five key accounts and a few engineers thought a POC would get the ball rolling. They might do the following:

- Research and determine whether a product with this function already exists.

- Research and identify AI and ML technology and trends to determine whether there is a solution that exists.

- Consider other internal technical tooling and technology that exists.

Condense this information into some artifacts to market the technical feasibility to internal management.

Prototype

Once the team has determined the tooling and technical feasibility, they may want to shift toward building the prototype, which will help stakeholders visualize the product and realize its real-world usage and value. As previously mentioned, this stage will likely have all the features and functionality that are critical to its success and were likely mentioned at some point of engagement with the five key accounts that initiated the request.

Following the process in this stage of development, for some solutions, will help the team refrain from "scope creep" and successfully transition into pilot and production development for a product in alignment with the customers' key use cases. This can also help to seamlessly and asynchronously begin the marketing and development stages.

Marketing

Once the prototyping stage has been completed and various personas are developed, the attention can shift toward the marketing stages. As it relates to the text in this chapter, think of the strategic planning process of backcasting, where the future state is defined, here via POC, and the development work is completed. Although mentioned here, prior to development, we'd consider beginning the phase asynchronously with the development work and holding the development process accountable for delivering what we are marketing. This may not be suitable for all initiatives or even industries.

It is also equally important to revisit the concept of personas from *Chapter 6*. We can create personas based on the type, i.e., buyer type, user type, and so on. At this stage, the team should have a solid understanding of those types, along with the target audience. Please revisit concepts in *Chapter 6* if needed. Your marketing strategy should incorporate enough data about targeted personas to further inform and shape your product during the development process.

When bringing a product to market, you'll hear the term go-to-market and sometimes product-led growth as the strategy. Product-led growth utilizes the product specifically to "acquire, activate, and retain customers" (Bush, 2019) while inheriting GTM core principles. Although marketing is not the primary focus of this book, it is relevant in the context of positioning SLI/SLO-driven reliability as a marketable service. Organizations that offer reliability as a service, reliability consulting, or reliability engineering platforms can leverage SLIs and SLOs as core value propositions, ensuring that service levels reflect achievable reliability guarantees. If not, then many of the tasks can only help your team formulate ideal selling points when attempting to elicit internal investors and stakeholders.

Within the marketing space, the GTM strategy will consist of several stages, as with the development processes. We will not go into depth about each stage but will highlight the purpose of each. Stages of the GTM strategy may include the following, in chronological order:

- **Research**: Research the current market to develop insights regarding market needs and trends. This should also include competitor analysis to understand what competitors exist and what features and functionality will set your product apart. This stage may also include reviewing past customer engagements and key business accounts.

- **Design**: Design, as it relates to productizing SLIs and SLOs, centers around understanding what specifically you want to bundle. Conceptualization was likely done during the ideation stage, which leaves this stage of the process for focusing on packaging for the target market. Building data surrounding what additional features are needed to make this a competitive seller will help to guide this phase.

- **Build**: The build process as it relates to the context of this chapter relates to external documents and digital assets for product branding. This stage may also include content development for initial training, project plans, and customer-facing contracts, if necessary. Internally, it can include similar artifacts that help to run a successful workshop, training materials, and pre-work documents.

- **Pricing**: Pricing heavily relies upon what you decide to sell or market. If the organization plans to schedule reliability engineering workshops, they might be interested in a la carte pricing. If the organization is interested in an SLI/SLO platform, they may be interested in subscription or pay-as-you-go pricing plans. If there is ongoing support, the team may want to implement contracts providing specific services for a cost for an explicit amount of time.

- **Sell**: Depending on the size of the team, organization, or individual goals, what does the sales plan look like? Does it include sales enablement, which requires training and enablement documentation? If sales agents are in a mix of things, how do we incentivize sales agents? What feedback loops can we create between the sales channel and external customers? If we are externally selling our product, how do we utilize sales tactics to internally market and create buy-in among stakeholders and engineering teams? These are examples of questions that you'd need to answer to aggregate the appropriate data for this phase.

- **Monitor**: In the later stages of the process, there will come an improvement stage where everything is up and running. During the improvement stage, how do we monitor the impact the product has within the organization, or within the customer's organization? The team may want to implement processes that tie into organization-wide KPIs and OKRs to better track improvements.

Development

The development process can begin after the success of a POC or prototyping event. Depending on the structure of the internal team and organization, it can take place asynchronously with specific stages of the marketing lifecycle.

During the development stage, you will likely develop an **MVP**, or **minimal viable product**, that represents the final product with the minimum number of features required to attract early adopters and encourage the team to develop actionable insights from the adopters. This includes creating the necessary artifacts, such as product roadmaps and internal backlogs for product management capabilities and future iterations of features that may not have made it into the MVP version.

Launch

The product launch is the period before releasing the product to the market. This might include social media advocacy, internet marketing ads, and various other communications to inform your target audience of the product's general availability. During this stage, you'd want to focus on the release aspects of the product.

Monitor improvements

The final stage is an ongoing and iterative process to monitor and identify gaps for improvement. This stage is dependent on the structure of the team and the internal workings of your organization. It includes the period where feedback is garnered through customers or users and implemented. This can be done via processes used in the earlier stages, such as interviews and surveys. More established organizations may have **NPS**, or **Net Promoter Score**, systems in place to capture customer temperature and feedback from using the system.

Despite the method used, it is important to capture data in a way that provides information related to the specific features of your product and actionable insights to respond to.

If your customer is an internal engineering team or business unit, you can still utilize similar processes that you'd implement for an external customer within the scope of your budget and resource allocation limits.

During this stage, you'd likely look at which users your product is attracting, what features they are most focused on, and what features they are requesting or submitting complaints about. This includes assessing your own team's communication methods and strategies for product rollout. This will also include a reassessment of the artifacts created, such as product roadmaps and product management systems for backlogs to iterate on the features that were initially conceived.

Now that we have briefly reviewed the various stages of the product development lifecycle and go-to-market strategy based on a product-led organization, let's focus on how we can use pieces of each lifecycle and transform service reliability into a product.

SLIs and SLOs product lifecycle

Service level performance to ensure your technical solutions meet the expectations and needs of the customer is crucial to the success of your business. Since we have briefly reviewed the product and marketing lifecycle as it relates to products in the technology industry, it's time to apply the lifecycle and processes to our SLI and SLO process, to understand how we can package it as a service for external customers and other internal engineering teams and related stakeholders, requiring customer-centric service level performance metrics.

As a brief reminder, it is important to understand that being sold internally does not mean your team or business unit is selling a tangible product to other internal teams. In some instances, if you are building a platform or application that solves a reliability engineering problem, this may be true. However, in the scope of this chapter, it is to foster a culture where if/when we decide to implement service level performance, we maintain a business mindset and encourage internal teams to increase their understanding of customer centricity from a business perspective.

To successfully achieve what was previously mentioned, we'd ideally consider and apply the necessary stages to the SLI and SLO ideated solution referenced in the upcoming sections. A high-level depiction appears in *Figure 14.2*.

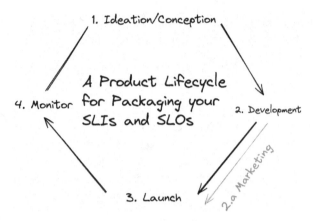

Figure 14.2 – A product lifecycle for packaging your SLIs and SLOs

At the time of writing this, I am grateful for the opportunity to have partnered with organizations that offered reliability engineering capabilities through SLI and SLO enablement, SLI and SLO development, and SLO management platforms as a solution for internal and external customers. My initial experience with SLOs began as a part of a platform team providing enterprise support to development teams using our platform for container orchestration, application development, and DevOps tooling. As a part of the platform team providing support, SLO dashboards for incident and ticket management were a solution for us.

Adding to that, joining another organization and attending another staff engineer meeting with the customer support team looking for ways to improve ticket management fostered an interest in the fundamentals related to reliability engineering. I include this to say, although the book focuses on service level performance for application services and platform environments, do not limit the context in which SLIs and SLOs can be used to improve the technical logistics within your organization. This leads us into the initial stage of ideation within the suggested lifecycle for packaging and selling service-level performance capabilities as a service.

Ideation/conception

During the ideation stage, it's important to conceptualize what components of service level performance you are looking to implement or sell. This can vary from consulting services on various topics previously mentioned, where one would be creating and running workshops to authentically help an organization with the initial stages of establishing what system components to measure. It can also result in building a platform solution providing SLI and SLO management and reporting capabilities to other enterprise businesses with a need for specific measurements.

In the previous section, we referenced research as a part of the marketing stage. However, upon creating a POC of your proposed solution, if applicable, you may want to conduct market research to identify organizations within your target market that currently have the same or a similar solution. This will help to better develop features that set your product apart from the rest.

If marketing internally, it may be in your best interest to research with other engineering teams to identify what monitoring solutions they have in place, bottlenecks, and other blockers to ensure your ideation is in alignment with the needs of the broader organization. Another team may have sufficient data to develop actionable insights and be more than willing to act as a customer throughout the various stages. This, ideally, will also help to ensure alignment prior to development, which leads us into the development phase.

Development

Once you, and your team, if relevant, can identify the capabilities that you would like to sell, you can then begin the development process. For this book's purposes, we will not limit development to the technical aspects. Whether you are attempting to develop internally or externally, there will be requirements for documentation, eliciting internal system designs, and taking physical action to build the features identified during the ideation stages.

At this stage, we will not incorporate many of the GTM phases previously mentioned. However, there are a few that we want to consider during, prior to, or asynchronously with the development process. The phases we should include are as follows:

- **Marketing**: How do we market the product prior to it being released to the public, or even to internal teams? Is the solution an industry-related solution that requires marketing ads and social media advocacy? If the product is centered around internal engineering teams, what does the marketing strategy look like to increase the level of buy-in? Do we create short demos and tutorials?

  As a part of this process, it is also important to think about and consider the selling approach. Does it warrant a top-down or bottom-up selling strategy? Bottom-down strategies tend to work better within product-led environments and focus on the product marketing and selling itself through customers using it (Bush, 2019). On the flip side, a top-down selling strategy will foster buy-in and approval via the executive pipeline and require a different marketing and selling strategy. Each approach will likely have some level of impact on the pricing strategy, which leads us into the next phase.

- **Pricing**: The features your team decides to sell and the packaging decision will depend on the pricing strategy. Is this an ongoing service that customers can subscribe to? Does the team want to offer an a la carte menu? Are we building a platform with service functionality that provides pay-as-you-go or freemium tiers? If we are providing workshops to the customer, we may want to charge for the workshop. However, does the relationship end with the sale or are we offering the ability for customers to bundle additional services and improve the customer account churn rate?

  The structure of the organization and budget of the team implementation will greatly impact the decision-making process within this phase. In addition, the top-down approach places a greater burden on the sales team. Neither is better than the other. It is a matter of opting for the solution that provides the appropriate sales cycle and will align better with your target users' needs and the future scalability of your customer base.

- **Sales**: If your customers are external facing and sales representatives or consultants are available, what does the ideal level of interaction with the customer look like? Does the business group or team have the budget to incentivize sales agents? Do we utilize the team as sales agents and perform demos or use proofs of concepts to attract early adopters and other future clients? Decisions made within this phase will help to set individuals not involved in the technical aspects of the product up for success.

Launch

The launch period is heavily dependent upon the method you are using to productize your SLI and SLO process. This includes the decisions made during the marketing phase. We'd expect many of the items in the marketing phase to have been implemented in preparation for "flipping the switch" to go live.

Another key consideration in the go-live phase is ensuring robust incident response and monitoring processes. SLIs should be established to measure key performance indicators such as request latency, error rates, and availability. SLOs should define acceptable thresholds to trigger alerts when service reliability deviates from expectations. This ensures that issues are logged, managed, and resolved efficiently with minimal downtime. In the event we are rolling out a workshop, are there any on-site logistics that could heavily impact the success of the workshop? If the workshop is being conducted in a virtual environment, how do we ensure there are no technical blips in the virtual meeting room or with the collaborative tools we are accessing via the web? These are all questions that need to be asked to ensure a successful go-live and launch day.

Monitor

Once the team has experienced a successful launch day or executed the first initial workshop, how can we better understand the value of the solution? What are the value metrics that will help to track this information over time to help customers and invested stakeholders understand the value? If we have a solid picture of the value that we hope or expect to bring, this offers the team a good starting point to understand what they need to monitor to start with. This is in addition to creating a solid foundation for maintaining increased visibility for iterating on what additional features to incorporate to continue to scale the solution.

The monitoring process does not merely include monitoring the technical features and implementations but also whether the product is meeting the needs of the customer. Remember, this is achieved through the initial development of the persona and persona journey to understand how components in the system work together to achieve an outcome for the ideal persona. If this is done as expected, our SLIs and SLOs should tell the expected story, help to establish a set of value metrics, and align the revenue model with the customer acquisition model (Bush, 2019).

At some point in this stage, we will pose a series of questions, such as the following:

- Is there a need to increase the capabilities and features of the system?

- Are customers satisfied and seeing a reduction in the number of problems that initially attracted them to our solution?

- Has implementation increased the ability of the customer to meet internal objectives, and thus short-term and long-term strategy goals?

- Are there processes in place that help to build this data and thus create actionable solutions to ensure we are solving problems that the customer is not immediately aware of?

There are various other questions to help formulate some hypothesis of the desired goals and shift the team in the direction of developing the processes to build and monitor the identified value metrics. Related to the text within this chapter, we might consider the following:

- The number of workshops scheduled within a month or a quarter, of which customers could implement SLIs and SLOs.

- The amount of revenue generated for a platform per annum.

- The monthly recurring revenue generated in a subscription environment.

Outside of the monetary aspects, if we are focused on the customer and metrics that help to gauge their behaviors and improve the customer experience, we'd consider the following:

- What is the customer acquisition cost as it relates to monetary and/or staff required to implement and maintain?

- Does the **customer lifetime value (CLV)** align with the numbers we are experiencing?

- What are the retention rates?

- Is there a positive correlation between newly released features and new adopters?

Apart from understanding how the product performs monetarily, we want to see a positive correlation between customer usage of the product and generating new customers, as well as low numbers in terms of customer churn. Your value metrics should help you to better understand how your product is performing, in addition to whether the way the team or organization is responding to the customer's needs is sufficient.

Summary

This concludes the discussion about creating an SLI and SLO sellable product. Although not the focus of the book, it is common to create a product or solution without the knowledge of how to bring it to market or how to internally garner the buy-in that is needed from the broader organization. This is especially common for individuals who might have the technical inclinations but not necessarily the business knowledge and execution to bring it to life. After reading this chapter, I hope your mind is stimulated in a way that brings about creative and innovative ways to contribute to the reliability engineering community, if for nothing more than to improve the reliability within your own teams and organizations.

Although this chapter concludes the book, it is only a single part of your journey with SLIs and SLOs. If you are just starting, I hope that it encourages you to get started in a structured and fun way. I hope that you couple this with other reliability engineering practices and materials to begin the transformation process within your organization.

Further reading

You can review and read the referenced article about concepts mentioned in this book:

- Bush, W. (2019). *Product-Led Growth: How to Build a Product That Sells Itself*. Waterloo: Product-Let Institute.

Index

`packtpub.com`

Subscribe to our online digital library for full access to over 7,000 books and videos, as well as industry leading tools to help you plan your personal development and advance your career. For more information, please visit our website.

Why subscribe?

- Spend less time learning and more time coding with practical eBooks and Videos from over 4,000 industry professionals

- Improve your learning with Skill Plans built especially for you

- Get a free eBook or video every month

- Fully searchable for easy access to vital information

- Copy and paste, print, and bookmark content

Did you know that Packt offers eBook versions of every book published, with PDF and ePub files available? You can upgrade to the eBook version at `packtpub.com` and as a print book customer, you are entitled to a discount on the eBook copy. Get in touch with us at `customercare@packtpub.com` for more details.

At `www.packtpub.com`, you can also read a collection of free technical articles, sign up for a range of free newsletters, and receive exclusive discounts and offers on Packt books and eBooks.

Other Books You May Enjoy

If you enjoyed this book, you may be interested in these other books by Packt:

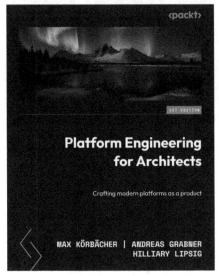

Platform Engineering for Architects

Max Körbächer, Andreas Grabner, Hilliary Lipsig

ISBN: 978-1-83620-359-9

- Make informed decisions aligned with your organization's platform needs
- Identify missing platform capabilities and manage that technical debt effectively
- Develop critical user journeys to enhance platform functionality
- Define platform purpose, principles, and key performance indicators
- Use data-driven insights to guide product decisions
- Design and implement platform reference and target architectures

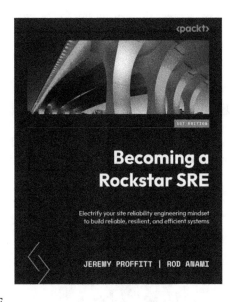

Becoming a Rockstar SRE

Jeremy Proffitt, Rod Anami

ISBN: 978-1-80323-922-4

- Get insights into the SRE role and its evolution, starting from Google's original vision
- Understand the key terms, such as golden signals, SLO, SLI, MTBF, MTTR, and MTTD
- Overcome the challenges in adopting site reliability engineering
- Employ reliable architecture and deployments with serverless, containerization, and release strategies
- Identify monitoring targets and determine observability strategy
- Reduce toil and leverage root cause analysis to enhance efficiency and reliability
- Realize how business decisions can impact quality and reliability

Packt is searching for authors like you

If you're interested in becoming an author for Packt, please visit `authors.packtpub.com` and apply today. We have worked with thousands of developers and tech professionals, just like you, to help them share their insight with the global tech community. You can make a general application, apply for a specific hot topic that we are recruiting an author for, or submit your own idea.

Share Your Thoughts

Now you've finished *SLIs and SLOs Demystified*, we'd love to hear your thoughts! Scan the QR code below to go straight to the Amazon review page for this book and share your feedback or leave a review on the site that you purchased it from.

`https://packt.link/r/1835889395`

Your review is important to us and the tech community and will help us make sure we're delivering excellent quality content.

Download a free PDF copy of this book

Thanks for purchasing this book!

Do you like to read on the go but are unable to carry your print books everywhere?

Is your eBook purchase not compatible with the device of your choice?

Don't worry, now with every Packt book you get a DRM-free PDF version of that book at no cost.

Read anywhere, any place, on any device. Search, copy, and paste code from your favorite technical books directly into your application.

The perks don't stop there, you can get exclusive access to discounts, newsletters, and great free content in your inbox daily

Follow these simple steps to get the benefits:

1. Scan the QR code or visit the link below

https://packt.link/free-ebook/9781835889381

2. Submit your proof of purchase
3. That's it! We'll send your free PDF and other benefits to your email directly

www.ingramcontent.com/pod-product-compliance
Lightning Source LLC
LaVergne TN
LVHW082125070326
832902LV00041B/2563